TURNSTILE ONE

TURNSTILE ONE

A Literary Miscellany from
THE NEW STATESMAN AND NATION

Edited by
V. S. PRITCHETT

TURNSTILE PRESS
10 Great Turnstile, London, W.C.1.

First published in 1948 by
Turnstile Press Ltd
10 Great Turnstile London W.C.1
Printed in Great Britain by
Latimer Trend & Co Ltd Plymouth
World Copyright All Rights reserved

FOREWORD

THE stories, poems, the essays random and critical, contained
in this volume have been taken from the literary pages of *The
New Statesman and Nation* and date, with one or two exceptions from the marriage of *The New Statesmen* and *The Nation*
in 1931. The exceptions are from *The New Statesman* prior to
1931. To attempt an anthology that was both historical and
representative, a literary record including all the names and
all the moods of the last twenty years or so, seemed too solemn
and egocentric: and why, indeed, not go back to 1913 when
The New Statesman was founded; why not make a detour into
the parallel life of *The Nation* (founded 1907) and thence back
to *The Athenaeum* (1828) and forward to *The Week-end Review*
(1930)? The historian of the weekly reviews has many years
of work in the archives of Great Turnstile, and we leave
him to his task; it will illuminate the cultural history of the
present century; he will come across original work by nearly
all the distinguished writers of the period. Our more modest
aim, in this present series—which we intend to continue—is to
entertain. When many of the items in the present volume were
first published, their authors were unknown or known only to
the few; like Mr. Desmond MacCarthy and Mr. Raymond
Mortimer, who in turn took on the literary editorship, they
have since reached the highest eminence in contemporary
letters. One or two things, like James Joyce's evocation of
Sullivan's singing, are valuable curiosities, and D. H. Lawrence's letter about pre-Nazi Germany has become a famous
example of historical prophecy. There is one serious omission:
Mr. Bernard Shaw, who was one of our founders and is our
oldest contributor, expresses an unalterable aversion from all
anthologies—and his work therefore remains unrepresented in
this volume.

V. S. P.

CONTENTS

Poems

Short Stories

Essays and Reviews

Art

Music

Letters to the Editor

ACKNOWLEDGMENTS

Thanks are due to the following for permission to reproduce items in this volume which have been re-published in book form since their first appearance in *The New Statesman and Nation*: Allen and Unwin Ltd. (and The Macmillan Co., New York) for "The Sentry" from *Raider's Dawn* by Alun Lewis. Edward Arnold and Co. (and Harcourt, Brace and Co. Inc., New York, and Longmans Green and Co., Toronto) for "Mrs. Grundy at the Parkers" from *Abinger Harvest* by E. M. Forster. Jonathan Cape Ltd. for "On the Road" from *The Black Boxer* by H. E. Bates; "Nerves" from *Quiver's Choice* by Sagittarius; "Tutty" from *Daylight and Champaign* by G. M. Young; Jonathan Cape Ltd. (and Reynal and Hitchcock Inc., New York) for "Naming of Parts" from *A Map of Verona* by Henry Reed. Chatto and Windus for "Matisse and Picasso" from *Since Cézanne* by Clive Bell; Chatto and Windus (and Henry Holt and Co. Inc., New York) for "What the Hell?" from *What the Sweet Hell* by Peter Chamberlain; Chatto and Windus (and Harcourt, Brace and Co. Inc., New York) for "The Président de Brosses" from *Portraits in Miniature* by Lytton Strachey. Constable and Co. Ltd. (and Harcourt, Brace and Co. Inc., New York) for "Last Words" from *All Trivia* by Logan Pearsall Smith. J. M. Dent and Sons Ltd. for "Seeking the Island" from *The Solitary Man* by Richard Church; "Princess Mary's Wedding Jewels and the Pied Minstrel" from *Collected Poems* by H. E. Palmer. Faber and Faber Ltd. (and Random House Inc., New York) for "What I Expected" from *Poems* by Stephen Spender, and "Song" from *Another Time* by W. H. Auden; Faber and Faber Ltd. (and Henry Holt and Co. Inc., New York) for "Making a Fire" from *The Fleeting* and *Collected Poems* by Walter de la Mare; Faber and Faber Ltd. for "The Zulu Girl" from *Adamastor* by Roy Campbell. Victor Gollancz Ltd. (and Random House Inc., New York) for "Miss Lee" from *Post D. Digging for Mrs. Miller* by John Strachey. The Hogarth Press Ltd. for "Πάντων γλυκύτατον μεταβολή" from *Poems* by Clive Bell; "December Night" from *Selected Poems* by V. Sackville West; "Bishop Thirlwall" from *Channel Packet* by Raymond Mortimer; The Hogarth Press Ltd. (and Random House Inc., New York) for "You that Love England" from *The Magnetic Mountain* by C. Day Lewis. The author and Faber and Faber Ltd. (and Random House Inc., New York) for "Les Sylphides" from *Plant and Phantom* by Louis MacNeice. John Murray for "Pot Pourri from a Surrey Garden" from *Old Lights for New Chancels* by John Betjeman. Oxford University Press for "Venus Anadyomene" from *Selected Poems* by W. J. Turner. George Routledge and Sons Ltd. (and Henry Holt and Co. Inc., New York) for "Actaeon's Lament" from *Collected Poems* by Sidney Keyes. Martin Secker and Warburg Ltd. for "The Raider" from *Awake and Other Poems* by W. R. Rodgers.

Peter Chamberlain

WHAT THE HELL?

I GOT most everything I want. Look at it all ways I have. Well, then . . .

I like to empty my pockets before I go to bed at nights. I got a gold fountain-pen cost three quid, and a pencil the same nearly as much. There's a little pearl knife with one blade and a thing for your nails. My nails look pretty good too. I got three lighters, one with a watch in; I use that most.

My gold cigarette-case is real class; it cost a mint of money in Regent Street. And I got a silver one; a big 'un with fine markings. Mostly I carry fags in the packet though. I can smoke expensive muck if I choose, but I like the twenty a bob best.

I got a gold wrist-watch which don't keep good time but looks swell, with a funny sort of face you can't read very well, but its smart, with a metal thing for a strap, gold, that Jim told me was nancy, only that's just his jealousy I guess. I got a gold chain and another watch and some of those bloody silly dangling things with seals and that. Keeps A1 time that one, but it's only for the evening. I mean I got pretty well everything I want.

The only ring I wear's the goods, with a greyhound crest on it. It's bad to wear more than one ring. I got a gold-bound pocket-book and a note-book with a gold-tipped pencil. And a gold case for matches.

I got some links I've never seen bettered, platinum and pearl they are, with a set of studs to match. The tops screw in. I only got two left now, a prostitute pinched one, the bitch! Not that it makes any odds 'cos my shirts, they're specially made for me, show only two studs, see?

So I like to arrange them all on the dressing-room table with my ivory hair-brushes before I go to bed.

I got twenty-four pairs of walking-out shoes and I use them all, and seven overcoats, some of them with belts at the back like the advertisements. There's no two ways about it my clothes are as good as any you'll find in London. And I know how to wear good clothes, double-breasted coats suit me. And a

bowler hat that don't look like the race-course. When I buy socks
or ties I go to the best West End shops and choose the best that
money can buy; sometimes I get twenty or thirty ties and as
many socks at the same time. I got expensive umbrellas like the
ones you see. I look A1. I know that.

I got a fitted suit-case cost nearly fifty quid and my other
bags were pretty well as expensive. I've never seen them
bettered. I got a cocktail cabinet which . . .

Well, look at this flat. You can see that everything's really
posh at a glance. Furnished complete by a bloke who knew
his job. He ought, he charged enough, Christ knows. And I got
taste, too; the girls in shops always tell me that. Pictures and orn-
aments and rugs and knick-knacks all in the very best style. But
nothing simply because it's expensive. It's a treat this flat; best
address in London, too; hot water and heating and everything.

When I give a party people come. No matter who they are,
and some of them are real swells, they come. And they're
always very civil to me. I go to all the smart places. I can order
a dinner in a restaurant that . . . Why, I'm even thinking
of getting a racehorse! I could buy one if I liked, it isn't the
money. I got a Talbot 105 Saloon which takes some beating.

And the girls! You should have seen the bit that I took
abroad last year. As smart a piece as any I saw in Nice. She
cost me a heap of money, but she was good value.

I've had the real goods throw themselves at me in this very
room. The better class they are the more loving they seem to
be. You'd be surprised at the things some of them do. And
finely built girls, too. Of course it's the money most of them
want—I'm not such a fool as not to know that—but after all . . .

My new dress suit set me back thirty-five guineas. A lot of money
you'll say, but worth every penny of the price. My man shaves
me every day. I got my monogram on my pyjamas. I got . . .

I got an electric coffee-pot and electric heater to keep the
plates warm. I got a radio-gram. I got a bathroom you couldn't
better at Grosvenor House. I got a gold match-box with my
initials in diamonds in one corner. I got . . . Well, I can walk
into a shop and buy pretty well everything I want. And I'm
generous with it. Nothing's too good for a friend of mine.

Yes, I've got pretty well everything I want. Well, then? Well,
then? What the sweet Hell?   [*1935*]

Rebecca West

RUDYARD KIPLING

THE chief tragedy of Rudyard Kipling's life was summed up
in two of the tributes published in the newspapers the morning
after his death. Major-General Dunsterville, the original of
Stalky, boasted: "In three-score years and ten no man's
outlook on life could have changed less than that of Rudyard
Kipling." Sir Ian Hamilton wrote precisely and powerfully:
"As one who must surely be about Kipling's oldest friend, I
express my deep sorrow. His death seems to me to place a full
stop to the period when war was a romance and the expansion
of the Empire a duty." Those two sentences indicate the
theme of that tremendous and futile drama in which a man,
loving everything in life but reality, spent his days loathing
intellectuals as soft and craven theorists, and yet himself never
had the courage to face a single fact that disproved the fairy-
tales he had invented about the world in youth; and who,
nevertheless, was so courageous in defending this uncourageous
position that he had to be respected as one respects a fighting
bull making its last stand. That drama explains why the
public regards Rudyard Kipling as one of the most interesting
men of our time. He stands among those Laocoon figures who
in pride and strength are treading the road to the highest
honours, when they are assailed by passions, which seem not
to be a part of the victim's individualities, but to have crawled
out of the dark uncharted sea of our common humanity. Such
men are judged not by their achievements in action or the
arts but by the intensity of the conflict between them and their
assailants. Such judgment had to recognize Rudyard Kipling
as a memorable man.

That, in part, explains his fame on the Continent. His
warmest admirers would have to admit that that is extrava-
gantly inflated. A short time ago I was present when one of
the greatest figures in European literature explained to our
most subtle living novelist that it could only be political prejudice which prevented him from recognizing *Soldiers Three*

3

and *They* as permament glories of English Literature, very
near its apex. "You think them very much better than anything Shaw and Wells have written?" "Oh much!" "Better
than anything Dickens and Thackeray have written?" "Of
course! Much better than anything else in your modern
English literature—except Oscar Wilde and Lord Byron!"
The just cataloguing of Rudyard Kipling with two other
Laocoon figures suggests that an imperfect knowledge of a
language may permit a reader to see the main pattern of a
fabric, which a reader of great linguistic accomplishment might
lose because of absorption in fine verbal touches. But it does
not explain the curious progress of his fame in this country.
That followed a course which it is hard to explain to a post-
war generation.

Those of us who were born in the first half of the 'nineties
remember a childhood shadowed by certain historical facts:
the gathering trouble in South Africa, the Home Rule question,
the Dreyfus Case, the Diamond Jubilee, and the fame of
Mr. Kipling. These were of not easily differentiated importance; and it must be remembered that Kipling was not thirty-
five till the turn of the century. He enjoyed the celebrity
and rewards of Mr. Noel Coward and Mr. Priestley put
together, at less than Mr. Noel Coward's present age, with
something of the more than merely political, almost priestly,
aureole of Mr. Baldwin. He had laid the foundation of this
fame principally with his volumes of short stories, *Plain Tales
from the Hills, Soldiers Three* and *Life's Handicap,* his novel, *The
Light That Failed,* and his volumes of poetry, *Barrack Room
Ballads* and *The Seven Seas.*

It will seem to anyone who now takes up these volumes for
the first time, or can read them in a state of detachment, that
their fame was not deserved. Those books are the work of
a preternaturally clever boy in his early twenties, of odd and
exciting, but limited experience, and they are just as good as
could be expected, and just as bad. *Plain Tales from the Hills*
are just the stories a young writer of parts will write when he
is mastering the bare elements of the story-teller's craft; when
he is teaching himself to get down on paper the crude sequence
of events, the mere mechanical movements of people in and
out of rooms and up and down stairs. *Soldiers Three* for all they

have stamped the imagination of a people, are anecdotes told with too much gusto and too little invention. *Life's Handicap* are better stories, for in them Kipling has perfected the art of hooking a reader's attention as neatly as an accomplished salmon-fisher casting a fly. I cannot believe that a young officer and his Hindu mistress would converse so exclusively in the manner of conscientious members of the Chelsea Babies' Club as is represented in *Without Benefit of Clergy*, but I shall not forget that story till I die. As for *The Light That Failed*, it is a neat, bright, tightly painted canvas, but it falls far short of deserving to cause a sensation. Dick Heldar is a boy's idea of an artist and a man; Maisie is a boy's idea of a woman; Bessie Broke is a boy's idea of a drab; Torp is a boy's idea of an adventurer. The verse is naturally better. Poetic genius makes a qualitative demand on experience; fiction makes a quantitative test as well. And indeed all his life long Kipling was a better poet than he was a prose-writer, though an unequal one. In his verse he was a fusion of Ella Wheeler Wilcox, Adelaide Proctor, Alfred Noyes, George R. Sims (*Gunga Din* is as bad as that), with a militarist A. P. Herbert, one of the grander Scottish hymnal-writers and a pure and perfect lyrist, who could distil a day of alien weather in a verse as bright and clear as a dewdrop. But it must be doubted whether an age that recited *Gunga Din* and *The Absent-minded Beggar* at the top of its voice was really swayed by admiration for that shy and delicate lyrist in its estimate of Kipling's genius.

Yet there was nothing at all fortuitous about Kipling's success. It could not be called a fluke. To begin with, his work then and all through his life had the curious property of seeming better than it disclosed itself after a few years. Some of his work was gold; and the rest was faery gold. Moreover, it had rare qualities which made it superbly relevant to its time. The first two were the emphasis on colour in his style, and the vast geographical scope of his subject-matter, which made his work just the nourishment the English-speaking world required in the period surrounding the Jubilee and the Diamond Jubilee. I do not find that the post-war generation realizes what marvellous shows these were, or how they enfranchised the taste for gorgeousness in a population that wore dark clothes, partly from a morbid conception of decorum and partly because cleaning was so expensive, and lived in drab and smoky times. Of the Jubilee I cannot speak; but of the Diamond Jubilee I have enchanting memories of such feasts for the eye as I do not think I knew again until the Russian Ballet came to dip the textiles of Western Europe in bright dyes. London was full of dark men from the ends of the earth who wore glorious colours and carried strange weapons, and who were all fond of small children and smiled at them in the streets. I remember still with a pang of ecstasy the gleaming teeth of a tall bearded warrior wearing a high head-dress, gold ear-rings and necklaces, a richly multi-coloured uniform, and embroidered soft leather boots. There were also the Indian troops in Bushey Park, their officers exquisitely brown and still, and coiffed with delicately bright turbans, the men washing their clothes at some stretch of water, small and precise and beautiful. They came from remote places and spoke unknown tongues. They belonged to an infinite number of varied races. They were amiable, they belonged to our Empire, we had helped them to become amiable by conquering them and civilizing them. It was an intoxicating thought; and it was mirrored in the work of Rudyard Kipling and nowhere else, for nobody could match his gift of reflecting visual impressions in his prose, and he alone among professional writers had travelled widely, and had the trick of condensing his travels into evocative runes which are almost as much magic as poetry. Hence he could restore confidence to a population that had slowly lost touch with their traditional assurances throughout the nineteenth century and give them a new sense of religious destiny. Since they were subjects of the British Empire they were members of a vast redemptory force.

And, indeed, that belief produced some not at all poisonous fruits. One night, when I was some years older, my mother returned from an expedition to town, and with flashing eyes described how she had come on a vast crowd standing round a hotel and raising cheer after cheer. Presently there appeared at the lighted window the stiff head and beard of Botha, woodenly bowing acknowledgments. The crowd had gathered to cheer the South African Generals, come to London to settle the peace, not (as one of the post-war generation startled me by assuming the other day on hearing this anecdote) because they were pro-Boer, but because they were full of the spirit of *parcere subjectis*. Uglier things have happened in history.

The third quality which made Kipling the presiding genius of his time was his passion for machinery. He assured the slaves of a mechanized world that what they tended were civilizing forces; that the task of tending them was a discipline and high achievement, and that the humblest who performed that task worthily could hold up his head among kings. Again, he brought a sense of religious destiny back into a disorganized world. He was able, in fact, to render an immense service to his age, and it is no wonder that in his later years, when it became apparent that that age had passed for ever, he refused to recognize the change, and raised a disgruntled pretence that nothing was happening save an outburst of misconduct on the part of the intellectuals and the lower classes. It is no wonder that he should want to do so, human nature being as frail as it is; but it is surprising that the writer of the masterpiece *Kim* should have found himself able to do so.

It was partly the consequence of a real incapacity for handling general ideas and grasping the structure of the world in which he lived. He was full of contempt for Pagett, M.P., the radical English politician who came out to India for a few months and then laid down the law to administrators who had known the country for a lifetime. But Sir Edmund Gosse, that wavering convert to the conventional, who could never be trusted not to lapse into dangerous penetration and sincerity, once pointed out that whenever Kipling wrote about England or any place but India he was simply a Pagett M.P. turned inside out. This was partly due to his Indian childhood, but it must also be laid to the charge of the kind of education which England provides for its governing classes. It is interesting to turn back to his very early travel book, *From Sea to Sea*, if only to see how carefully he hammered out that descriptive style which has had even more influence in France than here, since it is the foundation of the best in *le grand reportage*; but it is interesting also as an indication of just how well Stalky & Co. were taught. It begins with a chapter of jeers at a wretched young man from Manchester on a trip through India, who had bought some silly sham antiques and failed to understand the working of some wells on the plains. But in the later chapters Kipling himself travels through the Western States, only fifty years after the forty-niners, with not the faintest appreciation of what the settlement of the country meant. He gets off the train at Salt Lake City and has no word of reverence for that miracle of statesmanship which set a noble city and a stable State on a trackless and waterless desert. Merely he complains that the *Book of Mormon* is illiterate, that the Tabernacle is not pretty, and that polygamy is shocking. Could any young man from Manchester do worse? Surely the United Services College should have taught him better than that?

But the same wonder regarding the value of our English system of education arises when we look round at Kipling's admirers among the rich and great. He was their literary fetish; they treated him as the classic writer of our time; as an oracle of wisdom; as Shakespeare touched with grace and elevated to a kind of mezzanine rank just below the Archbishop of Canterbury. But he was nothing of the sort. He interpreted the mind of an age. He was a sweet singer to the last. He could bring home the colours and savours of many dis. tant places. He liked the workmanship of many kinds of workers, and could love them as long as they kept their noses to their work. He honoured courage and steadfastness as they must be honoured. But he was not a faultless writer. His style was marred by a recurrent liability to a kind of two-fold vulgarity, a rolling over-emphasis on the more obviously picturesque elements of a situation, whether material or spiritual, and an immediate betrayal of the satisfaction felt in making that emphasis. It is not a vice that is peculiar to him—perhaps the supreme example of it is Mr. Chesterton's *Lepanto*—but he committed it often and grossly. Furthermore, his fiction and his verse were tainted by a moral fault which one recognizes most painfully when one sees it copied in French books which are written under his influence, such as M. de St. Exupéry's *Vol de Nuit*, with its strong, silent, self-gratulatory airmen, since the French are usually an honest people. He habitually claimed that any member of the governing classes who does his work adequately was to be regarded as a martyr who sacrificed himself for the sake of the people; whereas an

administrator who fulfils his duties creditably does it for exactly
the same reason that a musician gives a masterly performance
on his fiddle or a house-painter gives a wall a good coat of
varnish, because it is his job and he enjoys doing things well.
But the worst of all was the mood of black exasperation in
which Kipling thought and wrote during his later years.
He had before him a people who had passed the test he had
named in his youth—the test of war; and they had passed it
with a courage that transcended anything he can have expected
as far as war transcended in awfulness anything he can have
expected. Yet they had only to stretch out a hand towards
bread or peace or power or any of the goods that none could
grudge them in this hour when all their governors' plans had
broken down, for Kipling to break out in ravings against the
greed and impudence of the age. Was this a tragedy to deplore
or a pattern to copy?

But perhaps the rich and great admired Kipling for retiring
into rage and shutting his eyes against his times, because they
were obscurely conscious of the dilemma that must have faced
him had he left them open. Supposing that one has pledged
one's imagination before the war to the ideal of a great Power
which would ruthlessly spread its pattern of civilization over all
conquerable lands so far as it could reach, without tenderness
for its executives or the conquered peoples; which would count
the slaves of the machines as the equal of kings, provided
they performed their tasks with competence, and far superior
to the intellectuals who are infatuated with the notion of
freedom; which asked of its children discipline, and discipline,
and then discipline, and stood proudly to meet the force of
the world with force—what power would claim one's allegiance
after the war, every year more surely? It has often seemed
fantastic that the author of *MacAndrew's Hymn* should have
feared and loathed the aeroplane. Perhaps he felt that, had
he given his passion for machinery its head, that and the
rest of his creed might have led him straight to Dnieprostroi.

[*1936*]

James Joyce

FROM A BANNED WRITER TO A BANNED SINGER

In this remarkable document, Mr. James Joyce gave his impressions of his friend, Mr. Sullivan of the Paris Opera, in several of his leading roles. Many competent critics have regarded Mr. Sullivan as the most extraordinary dramatic tenor that Europe has listened to for the last half century. Mr. Joyce complained that Mr. Sullivan was "banned" or at least unknown in England. The reflections written here were sent in a letter to Mr. Sullivan by Mr. Joyce after an occasion on which the singer was carried shoulder high by his Marseilles admirers after an astonishing performance in "Guillaume Tell". One knows of no other similar documents, no letters in a tone of intense admiration and sardonic banter sent by, say, Manzoni to Rubini, or by Flaubert to Gilbert Duprez, or by Ibsen to the Swedish Nightingale. Lovers of grand opera will recognize the operatic situations and phrases with which the text is studded and detect under the mask of their Christian names the three divi who figure in the final quartette.

HE strides, booted with anger, along the spurs of Monte Rossini, accompanied solely by Fidelion, his mastiff's voice. They quarrel consonantly about the vocality of the wind, calling each and its other claimant names.

*   *   *

Just out of kerryosity howlike is a Sullivan? It has the fortefaccia of a Markus Brutas, the wingthud of a spreadeagle, the body uniformed of a metropoliceman with the brass feet of a collared grand. It cresces up in Aquilone but diminuends austrowards. It was last seen and heard of by some macgilliecuddies above a lonely valley of their reeks, duskening the greylight as it flew, its cry echechohoing among the anfractuosities: *pour la dernière fois!* The black-bulled ones, stampeding, drew in their horns, all appailed and much upset, which explaints the guttermilk on their overcoats.

*   *   *

A pugilant gang theirs, per Bantry! Don Philip, Jay Hell,

Big O'Barry of the Bornstorms. Arthur, siruraganist who loosed that chor. Damnen. And tramp, tramp, tramp. And T. Deum sullivamus.

* * *

Faust of all, of curse, damnation. But given Parigot's Trocadéro for his drawing-room with Ballaclavier in charge at the pianone the voice becomes suburban, sweethearted and subdued. The heat to-day was really too much of a hot thing and even Impressario is glad to walk his garden in the cool of the evening, fanning his furnaceface with his sweltertails. *Merci, doux crépuscule!*

* * *

Who is this that advances in maresblood caftan, like Hiesous in Finisterre, his eyeholes phyllistained, his jewbones of a cross-backed? A little child shall lead him. Why, it's Strongman Simpson, Timothy Nathan, now of Simpson's on the Grill! Say, Tim Nat, bald winepresser, has not one air left? But yeth he hath. Regard! Auscult! He upbraces for supremacy to the potence of Mosthigh and calls upon his baiters and their templum: You daggones, be flat!

* * *

What was in that long note he just delivered? For the laib of me I cannot tell. More twopenny tosh and luxus languor about I singabob you? No such thing, O son of an envelope. Dr to J. S. Just a pennyplain loafletter from Braun and Brotmann and it will take no rebutter. You may bark Mrs. Liebfraumich as long as you love but you must not burk the baker. Pay us disday our daily bread. And oblige.

* * *

On his native heath, Speech! Speech! cry the godlets. We are in the land of Dan. But their words of Muskerry are harsh after that song of Othello. *Orateur ne peut, charlatan ne daigne, Sullivan est.*

* * *

11.59 p.m. *Durch diese hohle Gasse muss er kommen.* Guillaume's shot telled, sure enough. But will that labour member for Melckthal be able to bring off his coo for the odd and twentieth supererogatory time? *Wartemal!* That stagsquall has passed over like water off a Helvetian's back. And there they are, yodelling yokels, none the worse for their ducking and *gewit-termassen* as free as you fancy to quit their homeseek *heimat* and leave the ritzprinz of their chyberschwitzerhoofs all over both worlds, cisalpic and transatlantine. And how confederate of gay old Gioacchino to have composed this finale so that Kamerad Wagner might be saved the annoyance of finding flauts for his *Feuerzauber! Pass auf!* Only four bars more! He draws the breathbow: that arrownote's coming. Aim well, Arnold, and mind puur blind Jemmy in the stalls! But, great Scott, whas is thas for a larm! Half a ton of brass in the band, ten thousand throats from Thalwyl: Libertay. libertay lauded over the land. (Tay!) And pap goes the Calville!

*   *   *

Saving is believing but can thus be? Is this our model vicar of Saint Wartburgh's, the reverend Mr. Townhouser, Mus. Bac., discovered flagrant in a *montagne de passe?* She is obvious and is on her three-legged sofa in a half yard of casheselks, Madame de la Pierreuse. How duetonically she hands him his harp that once, biting him, whom caught is willing: do blease to, fickar! She's as only roman as any *puttana madonna* but the trouble is that the reverend T is informed. She, *simplicissima*, wants her little present from the reverend since she was wirk worklike never so nice with him. But he harps along about Salve Regina Terrace and Liza, mine Liza, and sweet Marie. Till she cries: bilk! And he calls: blak! O.u.t. spells out!

*   *   *

Since we are bound for a change of supper, was that really in faith like the reverend Townhouser for he seemed so ver-damnably like? *Ecco trovato!* Father Lucullus Ballytheacker, the parish priest of Tarbert. He was a songful soul at the keyboard and could achieve his Château Kirwan with cigar thuriferant, without ministrance from platform or pulpit, chase or church. Nor used he to deny his Mary neither. *Nullo modo.* Up to maughty London came a muftimummed P.P. Censored.

*   *   *

Have you got your knife handy? asks the bellman Saint Andy. Here he is and brandnew, answers Bartholomew. Get ready, get ready, scream the bells of Our Lady. And make

sure they're quite killed, adds the gentle Clotilde. Your attention, sirs, please, bawls big Brother Supplice. *Pour la foi!*
Pour la foi! booms the great Auxerrois.

*   *   *

Grand spectacular exposition of gorge cutting, mortarfiring
and general martyrification, bigleighted up with erst classed
instrumental music. *Pardie!* There's more sang in that Sceine
than mayer's beer at the Guildhall. Is he a beleaper in Irish
luck? Can he swhipstake his valentine off to Dublin and weave
her a frock of true blue poplin to be neat for the time Hugenut
Cromwell comes over, gentlest lovejesus as ever slit weasand?
Their cause is well sainted and they are centain to won. Still
I'll pointe half my crown on Raoul de Nangis, doublet mauve
and cuffs of buff. Attagirl! *Ah ah ah ah ah ah viens!* Piffpaff, but
he's done it, the bully mastiff again. And woops with him
through the window tallyhoed by those friers pecheurs who are
self-barked. Dominie's canes. Can you beat that, you papish
yelpers? To howl with the pups!

*   *   *

Enrico, Giacomo and Giovanni, three dulcetest of our
songsters, in liontamers overcoats, holy communion ties and
cliqueclaquehats, are met them at a gaslamp. It is kaputt and
throws no light at all on the trio's tussletusculums. Rico is for
carousel and Giaco for luring volupy but Nino, the sweetly
dulcetest, tuningfork among tenors, for the best of all; after
hunger and sex comes dear old *somnum*, brought on by prayer.
Their lays, blent of feastings, June roses and ether, link
languidly in the unlit air. Arrives a type in readymade, dicky
and bowler hat, manufactured by Common Sense and Co. Ltd.,
carrying a bag of tools. Preludingly he conspews a portugaese
into the gutter, recitativing: now then, gents, by your leave!
And, to his job. Who is this hardworking guy? No one but
Geoge, Geoge who shifts the garbage can, Geoge who stokes
in the engine room, Geoge who has something to say to the
gas (*tes gueules!*) and mills the wheel go right go round and
makes the world grow lighter. *Lux!* The aforesung Henry.
James and John stand mouthshut. Wot did I say? Hats off,
primi assoluti! Send him canorious, long to lung over us, high
topseasoarious! Guard safe our Geoge!   [*1932*]

H. G. Wells

ANSWER TO PRAYER

Written at the time of the Abdication of Edward VIII

THE Archbishop was perplexed by his own state of mind. Maybe the shadow of age was falling upon him, he thought, maybe he had been overworking, maybe the situation had been too complex for him and he was feeling the reality of a failure without seeing it plainly as a definable fact. But his nerve, which had never failed him hitherto, was failing him now. In small things as in important matters he no longer showed the quick decisiveness that had hitherto been the envy of his fellow ecclesiastics and the admiration of his friends. He doubted now before he went upstairs or downstairs, with a curious feeling that he might find something unexpected on the landing. He hesitated before he rang a bell, with a vague uncertainty of who or what might appear. Before he took up the letters his secretary had opened for him he had a faint twinge of apprehension.

Had he after all done something wrong or acted in a mistaken spirit?

People who had always been nice to him showed a certain coolness, people from whom he would have least expected it. His secretaries, he knew, were keeping back "open letters" and grossly abusive comments. The reassurances and encouragements that flowed in to him were anything but reassuring, because their volume and their tone reflected what was hidden from him on the other side. Had he, at the end of his long, tortuous and hitherto quite dignified career, made a howler?

There was no one on earth to whom he could confide his trouble. He had always been a man who kept his own counsel. But now, if only he could find understanding, sympathy, endorsement! If he could really put things as he saw them, if he could simplify the whole confused affair down to essentials and make his stand plain and clear.

Prayer?

If anyone else had come to him in this sort of quandary, he would have told him at once to pray. If it was a woman he would have patted the shoulder gently, as an elderly man may do, and he would have said very softly in that rich kind voice of his, "Try Prayer, my dear. Try Prayer."

Physician heal thyself. Why not try prayer?

He stood hesitatingly between his apartments and his little private oratory. He stood in what was his habitual children's-service attitude with his hands together in front of him, his head a little on one side and something faintly bland and whimsical about him. It came to him that he himself had not made a personal and particular appeal to God for many years. It had seemed unnecessary. It had indeed been unnecessary. He had of course said his prayers with the utmost regularity, not only in the presence of others, but, being essentially an honest man, even when he was alone. He had never cheated about prayer. He had felt it was a purifying and beneficial process, no more to be missed than cleaning his teeth, but his sense of a definite hearer, listening at the other end of the telephone, so to speak, behind the veil, had always been a faint one. The reception away there was in the Absolute, in Eternity, beyond the stars. Which indeed left the church conveniently free to take an unembarrassed course of action. . . .

But in this particular tangle, the Archbishop wanted something more definite. If for once, he did not trouble about style and manner. . . .

If he put the case simply, quite simply, just as he saw it, and remained very still on his knees, wouldn't he presently find this neuralgic fretting of his mind abating, and that assurance, that clear self-assurance that had hitherto been his strength, returning to him? He must not be in the least oily—they had actually been calling him oily—he must be perfectly direct and simple and fearless. He must pray straightforwardly to the silence as one mind to another.

It was a little like the practice of some Dissenters and Quakers, but maybe it would be none the less effective on that account.

Yes, he would pray.

Slowly he sank to his knees and put his hands together. He was touched by a sort of childish trustfulness in his own attitude. "Oh God," he began, and paused.

He paused, and a sense of awful imminence, a monstrous awe, gripped him. And then he heard a voice.

It was not a harsh voice, but it was a clear strong voice. There was nothing about it still or small. It was neither friendly nor hostile; it was brisk.

"*Yes*," said the voice. "*What is it?*"

They found His Grace in the morning. He had slipped off the steps on which he had been kneeling and lay, sprawling on the crimson carpet. Plainly his death had been instantaneous.

But instead of the serenity, the almost fatuous serenity, that was his habitual expression, his countenance, by some strange freak of nature, displayed an extremity of terror and dismay.

[*1937*]

E. M. Forster

LANDOR AT SEA

I STROVE with none, for none was worth my strife;
    Reason I loved, and, next to Reason, Doubt;
I warmed both hands before the fire of life;
    And put it out.   [*1938*]

Raymond Mortimer

BISHOPS

I AM one of the diminishing band who dearly love a bishop.
And are they not remarkably imposing, in gilt frames on the
linenfold panelling of College Halls, the Prelates of the Establishment, girt in the billowing majesty of rochet and chimere?
One may perhaps sometimes be reminded—how inappropri-
ately!—of glorious specimens of trout or salmon, preserved,
for their superior size, by the art of the taxidermist; for these
spiritual peers have an uncommonly well-fed look. And well
they might have, since their revenues were princely. They
could not compete, of course, with the Prince-Bishops of the
Continent. Lambeth and Farnham cut a poor figure in comparison with Würzburg or Saverne, and I think no English
prelate boasted a hunt of his own as well as an official mistress,
like the Rohan Cardinal-Archbishop of Strasbourg. But Winchester carried with it £50,000 a year, in days when money
went farther than it does now, and a Bishop of Derry could
be for twenty-five years an absentee from his diocese, spending
his stipend on Continental travel and bogus Old Masters.

*   *   *   *   *   *

In the nineteenth century the Bishoprics were less frequently
accaparated by the cadets of the great ruling families, and more
regard was had to the appearances of piety. Had not the
French Revolution exposed open irreligion as a grave danger
to property? But the Bishops remained very rich—and very
conservative. By voice and vote they resisted every possible
reform, such as Catholic Emancipation, the admission of Dissenters to the University, the Jews' Disabilities Bills, the Great
Reform Bill, successive attempts to repeal the Corn Laws, and
Home Rule Bills. Humane legislation, so long as it did not
affect the landed interest, did not usually excite their violent
antagonism: they were content to absent themselves, much to
Lord Shaftesbury's indignation. But they voted against abolish-
ing the death penalty for theft, and, of course, against the

opening of museums on Sunday. Indeed it is difficult to discover any reform, until recently, in which they took an active
part. Can one wonder that Carlyle called them "stupid, fetid
animals in cauliflower wigs and clean lawn sleeves, Bishops, I
say, of the Devil—not of God—obscure creatures, parading between men's eyes and the eternal Light of Heaven"? All that
is now changed. Gone are the princely incomes, the princely
palaces are meagrely maintained or put to other uses, the
tables no longer groan under massy viands, the cellars are
widowed of their ancient wines. The last Bishop, I think, to
boast of noble blood has lately died, and even the traditional
glories of classical scholarship are feebly represented on the
Episcopal bench. Our Bishops are become administrators,
Marthas too much burdened with diocesan business to linger
over the fine points of an Eclogue or even of a Burgundy. A
Chichester, who can write, and write admirably, a vast
biography, is almost unique. Even the delights of controversy
are smothered in the press of keeping solvent a Church with
diminishing returns. A Birmingham, believing less than has been
customary for Bishops, may feel obliged to attack those of his
poorer clergy who have the temerity to believe too much, but
the Bench as a whole has wisely accepted the comprehensive-
ness of the Establishment, and agree that the Prayer Book with
its Catholic Liturgy and Protestant Articles was designed to
include a variety of beliefs. It is now almost as safe (except in
so far as preferment is concerned) to adore the Sacrament as
to question the Divinity of Christ. And with decreased revenues
has come a decreasing conservatism: there is probably not a
Bishop in the House who does not deplore the political record
of his predecessors. They are anxious now in the interest of
better housing, of democracy, of peace. But while their en-
lightenment has expanded, their influence and stature have
dwindled. How many Bishops are there whose names even are
known to the general public? But the prelates of the nineteenth
century were among the most curious figures of that enigmatic
age. Consider the frigid Howley, the pugnacious Phillpotts,
the logical Whately, the politic Blomfield, the eloquent Magee,
the learned Stubbs, the adroit and humane Wilberforce, the
devout King, the intellectual Creighton, the apostolic Selwyn,
the erastian Tate, the ceremonious Benson, the autocratic

Temple, the sagacious Davidson—they are men salient by their energy and singularized by their characters. The inevitable contest between the ideals of the Gospel and the requirements of ecclesiastical statesmanship gives to their lives a peculiar and ironic interest. The contest, it is true, was usually unconscious, for awkward scruples may well find a sedative in the exquisite atmosphere of an English cathedral. The silvery intoning of Minor Canons and the dulcet concent of choir and organ purify the Liturgy from any over-urgent meaning; in so general a manner and so sonorous a prose do we confess our sins that they scarcely seem sinful; and the flawlessly performed ceremonial, stripped of the symbolism that gives to the most pompous Roman function an awful significance, seems designed to transport us into an ideally comfortable world, where there is nothing disquieting, unseemly or actual.

*   *   *   *   *   *

The life of a great Victorian Bishop has lately been written by an American member of his family.[1] Born in 1797, the son of a curate, he was comparable in precocity with J. S. Mill, for he read Latin at three, Greek at four, and when he was eleven a volume of his verses, moral tales and sermons was published which enjoyed very favourable notice. Charterhouse, Trinity, Cambridge, and a Continental tour during which he came under the influence of Baron Bunsen continued his education. He was called to the Bar, and showed his interest in advanced biblical criticism by translating Schleiermacher's *Luke*. In 1827 he was ordained, in order to retain his Trinity fellowship, and returned to the College, where he guided the steps of Monckton Milnes, and the first "Apostles", Tennyson, Hallam, Stanley and Maurice. Unorthodox, and at this time only dubiously a Christian, he was inspired by a fiery love neither of God nor of his fellow-men: he merely required leisure to write. "Society", he explained, "possesses two or three strong stiff frames, in which all persons of liberal education who need and desire a fixed place and specific designation must consent to be set." This view of the Church as a gentlemanly career was not unusual, but soon he gave real ground for complaint. A pamphlet in favour of the admission of Dis-

[1] *Connop Thirlwall* by John Connop Thirlwall, Jr.

senters to the University, in which he attacked compulsory
chapel, infuriated the orthodox. Christopher Wordsworth, the
Master of Trinity, demanded his resignation with what
Macaulay called "unutterable baseness and dirtiness". Thirlwall obeyed, but was swiftly rewarded by the Whig Government with a rich living, and devoted himself to writing a
history of Greece. (Grote was simultaneously at work on the
same task, and the respective merits of the two histories were
energetically canvassed. To-day they appear almost equally
unreadable.) In 1840 Melbourne gave Thirlwall the Bishopric
of St. Davids, to the consternation of conservative churchmen.
He was a good scholar in Latin, Greek, Hebrew, German,
Dutch, Italian, French, Spanish and Portuguese, and now he
learnt Welsh, the first occupant of his See since the Reformation
to attempt this necessary task.

                *   *   *   *   *   *

His biographer admirably sums up his career:

Practical irony dominated Thirlwall's life as it filled his writings.
He was morally forced into the four "frames of society" which he
filled. Hating the law, he studied it for six years; contemptuous of
the clerical profession, he took Orders to teach at Cambridge; not
designed for parochial work, he was given a fat benefice after his
expulsion from Cambridge: Liberal in politics and unorthodox in
theology, he was induced to abandon all his scholarly productivity
for a bishopric in the National Church.

In his earlier years he seems to have seen in Christianity little
more than the philosophy of his favourite Cicero purveyed in
a form more effective and possibly more refined. And he never
attained any feeling for the mysteries of the Faith. (But I think,
from his writings, that he later came sincerely to a more
definite churchmanship than his biographer allows.) Thus
admirably suited to the Established Church of the eighteenth
century, he found himself rather isolated in his own time. As
a diocesan he was unsuccessful. The Welsh clergy and parish-
ioners were unintellectual, ungentlemanly, and often drunk.
"His horror of the manners of his flock soon grew into a horror
of their persons, and, brutally frank as he was, he took small
pains to conceal his contempt." The story went that the
Bishop was accompanied by a large dog trained to know and

bite curates. Freezing and repellent to men who did not share
his intellectual interests, he was devoted to animals and children,
and walked out in the harshest weather to feed his favourite
geese. The last years of his life were sweetened by a friendship
with a charming and accomplished girl, Miss Betha Johnes,
and a selection of his letters to her, edited after his death by
Dean Stanley under the title, *Letters to a Friend*, may be recommended as remarkably agreeable reading to anyone interested
in the Victorian *Stimmung*. He never married; almost the
only personage to excite him to passionate admiration was
Alexander the Great; and the Bishop of Winchester wrote of
him that "for all the vast power and intellect which he possessed, and that habit of speaking strongly which he sometimes
exhibited, his heart showed all the feelings, almost the sensitiveness, of a woman". Above all, his was the saving, if unchristian,
grace of irony. The story remains of a dinner-party at which
his neighbour had to repeat some banal remarks several times
before it penetrated to Thirlwall's failing ears. "When the
Bishop finally grasped the remark, he dignified it by remarking
sotto voce, 'Strange, how little one loses by being deaf!' "

* * * * * *

Thirlwall succeeded the casual Bathurst and anticipated the
strenuous Percival, as a solitary supporter of Liberalism on
the Bench of Bishops. Alone among them he supported in
1845 the Maynooth Grant; alone he voted in 1869 for the
Disestablishment of the Irish Church. His maiden speech in
1841 was in favour of the admission of Jews to civil rights,
and he was more tolerant than most of his fellows even of
the Tractarians, though he voted for Dizzy's foolish Public
Worship Regulation Act. Mr. Gladstone, despite his detesta-
tion of Latitudinarianism, declared that his was "one of the
most masculine, powerful, and luminous intellects that have
for generations been known among the Bishops of England".
The annual charges with which he bewildered the bucolic
clergy of his diocese were widely prized as the most weighty
and thoughtful of episcopal utterances. They are read now
by only the most determined of antiquaries. The tolerance
that was the positive contribution of Broad Churchmen like
Thirlwall, Stanley, Arnold and Hare, has triumphed, though

they are disqualified for the sympathy of most Anglicans by their blindness to the poetry and pragmatic efficacy of the traditional Christian mysteries. What Thirlwall would have considered superstition has proved more fruitful in works than his respectable rationalism. And Bishops, who outdo him in Latitudinarianism, are now happy to be censed and to vest themselves in mitre and cope or even chasuble. This scholarly, well-written and well-proportioned *Life* of Thirlwall therefore appears (as indeed did Thirlwall himself) fifty years too late. Lancelot and Pelleas and Pellenore are hardly more remote from us than Hoadly and Harcourt, Phillpotts and Thirlwall. But does not this remoteness lend to the majesty of lawn sleeves a new and as it were romantic charm? Mrs. Proudie in her crinoline is evidently picturesque, and I suggest to Mr. Ashton that he make a ballet of *Barchester Towers*. Now, when the literature of escape is more than ever necessary, how soothing to take refuge among faded controversies in the company of these extinct but thoughtful, vigorous, and dignified mammoths.   [*1936*]

Michael Roberts

NOTE ON θ, ϕ AND ψ

WHEREAS my lady loves to look
On learned manuscript and book,
Still must she scorn, and scorning sigh,
To think of those I profit by.

Plotinus now, or Plutarch is
A prey to her exegesis,
And while she labours to collate
A page, I grasp a postulate,

And find for one small world of fact
Invariant matrices, compact
Within the dark and igneous rock
Of *Comptes Rendus* or *Proc. Roy. Soc.*

She'll pause a learned hour, and then
Pounce with a bird-like acumen
Neatly to annotate the dark
Of halting sense with one remark;

While I, maybe, precisely seize
The elusive photon's properties
In α's and δ's, set in bronze-
bright vectors, grim quaternions.

Silent we'll sit. We'll not equate
Symbols too plainly disparate,
But hand goes out to friendly hand
That mind and mind may understand

How one same passion burned within
Each learned peer and paladin,
Her Bentley and her Scaliger,
My Heisenberg and Schrödinger.   [*1935*]

W. J. Turner

BACH

THE golden age of music may be said to have concluded with
Brahms, who died in 1897. I fix the death of Brahms as a finger-
post in musical history marking the dividing of ways, not
because Brahms was the "austere classicist" most encyclo-
paedias and works of reference represent him to be, but because
he was soaked in the old German religious tradition. Again, I
use the word "religious" without reference to any particular
creed or faith, but as signifying an emotional attitude towards
life, namely, the emotional feeling that all men are brothers
and that man is a spirit. This attitude has often been called the
Christian attitude, but since it is not peculiar to Christianity it
is preferable to call it the religious attitude.

B

Now Bach, Beethoven, Brahms and, surprising as it may seem, even Wagner were saturated with this spirit. Bach was the most orthodox and least personal in his belief. To him man was infinitely the most important creature on this planet. In fact, it is doubtful whether he ever even contemplated the fact that man lived upon a planet and a small planet at that; certainly it was no part of his consciousness that man was the cleverest and most successful of the mammals. Historically, that conception had not yet dawned upon the world. To Bach man was the direct creation of God; he had free will, the choice of good and evil, and alone of all the creatures of this world he partook of the Divine spirit. In other words, each man was a dusty envelope, a "veil of flesh", clothing a divine soul, and was in consequence infinitely important.

Although a Lutheran Protestant brought up in the pious atmosphere of South German family life, Bach had more than a touch of genial vivacity. That he had enormous vitality needs no proof beyond his music, but there are his two wives and his numerous children as an additional testimony. There is also the fact that his eldest son, Wilhelm Friedemann, had a touch of genius and that his second son, Carl Philip Emmanuel, was a quite exceptionally gifted musician. But vitality does not necessarily mean gaiety or vivacity; in the early Bach, however, there was a spark of gaiety, as may be seen from the complaint made by the consistory of the church at Arnstadt, that he "bewildered the congregation by many strange sounds", that his preludes were too long, and that, when remonstrated with, he had made them too short, that he went to a wine shop during the sermon, that he had not had any choir practices, and that a "strange lady" had been admitted into the choir and had been allowed to "make music".

It must be added that he was only twenty-one when this indictment was drawn up and that as he grew older he became more and more serious, until his personality became well-nigh submerged in that profound solemnity which stares at us from his portraits. This solemnity, this heavy, portentous seriousness which settled upon his genius like a cloud was, I imagine, the result of that Protestant environment on a man of musical genius, tremendous vitality, but of little spiritual originality. It has been the custom during the last hundred

years all over the civilized world to think of Bach as a great
religious composer. The Protestant churches of Europe and
America, fortified by assurances from the highest professional
authorities as to his purely musical genius, have united in
struggling to perform some part of that cataract of cantatas
and motets which flowed from Bach's pen with the "monotonous periodicity of a Sunday sermon", and on festival
occasions have struggled with his John or Matthew Passions or
his B minor Mass. This attitude to Bach persists to-day. It
culminated in the late Sir Hubert Parry's book, which is full
of such passages as:

The cantate *Herr, wie Du willt*, is a very remarkable example of
the depth of insight which is so often shown in Bach's musical
interpretation of words. If superficially interpreted these particular
words may be seen to be beset with pitfalls. They do indeed actually
suggest an incomplete submission to the Divine will as the soul is
made to express itself in the words, "Ach! aber ach! wie viel lässt
mich dein Wille leiden", etc. The danger obviously is to accentuate
the harshness of "the Lord's will" in order to enhance the credit
of submission. In the text each pair of lines of the hymn relating
to the Divine will is followed by a passage in which the soul in a
sort of aside expresses its real opinion. Therefore, if the words
were quite frankly interpreted in musical terms, they would express
but a formal and superficial submission. Bach had in a sense to
accept the situation which was provided for him and to write in a
minor mode rather than the major, which would have expressed
more frankly the loyal and unstinted submission to the will of the
Supreme Being whose wisdom passes all understanding. . . . To
suggest the insignificance of the human creature in relation to
the Divine will, the music is at first confined to the highest part
of the scale, the bass being supplied by violins and violas pizzicato.

Now, my first instinct is to translate the words, "Ach! aber
ach! wie viel lässt mich dein Wille leiden" into an ironic "My
goodness! how much thy will lets me suffer", which is enough
to show how different is the modern spirit. We have not got
in the twentieth century that calm assurance that we know
exactly what the Divine will demands of us which the eighteenth-century Protestant Christians had. We—I am speaking
of people who have an inner activity of their own, and are
not mere imitators of the activity of others, past or present—
are, probably, not even sure that there is a Divine will, but we

are certain that any Divine will that we can make contact with
is infinitely more complicated and more difficult to understand
than that referred to by the authors of the words of Bach's
cantatas. But Bach set these German hymns to music without
any apparent consciousness of their painful inadequacy as an
expression of the spirit. Parry admits that Bach's Leipzig
cantatas were in many cases less interesting than his earlier
works; he even stumbles surprisingly near a perception of
what was lacking when he suggests in explanation that Bach
was accommodating himself to the "necessity of addressing
people who had somewhat lost touch with the primitive poetry
of religion". Here several points immediately suggest themselves. First, it is not the business of a great composer to accom-
modate himself to any audience. Secondly, what Parry so mis-
leadingly calls the "primitive poetry of religion" is just "religion", that is all. For either religion is an activity of the spirit,
i.e. "poetry", or it is a perfunctory imitation of that activity,
a collection of formulae or dogma, a "mumbo-jumbo" intellectually remembered and publicly jabbered on Sundays with
"monotonous periodicity".

Now, when I said that Bach seemed to me a composer of
great vitality but of little spiritual originality, this is what I
meant. Those Lutheran Christians were a vigorous stock: they
could listen to immensely long sermons and cantatas with a
dogged indifference to physical distress. This indifference to the
weariness of the body may be regarded—has been regarded—
as a triumph of spirit over matter, but it is just my point that
their spirituality consisted of no more than this and that they
imposed it intellectually upon themselves.

Their religious activity was an "imitation", and, like all
imitations, materialistic; so it is noteworthy that when Bach
shows some sign of life in his religious music it is when he is
personally touched by some everyday human sentiment. Parry,
speaking of the superiority of the St. Matthew Passion to the
bulk of the cantatas, says that the theme with which the music
deals is the brotherhood of man:

It sets aside the glamour of Divine origin and appeals to men's
hearts direct, to look upon the story of unsurpassable human
goodness, patience, endurance, loving-kindness and suffering, to
dwell upon every moment of it and set it before mankind as the

highest state to which mankind can attain, redeeming humanity itself by the proof of its supreme possibilities of selflessness, and winning the title to divinity by a life and death which surpassed all the experiences of mankind.

This, after the first sensible distinction, is a fair sample of the shallow, sentimental gush which gets written by clever men of religious instincts but of no creative religious originality. It is shallow gush because it will not stand the test of the experience which a profound mind can bring to it. We moderns will not accept complete selflessness, complete self-sacrifice as the ideal expression of the human spirit. The story which Parry sets before us as "the highest state to which mankind can attain", we will accept as an expression of a precious truth, but not as the whole truth. Now, I maintain that Bach's religious music is, from the religious point of view, shallow because it is a mere perfunctory adornment of a religion, not the expression of a fresh religious activity.

A religion is a dead religious activity, mummified and preserved as a method of spiritual life which those who have no spiritual life can imitate. In this sense alone is Bach's church music religious. It is admirable in its perfunctory imitation, but whenever it is alive it is just expressing the ordinary feelings of human animals towards one another. But Parry was quite right in selecting Bach's "religious" music as necessarily his greatest. The modern reaction against the spiritual is really a reaction against the sham spiritual, against humbug. It does not in the least succeed in satisfying me with the jazz-music of Stravinsky or the sensual bravura of negro sculpture. That sort of thing can give all unprejudiced people pleasure, but only half-developed erotic women (and men) will find it satisfying. If, however, we are incapable of genuine original religious activity, if we are spiritually numb, far better enjoy what live faculties we have got than deceive ourselves with sentimentalism and moral and humanitarian heroics. There is no harm in admiring Bach's Cantatas and Passions, Wagner's *Parsifal* and Puccini's *Madam Butterfly*, so long as we keep our tongue in our cheek. There is even virtue in recognizing that Bach had more intellectual and emotional power than an infinite number of Puccinis and Stravinskys. But Bach a great religious composer! Oh, dear no! [*1922*]

H. N. Brailsford

THE GOLDEN BOUGH

THE news of Sir James Frazer's death brought to many of us who
have reached middle life, or passed it, a painful nostalgia. Once
upon a time there was an era when men could speculate on the
origins of religion and the infancy of the human mind in the
profound calm of a continent that believed it had attained
civilization. To-day, as we recall it, it is as if we were dragging
the mangled corpse of a parent from the rubble and debris of
our ancestral home. In those days the only Germans with whom
we reckoned were such men as Haeckel, whose entrancing
volumes stood beside Darwin's on our shelves, or that pioneering
scholar, Mannhardt, whose work Frazer continued to such purpose. The old man is gone, burdened with years and honours,
his work rounded and complete, and over his grave we must
struggle with barbarians for the right to think and speculate
with free minds. He knew, as he often said, that the primitive
savage whose thinking he traced in our still surviving supersti-
tions is alive in the dark places of our hearts. That savage has
armed himself with wings and high explosives and our worst
peril is that when we hear his war-cry in the enemy tongue it
may awaken an echo in our own.

To his own generation and the next, Frazer was much more
than a great scientist who endeared himself to us by the humanity and the literary grace of his style. Under the dry reserve of
his shy Scottish manner there lay concealed a gift of imaginative
sympathy that was for ever performing its miracles by penetrating the ways of thought of hairy Ainus and Australian black-
fellows, while it moved as if it were at home, in spite of its
Calvinist ancestry, amid the gracious paganism of Hellenes and
Syrians. "Without poetry and tenderness," as he once wrote,
"it is impossible to form a true understanding of the human
mind and its creations." With all his scholarly restraint, and that
formidable patience which never wearied in the collection of
facts, half of Frazer, as he said of his master Renan, was a

romantic Celt. With a plodding industry that no Teutonic
scholar ever surpassed, he managed to combine an artist's sense
of form, and even when it grew into twelve big volumes, packed
with innumerable notes, *The Golden Bough* moved from the in-
triguing question of its opening pages to the triumphant solu-
tion in its last book with a sureness and grace that resembled
rather a musical composition in strict sonata form than a scientific treatise.

We read this great book with insatiable curiosity and un-
flagging pleasure, but there were solider reasons than these for
our gratitude. The rationalism of the Mid-Victorian Age had
never been happy or at ease in its rejection of revealed religion.
A haunting sense of guilt dogged it, even while it battled bravely
for its intellectual freedom. It felt that its agnosticism was a sort
of parricide. That was inevitable so long as our rationalistic
convictions were the fruit of a bitter controversy, won by
denials, revolts and exposures, that had raged from Voltaire's
day to Darwin's. When at length we read *The Golden Bough* the
dust of the battle settled, and with the serenity that comes only
from scientific method religious beliefs took their place among
other natural phenomena, as a subject for dispassionate investigation. Frazer knew very well what he was doing, but with
confident tact he left his readers to draw their own conclusions.
Long before we reached the end of the book, the creed and
mythology which had once seemed to us unique in their impera-
tive appeal to our flagging capacity for faith, had taken their
due place as one manifestation among many of an all but universal cult, which had its origins neither in Judaea nor in
revelation, but in the first efforts of primitive man to influence
by magic for his own immediate ends the seasons and the stars
in their courses, the bounty of vegetation and the fertility of his
flocks. Why the god must be slain and why it was an obligation to
partake of his flesh was theological mystery no longer, but an
intelligible fact in the life-history of agricultural peoples. Frazer
contrived to do his work without arousing in any embarrassing
degree the fury of the fundamentalists, yet to none of the libera-
tors do we owe a greater debt. He did for our time what Lucre-
tius did for his; he emancipated us from the most crushing form
of fear. As the sense of oppression lifted, our indignation and our
partisan resentments vanished also. In Frazer's words we could

feel "the tender charm of the idols which our poor human species had so long cherished as its gods".

It would be difficult to exaggerate the influence of this man's life-work upon his own generation and the next. He pushed back history several thousands of years. If the primitive farmers who grew their grain as a daring experiment on irrigated terraces beside their megaliths left no written records, we could now guess what hopes and anxieties and quasi-scientific reckonings occupied their thoughts. We had a clue to the ideas that dominated our own ancestors when they hewed a way through the primeval forests towards the seashore and this island. We could now hear and distinguish the overtones of obsolete belief just audible in the vocabulary even of our modern languages. This work of Frazer's on what he called "mental anthropology" was doubly fruitful because at the same time the archaeologists were uncovering for us the stones and the paintings of these same primitive men whose thought Frazer was reconstructing by inference from the contemporary ideologies of the South Seas and the African bush. Primitive man was an hypothesis no longer: we can visit his picture galleries in the caves of the Dordogne and the Pyrenees. Men gained in this brilliant generation a new sense of the continuity and intelligibility of human life. Darwin, whose disciple and continuer Frazer felt himself to be, had traced the origins and the evolution of our physical body: he gave us the record of our mental growth. He consciously used the same comparative method, and with Marx and Freud he ranks only after the founder of modern biology among the influences which have fixed the thinking of our day.

Criticism, needless to say, has been busy on Frazer's work, its assumptions, its limitations, its methods and its results. His interest in ritual was always slighter than his interest in myth, yet ritual is certainly the more fundamental of these two. He ignored almost entirely the play of economic motive in the shaping of primitive society, a gap which Malinowski and others are filling. The schools of Freud and Jung are now offering their interpretations of symbol and myth with disturbing results as yet difficult to estimate. The comparative method, as Frazer followed it, had its pitfalls, for it was dangerous to tear fragments of mythology and custom out of the rich context in which they stood. The "primitive man" whose ways of thought he investigated was an abstract and hypothetical being, who never in fact existed. The inevitable reaction set in with the encouragement of scientific field work. Frazer was the typical sedentary scholar who had travelled only in his library, pillaging all the records from Herodotus and Plutarch to the early Jesuits and his contemporary Bishop Codrington. To-day it is the concrete individuality, the peculiarity of each separate primitive society that Franz Boas and Ruth Benedict have emphasized, until they have almost ceased to generalize or to search for any connecting threads in the rich variety of their discoveries. From another angle Rivers and the diffusionists challenged the assumption which Frazer inherited from Tylor —that if the thinking and institutions of primitive societies the world over reveal startling similarities, the explanation must be sought solely in the identical working of the human mind. If the anthropologists of the last century had known all that we now know about the possibility of navigation in primitive times, they would have been less sceptical about the diffusion of early cultures. As Professor Childe has put it, the Megalithic Cult was a missionary church which carried its beliefs and rites round the world with its colossal architecture. The comparative method, as Frazer used it, painted flatly in two dimensions. Rivers brought into it the factor of history and time: here he traced migration and conquest ,there degeneration, oblivion and decay. In short, the science that Frazer did so much to shape is still a living body of thought, with its fashions and its rivalries, its fresh tendencies and its experimental lines of development. But however it may grow, the immense mass of Frazer's creative work will remain its proudest classic. If here and there he was mistaken, if on this doubtful detail or the other his guess has been discarded, the substance of his argument stands erect among the noblest scientific monuments of a century that knew how to build in the grand manner.   [*1941*]

C. Day Lewis

YOU THAT LOVE ENGLAND

You that love England, who have an ear for her music,
The slow movement of clouds in benediction,
Clear arias of light thrilling over her uplands,
Over the chords of summer sustained peacefully;
Ceaseless the leaves' counterpoint in a west wind lively,
Blossom and river rippling loveliest allegro,
And the storms of wood strings brass at year's finale:
Listen. Can you not hear the entrance of a new theme?

You who go out alone, on tandem, or on pillion,
Down arterial roads riding in April,
Or sad beside lakes where hill-slopes are reflected
Making fires of leaves, your high hopes fallen:
Cyclists and hikers in company, day excursionists,
Refugees from cursed towns and devastated areas;
Know you seek a new world, a saviour to establish
Long-lost kinship and restore the blood's fulfilment.

You who like peace, good sticks, happy in a small way
Watching birds or playing cricket with schoolboys,
Who pay for drinks all round, whom disaster chose not;
Yet passing derelict mills and barns roof-rent,
Where despair has burnt itself out, hearts at a standstill—
Who suffer loss, aware of lowered vitality:
We can tell you a secret, offer a tonic; only
Submit to the visiting angel, the strange new healer.

You above all who have come to the far end, victims
Of a rundown machine, who can bear it no longer;
Whether in easy chairs chafing at impotence,
Or against hunger, bullies and spies preserving
The nerve for action, the spark of indignation—
Need fight in the dark no more, you know your enemies;
You shall be leaders when zero hour is signalled,
Wielders of power and welders of a new world.   [*1932*]

32

H. E. Bates

ON THE ROAD

THE wood was flooded with April sunlight, but shallow pools of rain lay wherever there were hollows in the black earth under the oak trees. Black rings of ashes were dotted about the ground where tramps had made their fires and rested, and primroses were blooming everywhere at the feet of young hazel trees. The wind that blew the hazels with a soft sound one against another was sweet and warm and laden with the scent of the primroses. It was like the breath of a new life.

A man came into the wood from the road and strode a hundred paces into it at random among the hazel trees. He was tall and black-haired and powerfully broad at the shoulders; he carried himself superbly, with a slight swagger of his hips, holding his head high up, and sometimes throwing it slightly backward, with unconscious motions of arrogance and pride. He looked less like a tramp than a fighter, but less like a fighter than some proud, sardonic Indian. His face was muscular and powerful, the skin was burnt tough and dry by the sun, and there was a glimpse of a tattoo mark of a purple and crimson flower on his naked chest. He was dressed in light brown trousers, a black jacket slung over his shoulder, a soft grey hat and a blue shirt faded and washed to the colour of the sky. He stood and nicked off a primrose with a finger-nail and put the flower in his mouth. He was looking for a place to rest.

He took another twenty paces into the wood and saw the white smoke of a fire among the trees. He stopped and gazed at the smoke for one moment and then walked on. In another moment he came upon a woman and man sitting by the fire on a space of earth between a sallow-bush and an oak tree. The man was asleep, with his head against the oak tree, and the woman was boiling a can of water on a heap of smoking wood. He saw a black bundle on the earth and an old perambulator pushed back against the sallow.

He stood perfectly still and gazed at the woman without a flicker of his dark eyes. She was dressed in a short black skirt and an old stained orange-coloured jersey stretched as tight as skin over her big breasts and shoulders. Her hair was very thick and blonde, and there was something about her that recalled a lioness: the tawny eyes sleepy and rich with changing lights, the lips ripe and heavy, the large strong face superb with its passionate languor. She had a newspaper open on her knees, but she put it down on the earth as he looked at her. Her hands were strong and handsome, and the skin was a beautiful golden colour, smooth and with tiny blonde hairs that gleamed in the sunshine.

"Sit down," she said. She waved her hand. There were no rings on her fingers. Her voice was low, and careless and husky.

He looked at the man lying with his head against the oak tree. She half-smiled.

"He's asleep," she said. "He's all right. You won't wake him."

He sat down on the black earth. He sat so that he could see both the man and the woman at one glance. In an instant he saw astounding differences between them. The man was haggard and white, and the bones of his cheeks stood out clear and sharp as knuckles under his dark eyes. His face was dirty and dissolute and strengthless, and he lay like a man who had received a stunning blow, his closed eyes dark as two deep bruises under his narrow brows. He looked as if he would never wake again, and the woman looked at him with one hasty glance of indifference as if not caring whether he woke or not.

The water in the can began to bubble, and the woman slipped a stick under the handle and took the can from the fire. The man leaned across without hesitation and quickly shook something brown from a packet into the water.

"You're very smart," she flashed, looking up. "What was that?"

He leaned over and stirred the water with the stick, which he took from her own hands. "Coffee."

He spoke the word with the primrose in his mouth, and then leaned back and took the flower from his mouth and spat away an inch of bitten stalk and put it back again. There was something about the paleness of the primrose against his dark face that made him doubly arresting.

They stared at each other in silence, their eyes languid and bold and unflickering.

"Where are you making for?" he asked suddenly.

"Liverpool," she said.

He looked at the perambulator. Then he glanced at her shoes. He noticed for the first time her blistered feet through the soles. He looked at her sharply.

"You're a hell of a way from Liverpool. A hell of a way," he said.

She did not answer. The smell of the coffee was strong in the wood, and there was no sound except the whistling of a blackbird and the bees booming softly in the yellow dusty sallow blooms. She reached over to the bundle and brought out two blue enamel cups and poured out the coffee and handed a cup to him.

"No sugar," she said in a languid voice.

He fumbled at his pocket and brought out a packet of yellow sugar, and set it on the earth between them and nodded towards the sleeping man.

"Going to wake him?" he said.

She crooked her elbow and smiled ironically and took a deep drink of her coffee.

"Like a fish," she said.

He nodded and looked at the thin white face more closely. It seemed very young.

"Twenty-five," she said. "And he was a fine kid. But now——" She laid her two hands just above her breasts and shook her head.

The man took the primrose from his mouth and threw it on the earth and began to drink his coffee. The sunshine came warmly down on his face, and as he tilted back his head he felt the intent and sleepy gaze of the woman on his face too.

"Where are you going yourself?" she said.

He finished drinking and wiped his lips and stared at her, boldly admiring her.

"I want to get to Bristol and find a ship and get to Valparaiso," he said. "I'm sick of this country. I used to know a man in Valparaiso; I made some money there at one time."

She nodded her head and took another drink of her coffee, and repeated thoughtfully:

"Valparaiso."

He drained his coffee and spat the grounds from his mouth and leaned back on one elbow. The place where they were sitting was for a space of a foot or two without shadow, and the spring sunshine poured full on the woman's head, so that her hair seemed more than ever golden and the strength and passion in her face finer in the yellow light. The old orange jersey had a row of buttons at the breast, but the first was missing and the second had slipped from its buttonhole. Her breast gleamed soft and fair against the dirty orange stuff, and half-unconsciously her hand moved and she did up the button afresh. But when her hand dropped back to her knees the swelling of her breast burst it apart again.

"What's it like in a place like Valparaiso?" she said suddenly.

"You know as well as I do."

She nodded.

"If the good God just thinks fit it can be wonderful. In one month in Valparaiso I made five hundred pounds. And easy, too. I made it too easy. I wasn't satisfied. I thought I could go down to Buenos Aires and make a lot more. I lost every penny in a fortnight. Then I went up to Panama and on to Cuba and over to San Francisco. I made a bit of money sometimes, but I could never keep it long. Now I want to get back to Valparaiso. But if things go wrong I daresay I shall want to get back here again."

His voice was deep and easy, and there was something nonchalant and ironical and dreamy about his words. The woman sat watching him with an expression of undisguised intensity, contemplating his dark face with a marvellous steadiness of her sleepy eyes, lost in thought; she seemed in that moment extraordinarily young, her face transformed by a moment of the strangest rapture. She looked at him candidly, enviously, and then suddenly with a glance of full-blooded passion too, her eyes wide and perfectly child-like, her bosom falling and heaving rapidly.

They sat for a moment and watched each other like two animals. His lips gradually assumed a little sardonic smile, but she never changed her expression of marvellous intensity. The sun was warming the primroses and the sallow-bloom, and the air was filled with the soft scents of them, the smell of woodsmoke and the strong odour of earth.

The man beneath the trees stirred suddenly in his sleep and began to breathe heavily, like someone drunk, without waking.

The sound upset the woman. In a moment the fine expression on her face was lost. The sardonic, dreamy smile vanished from the lips of the man too. He stood up.

"I'll push on," he said.

The woman rose to her feet also and stretched her arms over her head with a motion of weariness. In the moment that the orange jersey and the black skirt were pulled skin-tight over her rigid body he saw that she was pregnant.

She lowered her arms with a sigh, her magnificent body all languorous and heavy with its burden of strength and life. She yawned and then smiled at him when she had finished the yawn.

"You're not so very old?" he said.

"Twenty-nine."

"And some," he guessed ironically.

"No," she shook her head. "Twenty-nine."

"I believe you," he said.

He looked straight into her eyes and nodded, thinking for one moment of the sleepy man, the perambulator, her shoes and her pregnancy. She returned his look with some of the old intensity, but now as though she were thinking of something else, very far away.

"Well, I'll get," he said. "What'll you do if you get to Liverpool?"

She lifted her face a fraction towards the sun and shook her head. Instantly he looked as if he regretted bitterly having spoken the words.

"So long. Good luck for Valparaiso," she said.

"So long," he said. "Good luck."

They looked at each other for a single instant and something warm and tender flashed between them before he turned away and began to stride through the wood towards the road.

The wands of hazel trees kept whipping back as he passed, the pollen was shaken from the thick catkins and a golden dust came falling through the beams of sunlight slanting between the trees. The sound of the swaying branches and cracking twigs grew rapidly farther and farther away, and the hazel trees trembled less and less and finally became still again. The woman sat down and rested her face in her hands and stared in thought at the primroses and the sleeping man. The last of the branches swayed to rest in its place again and soon the wood was silent.   [*1931*]

David Garnett

THE DAWN IN BRITAIN

EVERYONE now knows of C. M. Doughty through his prose masterpiece, *Arabia Deserta*, which from being a very rare book has passed into the hands of a large and appreciative public. Knowing *Arabia Deserta*, its readers know Doughty's character, his nobility, his gentleness, his tenderness to all weak creatures, his delight in natural beauty and his deep feeling of common humanity. Of a solitary temper, a student of geology and archaelogy, with an absorbed interest in the history of languages, he went out into the Arabian peninsula where he wandered, poor and ill, at the mercy of every cut-throat robber or crazy fanatic, calling himself a Christian but overcoming the universal Moslem suspicion and hatred of the heathen stranger by his obstinate mildness and his lack of fear, bearing blows and threats, treachery and mal-treatment, as he bore with sickness and hunger until he came through his greatest danger safely, at last, out of the desert to a humane *sherif*, who succoured him and sent him to the coast. His whole mind and attitude to life was changed by this experience and he spent nine years in writing his book which has the whole of Arabia in it, the pilgrimage going down to Mecca from Damascus, the life of the Bedawy in their tents, of the townsmen in the oases, as well as the physical features of the land with its geology and ancient monuments, all told in a personal style, with so rich a vocabulary that the book which is difficult at first, gains with every re-reading. After writing *Arabia Deserta*, Doughty gave up the rest of his life to writing long, pre-Miltonic, narrative poems. They were lucky to find a publisher and found few readers. Edward Garnett, Edward Thomas, W. H. Hudson and I myself, at the age of sixteen, were among the small band who read every word of the six volumes of *The Dawn in Britain*. I rejoiced in such passages as this of the Sea-God:

> In towards the land,
> He turns, with fury, his triple-teamed chariot;
> And tumult great, of rushing wild-waves' spirits;

That ride, as foaming steeds, sea-billows' croups.
And follow (an infinite spume-sprinkling train);
The, on golden axe-trees, rolling, broad divine
Wheels, in wide salt sea-flood, of stormy god;
And play him round, and do on him attend.
Blowing then his sea-children, all, at his
Command, in whelky horns, grave note! he leads,
Vast waters' wall, with plunging foot, on Romans!
Those taken, in angry surges, twixt sharp cliff,
And folding flood, in *turmae* and cohorts, perish!
Ooze covered them, on that deceitful strand.

*   *   *   *   *   *

I used to believe that Doughty's poems would never become
fashionable, or widely known because people would not take
the trouble to accustom themselves to the difficulties of his
language and his syntax. I do not think so now, as I have
learned that people like taking trouble to tease out a writer's
meaning. Joyce is fashionable, though *A Work in Progress* is
written in an invented punning jargon of words with no meaning at all. Doughty's words are all exact. I think now that it is
partly the qualities which brought Doughty alive out of the
desert that have led to his neglect as a poet. Doughty is the most
serene, the least tormented of poets. Though almost as lonely
as Blake, he was spiritually at peace and for that reason has
been neglected by a generation which feels that it has no roots
in the past. Moreover, literary movements are connected with
the political movements of the time. The poetry of the last
fifteen years presents a parallel to the frustrated aspirations
towards a radically different form of society of a generation
that would have liked to abolish national and class differences,
but which has only succeeded in intensifying them. Doughty's
only message was a patriotic one: he foresaw 1914 with
something that seems now like second-sight and two of his
poems, *The Cliffs* (1909) and *The Clouds* (1912) were intended as
trumpet calls to rouse Britain to arms before it was too late:

War will, 'mongst World's new Nations, rage again.
War, hell of man's devising; whence babes are
Made orphans, wives left widows. War shall slay
Five times ten thousand men, the flower of Britain;
In his first days. Then shortly shall be changed;

(Whereof a memory only shall remain;)
Your liberty to Enduring Servitude!
. . . Were they not six times utterly undone?
Vanquished and dispossessed, thralled, servants made,
In this Home Soil, to strange invading enemies?
And, in those fathers's loins, ye yourselves were.
How boasted thou thyself, son of a Jute?

One of the most striking of his prophecies in *The Cliffs* (1909), describes an airship falling in flames on the Suffolk coast and of the burial of the bodies. The visitor to the Saxon church, full of the Doughty family memorials, at Theberton will find the grave of the crew of a German Zeppelin in the churchyard. If the U-boat campaign had been successful and England had been starved into surrender, these patriotic poems would be read with a very different emotion to-day and Doughty would be honoured, not for his prose, but for his weakest poetry.

*   *   *   *   *   *

Two books should do much to attract attention to Doughty's poetry. *Selected Passages from The Dawn in Britain*, arranged, with an Introduction, by Barker Fairley is excellently devised as "a sort of decoy dangled before the running reader" which is exactly what is needed. It is perhaps a pity that Professor Barker Fairley's selections are not taken from the whole body of Doughty's poetry, for *The Dawn in Britain* is the most difficult of the poems as well as the greatest. *Charles M. Doughty, a Study of His Prose and Verse*, by Anne Treneer is a most admirable exposition and valuation of all Doughty's work. It must be confessed that, even when he has grown acclimatized, Doughty's verse may give the reader a shaking-up:

> Stripped of harness,
> She, ah! Ligorix, in the high-starred, ghastful, night;
> Found 'mongst slain corses, fallen all him around.
> Was none there, with her, but a little maid.
> Then, long, they, on her back, great poise, assayed,
> To hoise, such power hath love!

Miss Treneer admits frankly: "There is a demon in Doughty, the demon which seems to lurk about all students of the history of words." It shows itself (in my opinion) because "he hated words which merely indicated relationship", and especially in the habitual omission of the definite article; "'neath dogstar" jolts me like a cruel rider's jerk at the reins. Moreover, as Miss Treneer says: "his wilfulness in twisting the natural word-order of English was his poetic bane". Professor Barker Fairley would not admit this. He sees Doughty not a left-handed or cranky poet who would not listen to reason, being headstrong and even fanatical in his self-isolation, but one of the great masters of English poetry, who did a great thing well, a poet who can be read for sheer style, as we read Milton. All that is needed is the approach—Doughty's approach—through his word-sense, his sense of the individual word. It will be clear that Doughty feels his words differently, more separately than other poets and that, if he could, he would just set the large words down and let them speak for themselves. . . . It is not the fault of Doughty's lines that they frequently fail to run smoothly like Spenser's. This is their virtue.

That is perfectly true. The individual word was all-important to Doughty. Miss Treneer deals at length with his vocabulary. Occasionally she reveals an ignorance of everyday rustic English. Thus *chitty-face* for a pert girl is current, *windrow* is used by every farmer at haymaking (and by D. H. Lawrence), *swapt off his head* is not merely "better than swept", it refers to the swap-hook used for cutting brambles and hedges. Nor did Doughty call beasts "by their half-forgotten names" when he used the words elk, water-vole and newt. The older word for newt is *effet*; surely it must be somewhere in the *Dawn in Britain*. Doughty's most tiresome habit, as Miss Treneer points out, was to use current words in their ancient meanings: *libertine* for a freed slave, *dissolute* for disunited, *superfluous* in the sense in which the Douai Bible refers to "worshipping superfluous beasts". Doughty went back, as Miss Treneer says, to Spenser and Chaucer because he did not want his words, in Professor Herbert Read's phrase, "to flash with interverbal meanings" like Shakespeare's. He regarded himself, not only as a poet but as a champion rescuing English words from the foul captivity in which they had languished, forgetful of their primitive virtue, for nearly three centuries. His demon led him also as Miss Treneer says, to the use of harsh names, Adama instead of Eve, and there is a likeness here to Blake's prophetic books. Gol- gonooza, Guledig, Cogidubnos, Goibniu, Ololon, Dagda, and Palamabron were given their names by poets writing in unrelieved solitude.

*   *   *   *   *   *

I have indicated some of the difficulties, but there are commensurate rewards. Doughty has the gift of writing lines that remain fixed in the memory. Thus love is

> A flower whose stem is fire, whose leaves are frost.

More than any poet of modern times, his words, speaking for themselves give a realistic image of the majesty of nature.

> Go up the Gauls in mighty shadows, cold;
> Where trembles the air, with drone of waterfalls;
> And sinks, upon their sense, crude mizzling reek.
> From darksome pines, they mount to snow-fleckt crags,
> Whence solemn mountain spires soar, and pierce heaven.

It is in such passages that one is aware that, as Professor Barker Fairley points out, "Doughty and Hopkins are as natural a pair to name together as Wordsworth and Coleridge. . . . When one considers the difference between them in temperament, Hopkins as tortured as Doughty is serene, and in theme, Hopkins intensely lyrical and personal, Doughty impersonal and detached, it is astonishing to discover how much they share in technique." For most readers to-day the tortured and the personal inevitably mean more in poetry than the serene and the detached, because poetry is not their daily preoccupation, but something to which they turn in moments of acute unhappiness and emotional unrest. Such readers will never find *themselves* in Doughty but they may find peace, particularly in the pastoral and lyrical passages. But, for myself, I like Doughty best when he is least contorted:

> In my weariness, I long hour;
> Fulfilled with joy of heart, have rested here;
> Since when in yonder field, his sweaty team,
> The ploughman loosed, lifted the shining share,
> From long cleft clod; and on his wheelers chine,
> Rode sideways whistling to his horses stalls.   [*1935*]

G. M. Young

TUTTY

FOR many years I was haunted by a ghost word, which has suddenly come back at me again. I first met it in a Dutch-English Dictionary in the form:

niet: nothing, naught, tutty.

I consulted W. P. Ker who knew everything, only to find that it was the one thing he did not know. Growing interested, I pursued it into other languages, always with the same result. The Portuguese lexicographer believed that *tutty* was the English for *nada.* The Spaniard, the Italian, the Swede, all entertained the same curious conviction. Clearly there must be in the world some archetypal dictionary in which *nihil,* or *rien* or *niente* is glossed: Anglicé *tutty,* and from which all pocket dictionaries are derived. Where is it?

Tutty returned to me in this wise. An enterprising dealer, some years ago, seems to have bought up the sheets of an English and French dictionary

containing
the pronunciation of the english in the french sounds,
scotch words from
W. Scott's novels, etc., etc.
BY SMITH.

My copy is dated 1907, but from internal evidence I should date the original to the eighteen-thirties. The Iron Road has been invented, but *gare* does not yet mean a railway station, only a wet-dock. I should rather like to see the conversation of Andrew Fairservice, the ejaculations of Mause Headrigg, of the classical periods of

Ride your ways, Ellangowan,

with all the scotch words rendered into french BY SMITH. *Voici la dernière baguette qui je couperai dans les bois estimables d'Ellangowan.* But contemporary french readers, baffled by

43

Stamach, were no doubt relieved and encouraged by learning that it was only *écossais pour Stomach*.

However, this has nothing, or tutty, to do with my ghost. Smith has got it, pronounced teut'-ti, and it means tutie. Tutie, pronounced too-te, is there also, and it means tutty. We seem to be moving in a circle. But about this tutty there is no mystery. Littré and O.E.D. are agreed that it is a crude oxide of zinc. It was formerly used in astringent ointments and lotions. Elizabethan soldiers laid in lots of it before going forth to war. It is good for Rhewms in the Eyes. The better sorts are ponderous and somewhat sonorous. *Cf. pompholyx*. But it is a hot day, O.E.D. too, is somewhat ponderous, and I feel I know enough. It is pleasanter to read on about the other Tutty, the nose-gay or Tuzzy-muzzy; about the Heath, which beareth his flowers in tutteys or Tufts; and the tything men of Hungerford who carry Tutti-poles or wands wreathed with flowers. But of my tutty—nada, niet, naught.

It is a very hot day, and I can do no more. I sincerely hope that it is not a Bad Word, but on that the character and experience of various persons whom I have consulted satisfy me. If it were, they would know it. But I should be really grateful to anyone who would solve the riddle and so lay the ghost, because Tutty is becoming like one of those words heard in dreams, words of incomprehensible and infinite significance, which seem to impart at once the secret of the Universe and the winner of the next Grand National. I can only offer one conjecture, and that is, that it arose out of a misreading of nosegay as no segay. *Cf.*, as the lexicons say, Nosmo King. The poor foreigner asked an English friend what no segay meant, and the friend replied, "It means nothing." Candidly, my conjecture seems to me to be pretty putid, even as conjectures go. But I have known worse. I have read *The Place Names of Kent* by Dr. Wallenberg of the University of Upsala. And, as I have twice observed, it is an exceedingly hot day.

Sɪʀ,

According to Hexham's Anglo-Dutch Dictionary (*Groot Woordenboek*, Rotterdam, 1658) *niet* meant "The Soil that runneth of Brasse, also a kind of Mettall"; this is printed as, and obviously is, something quite distinct from Dutch *niet* =English *nothing*, etc., and akin to the *tutty* which the *New English Dictionary* defines as a "crude oxide of zinc found adhering to the flues of furnaces in which brass is melted; also occurring in some countries as a native metal". The linking of the words *niet* and *tutty* is effected in Sewel's *Large Dictionary English and Dutch*: "Niet, Oogenniet, *Tuty*." "Oogen" is equivalent to "eye" and brings the investigation back to the eye-ointment, Sanskrit *tuttha*, from which the English word is perhaps derived (*N.E.D.*). The "archetypal dictionary" Mr. Young is looking for must, I think, be a Dutch dictionary, perhaps Sewel's, of which I have only seen the third edition (Amsterdam, 1735).

BRIAN W. DOWNS.

Christ's College, Cambridge. [*1935*]

Arthur Waley

NO DISCHARGE

I DO not believe that Heaven and Hell are in different places,
I do not believe that the utmost anguish of the damned
Could ever damp the bliss of neighbouring Saints.
I do not believe there have ever been complaints
From any of the Twenty-four Elders or Seven Spirits
About things like the smell of brimstone. "At first it seemed strong,"
They confess, "but one does not notice it for long,
And we keep our incense burning night and day."
"While as for groaning and gnashing of teeth," the angels say,
"What with the noise of golden harps and new song

"They scarcely worry us at all." To a recent guest
Shy at first amid so much goodness, wondering
Whether one can ever really be friends with the Blest,
Gazing down at the unconsumable Phoenix nest . . .
At the obstinate host whose daily bread is destruction,
Yet none can cease to suffer by being destroyed . . .
To such, a hospitable Elder will often come
Saying, "Meet me here when it's dark. You have never enjoyed
Beauty on earth such as I will show you to-night,
The fires of Hell reflected in the Glassy Sea."
The hours of evening pass; his golden crown, a little tight,
Tires him at first, his unaccustomed wings
Bewilder him, his fingers on the golden strings
Find disconcerting music, and his own voice
Startles him with its raptures when he sings.
Darkness drops; he stands by the smiling Elder
Wing to wing. Shall he look up, or down?
At the rose-leaf Phantom caught in this glacier of Heaven?
At the scarlet Fury prancing over Hell-town?
"It's wonderful to look at, isn't it?" the Elder said,
"Surely this alone makes it worth while to be dead!"

So Heaven and Hell live side by side
And such troubles as happens are of the mildest kind.
Now and again the dull, the gentle damned
Stir, and some salvaged Lucifer will try
To organize revolt. Which Heaven does not mind.
What does it mean? A few lost spirits clutching
Charred banners with the motto "We Want Wings",
Or "Harps for Hell", or "Golden Crowns for All".
The unpresentable, scrap-heap Lucifer flings
A written protest over Heaven's wall.
"They're bound to answer," "This time they must do some-
    thing . . ."
The meek spirits whisper, waiting outside.
Hours go by. Suddenly a terrible light
Flashes over them. Is it some new device
For blistering Hell . . . for cutting off their retreat?
No! That transcendant whiteness is the Angel of Day
Telling them quietly but firmly to go away.   [1941]

W. J. Turner

VENUS ANADYOMENE

'Tɪs said the planet Venus is
Compact of foaming seas
That roll abyss upon abyss
In shoreless melodies:

No deep cliff-thunder, no soft kiss
Upon a sparkling sand,
But clashing, frothing, shipless seas
Where no look-out cries "Land"!

Or else in leagues of silent calm
Her vast horizons lie,
Dim plateaux of wide shimmering grey
Beneath a feathery sky.

It may be there the mermaids comb
Bright hair to foaming scrolls;
In curving billow, waving plain
The *ssh* of shadow-souls.

It may be there the sirens fill
The night with silvery cries
As darkling hollow and bright hill
In soft procession flies.

It may be there the calm sea wreathes
To Venus' scallop shell,
And sound to her voice raindrop-falls
Like a small distant bell.

But has she also such cruel hands
And such a bitter smile?
And has she watery worshippers
Whom beauty shall beguile?

Her body is not rosy-white
Faint-fanned by golden bees;
There is no dark, warm Asian night
Obscure above her knees;

Pale soft sea-shadows cool her limbs;
Her eyes are like twin isles
Jangling with the music of paradise
In her enchanted smiles.

But those who kiss her sacred mouth
Are purified of dreams,
Freed from vague rhapsodies of sound
And Phosphor's mocking gleams

Their love is like a white, white pearl
Beneath a moonless night,
Drowned in the fathomless serene
Of faint, star-scattered light;

Their love is like a deep-sea flower
Remote from wind and wave,
Expression of the same sun's power
That earthly roses have;

Their love is like a strange sea-bird
That, wandering alone,
Passes, but once, and with wild eyes
For evermore is gone.

There is no telling of their love
On Venus or on Earth;
It is incomprehensible,
Even as death and birth.   [*1929*]

Mikhail Zoshchenko
(*Translated by* I.M. *and* S.S.N.)

THE FINE LADY

SKIRTS with hats, boys, mean nothing in my young life. If a skirt wears a hat, if she wears silkified stockings, or carries a Pekinese on her arm, or has a gold tooth, a fine lady like that, boys, is no skirt for me, but just an empty spot.

Yes, boys, certainly I've fallen for a fine lady in my time. Paraded down the street with her and taken her to the theatre. And it was in the theatre it all happened. In that very theatre, boys, she unfolded her ideology full volume.

Yes, I met her in the courtyard of our block. At a meeting. I look—there she is, all dolled up. Stockings and all that, a gold tooth.

"Where", I say, "do you come from, citizeness? What number?"

"I", she says, "am from No. 7."

"Very well," say I, "carry on."

And somehow, you know, from that very moment, she looked terribly good to me. I began popping in and out of her place. No. 7. Used to call there, of course, on official business. "How," let us say, "citizeness, do you stand about breakdown in your pipes and lavatory? All in working order?"

"Yes," she answers, "all in working order."

And she there, just nestling into a comfy shawl, and not another sound out of her. Only her eyes flashing. And the tooth glittering in her mouth. After I'd been calling for a month—she got used to it. Began to answer me back more in detail. "My pipes", she would say, "are working all right, thank you, Grigori Ivanovitch."

Further—friendlier. We started, she and I, parading about the streets. We'd come out on the street, now, and she'd tell me to take her arm. I catch hold of her under the elbow and trail around after her like a blooming hyena. And what to talk about—I haven't the faintest, and I feel embarrassed in front of everybody.

Now once she up and says to me:

"For why", she says, "are you forever trailing me about the streets? I get quite dizzy. You should," she says, "being a gentleman with a lady friend, and in power, take me somewhere—to the theatre, for example."

"Can do," I say.

And the very next day the com-cell sends tickets for the opera. One ticket I got, and the other Johnny—you know, the fellow who mends the doors in our block—subscribed.

I didn't look at the tickets and they turned out different. My one was to sit downstairs, and Johnny's one was right up in the gallery.

And so we went. Sat in the theatre. She sat on my ticket and I on Johnny's. I sat right up in the sky and couldn't see a ruddy thing. Only if I leant right over the railing I could just manage to see her. But not too well.

I got bored, and bored, and went down. And I look—entr'acte. And there she is, walking about amidst the entr'acte.

"Howdyoudo?" say I.

"How do you do?"

"It'd be interesting to know", say I, "whether your pipes are still in working order."

"Don't know," she says.

And all the time she keeps edging towards the buffet. I traipse after. She keeps wandering about the buffet and staring at the counter. At a tray on the counter. And at cakes on the tray.

And I, just like a blinking peacock, like one of the unslaughtered bourgeoisie, float all round her and offer her:

"If", I say, "you feel a craving to eat one cake, please do not hesitate. I'll pay."

"Merci," she says.

And then suddenly she walks straight up to the tray with the most depraved walk, swipes a big one with cream and starts stuffing.

Every penny I had on me was three cat's tears. Enough at the most for three cakes. She stuffs, while I frantically feel in my pockets, trying to tell how much money I have. And every penny—didn't amount to a blob nose.

She finishes the one with cream and swipes another. I even

managed a cough. But I didn't say a word. That damn-foolish bourgeois shame came all over me. You know, gentleman with a lady sort of thing, and no money.

I go sparring round her like a bantam, and she just giggles and fishes for compliments.

I say:

"Isn't it time for us to go and sit in the theatre? Wasn't that the bell?"

But she says:

"No."

And takes a third.

I say:

"Isn't that a lot, on an empty stomach? Won't you be sick?"

And she:

"No," she says, "we're used to it."

And takes a fourth.

Then the blood rushes to my head.

"*Put-that-back!*" say I.

And she gets frightened. Opens her mouth. And her tooth glitters in it.

It was like the reins getting under my tail. It's done anyway, I think, no more walking out with her.

"*Put-it*—to the devil's mother!" say I.

She puts it back. And I say to the proprietor:

"How much do we owe for three cakes eaten?"

But the proprietor displays indifference—he plays the fool.

"You owe me", he says, "so much for the four cakes eaten."

"How", I say, "for four, when the fourth is there on the tray?"

"No," he replies, "though it may be there on the tray, yet a bite has been made in it—and besides, it's been fingered."

"What," I say, "a bite? Allow me! It's your silly fantasies."

But the proprietor maintains indifference, and gives my face a shove with his fist.

Well, people, of course, collected. Experts. Some say a bite has been made, others say no.

I turn my pockets out, naturally, all sorts of thingummy-bobs topple all over the floor—everyone laughs. But I didn't see anything funny. I was counting my money.

And when I'd got it all counted—I just managed to scrape together enough for four cakes, just. All that row, mother believe me, for nothing.

Settled the bill. Then turned to the lady:

"Finish it up, citizeness," I say. "It's paid for."

But the lady doesn't move. She's shy of finishing it.

And just at this moment some great loafer butts in:

"Let me," he says, "I'll finish it up."

And he finishes it, the great bum. On my money, boys!

We sat back again in the theatre. Saw the damn opera through. And so home.

At the door she says to me:

"I've had enough piggery from you. Those with no money —don't go out with ladies."

I answer back:

"Not in money, citizeness, is happiness. Excuse the expression.'

That's how we split.

I don't care for fine ladies.   [*1932*]

W. H. Auden

SONG

As I walked out one evening,
   Walking down Bristol Street,
The crowds upon the pavement
   Were fields of harvest wheat.

And down by the brimming river,
   I heard a lover sing,
Under an arch of the railway:
   "Love has no ending."

I'll love you, dear, I'll love you
 Till China and Africa meet,
And the river jumps over the mountain,
 And the salmon sing in the street.

I'll love you till the ocean
 Is folded and hung up to dry,
And the seven stars go squawking
 Like geese about the sky.

The years shall run like rabbits,
 For in my arms I hold
The flower of the ages,
 And the first love of the world.

But all the clocks of the city
 Began to whirr and chime:
O let not Time deceive you,
 You cannot conquer Time.

In the burrows of the Nightmare
 Where Justice naked is,
Time watches from the shadow
 And coughs when you would kiss.

In headaches and in worry
 Vaguely Life leaks away,
And Time will have his fancy
 To-morrow or to-day.

Into many a green valley
 Drifts the appalling snow;
Time breaks the threaded dances
 And the diver's brilliant bow.

O plunge your hands in water,
 Plunge them in up to the wrist;
Stare, stare in the basin,
 And wonder what you've missed.

The glacier knocks in the cupboard,
 The desert sighs in the bed,
And the crack in the tea-cup opens
 A lane to the land of the dead.

Where the beggars raffle the bank-notes,
 And the Giant is enchanting to Jack,
And the Lily-White Boy is a roarer,
 And Jill goes down on her back.

O look, look in the mirror,
 O look in your distress;
Life remains a blessing,
 Although you cannot bless.

O stand, stand at the window
 As the tears scald and start;
You shall love your crooked neighbour
 With your crooked heart.

It was late, late in the evening,
 The lovers, they were gone;
The clocks had ceased their chiming,
 And the deep river ran on. [*1938*]

Leonard Woolf

THE ECONOMIC DETERMINATION OF
JANE AUSTEN

CLIO, we all know, thanks to Marx and his disciples, is economically determined. But the lady is so old and her character so terribly complex that the details of her economic determination are by no means easy to disentangle. Jane Austen, poor lady, is, I suggest, a better subject for the third degree of Marxian dialectic. If there is truth in the Marxian doctrine, every novelist must bear on mind and imagination the imprint of the economic system in which he lived; and, since in the novel he gives us a picture of society as he saw it, and often an implied criticism of it, we ought to be able to see very clearly in that mirror how economics determined both his mind and his environment. If you look into the mirror of Miss Austen's six great novels, that is in fact what you do see, and the reflection is to me, at any rate, a little surprising.

Jane Austen lived in the transition period between the eighteenth and nineteenth centuries, but she belonged much more to the eighteenth than to the nineteenth. Three of her novels were written before 1800 and the other three between 1812 and 1816. When she died in 1817, the new age of living, thinking, and writing, had hardly begun, and she at any rate had not been touched by it. One can see this, not only in her language and style, but in the books she had read. Her poets were Shakespeare, Pope, Gray, Thompson, Cowper, and Crabbe; her novelists Fanny Burney, Mrs. Radcliffe, Miss Edgeworth, Lewis, Fielding, and Richardson. The nineteenth century was just about to break into literature with Wordsworth, Coleridge, Byron, Shelley, and Keats, but she never felt the breath of the wind before the storm. There is no evidence that she read even *Lyrical Ballads*, which was published when she was twenty-three, and the most "modern" books she read were Scott's poems, *Waverley* and *The Antiquary*, and the very early poems of Byron.

Her father was a country clergyman, and she lived all her life in the country. The class to which she belonged was the lesser country gentry, but her family was rising socially. Her paternal grandfather was a surgeon and a surgeon was barely a gentleman; her father and her maternal grandfather were both clergymen, and therefore just within the charmed circle. In her own generation the family climbed well away from the surgeon. It became clergymen and admirals, won titles, and married the children of baronets and even, in one case, the granddaughter of a duke.

Jane Austen's social and psychological environment was therefore that of the eighteenth century country gentleman. The industrial revolution and nineteenth-century capitalism had not impinged upon it or upon her, and not a breath from them ruffles the surface of her novels. Whatever determined her economically was not the Victorian type of capitalism which left

C

such clear marks on the novels of Dickens and Thackeray. That is why I find it surprising that her social and economic standards should be, except in one important particular, those which we associate with a capitalist bourgeoisie rather than with country gentlemen and aristocrats. Charlotte Brontë, the daughter of another country clergyman, was born a year before, and her sister Emily a year after, Jane Austen died; *Jane Eyre* and *Wuthering Heights* were published in 1847 and *Villette* in 1853; but, if I did not know the dates, I should have said that it was Jane rather than Charlotte and Emily whom capitalism had economically determined.

I will begin, however, with the exception referred to above. Jane's attitude to "work" is the antithesis of that of a capitalist, and pre-eminently of the Victorian, bourgeoisie. There is hardly a single male character in her novels who does any work; to work at all is, indeed, almost incompatible with the status of a gentleman. She recognizes as socially possible only the following professions: the army and navy, the Church, and, with some reservations, the law. Of these professions only the army and navy are usually considered to be unobjectionable. Even so, it will be remembered, Anne Elliot was prevented by her family from marrying Captain Wentworth, because her father "thought it a very degrading alliance". "The profession", says Sir Walter Elliot, "has its utility, but I should be sorry to see any friend of mine belonging to it"; and his reasons are two, the profession is offensive, "first, as being the means of bringing persons of obscure birth into undue distinction", and second, because sailors "are all knocked about and exposed to every climate, and every weather, till they are not fit to be seen". "A man", he sums up, "is in greater danger in the navy of being insulted by the rise of one whose father, his father might have disdained to speak to, and of becoming prematurely an object of disgust himself, than in any other line." In applying the Marxian dialectic to Jane Austen, one must, of course, always remember that she is one of the greatest and subtlest of satirists, and the remark of Sir Walter Elliot, of Kellynch Hall, must not be treated quite as seriously as "facts" are dealt with—sometimes perhaps with equally small reason—by Marxists. But if Jane's smile hovers over Sir Walter, Lady Russell, who is represented as an unusually sensible woman, supported him in preventing the match, and the mature Anne, who had lived to regret having been persuaded by Lady Russell, still admitted her prudence.

As a profession, the navy is regarded by Jane Austen and her characters almost exclusively as a means to obtaining either a position or money. No other profession receives any consideration but the Church and the law. She knew that a gentleman might be a lawyer, but she hardly takes the profession seriously. It enters the novels, I think, three times. Mr. John Knightley was undoubtedly regarded as a gentleman and he was also undoubtedly a lawyer; he is the only major character of whom it is recorded that he "worked" in the Victorian sense, and he and his elder brother actually discussed legal questions, practically the only example in the novels of "serious" male conversation. Mrs. Bennet's father "had been an attorney in Meryton", and her sister, Mrs. Phillips, had married her father's clerk, and these facts, no doubt, were intended to account in part for the incorrigible vulgarity of the two sisters. Their brother had settled in London "in a respectable line of trade"; Mr. Gardiner in *Pride and Prejudice* and Mr. Weston in *Emma* are the only representatives of "trade" who are admitted to respectable society, and it is clear that Jane herself, as well as the Netherfield ladies, "had difficulty in believing that a man who lived by trade, and within view of his own warehouses, could have been so well-bred and agreeable" as Mr. Gardiner.

The only other reference to the law is a little surprising. Miss Crawford tries to persuade Edmund to become a lawyer rather than a clergyman, but I think that this is really intended to be an example of Miss Crawford's distressing pertness and levity. For there is no doubt that in the social and economic hierarchy of the novels the parson is normally considered to be well above the lawyer. The Church was, however, not a profession, nor did the parson work, in the nineteenth-century sense. Out of six heroes three are clergymen or prospective clergymen. But none of them seem to *work* as clergymen. Henry Tilney presumably occasionally preached a sermon when he happened not to be dancing in Bath, but unless one had been told so explicitly, there is nothing in the novel which could lead one to know that he is in Holy Orders. *Northanger Abbey* was written in the eighteenth century, before the Evangelical Movement had touched Jane

Austen. It had certainly touched her when she wrote *Mansfield Park* fourteen years later, but even Edmund regards his future profession almost entirely from its social and economic position, and one feels that Miss Crawford is nearer the truth than he when she says: "A clergyman has nothing to do but to be slovenly and selfish—read the newspaper, watch the weather, and quarrel with his wife. His curate does all the work, and the business of his own life is to dine."

This attitude towards "work", professions, and trade is, I suppose, characteristic of a landed aristocracy or gentry. Otherwise the economic determination of Jane Austen is of the type which one usually associates with a capitalistic bourgeoisie. The social standards are almost entirely those of money and snobbery. It is remarkable to what an extent the plots and characters are dominated by questions of money. The whole opening of *Sense and Sensibility* turns upon the finance of the Dashwood will and the avarice of Mrs. John Dashwood, whose income is £10,000. The finances of the Bennet family and the entail in *Pride and Prejudice* have an equal importance. The axis of the plot in every novel except *Emma* is money and marriage or rank and marriage. The social standard, ideal, and duty of a woman is assumed to be to marry as high or as rich as possible, and we know, on Mrs. Bennet's evidence, that, according to the tariff, £10,000 a year was as good as a lord. Sir Thomas Bertram, a man of the highest morality, considers Fanny's refusal of the rich Crawford positively immoral, and it is immoral because Fanny is poor and Crawford rich. Edmund, one of her most priggish and also, it is to be feared, one of her favourite heroes, takes much the same view as his father. It is true that Jane Austen herself was too sensitive to approve a system which reduced personal relations to a question of pounds, shillings and pence. The sale of Maria for Mr. Rushworth's £12,000 a year in *Mansfield Park* is the antistrophe to Fanny's refusal of Crawford—her plots are always carefully based upon a strophe-antistrophe theme—and leads to disaster. Elizabeth in *Pride and Prejudice* is really shocked by her friend Charlotte's acceptance of Mr. Collins for purely mercenary reasons, but there is no doubt that Charlotte Lucas accurately defines the ordinary economic standards of Jane's environment: "Without thinking highly either of men or matrimony, marriage had always been her object; it was the only honourable provision for well-educated young women of small fortune, and however uncertain of giving happiness, must be their pleasantest preservative from want." The corollary of this attitude of the lady and her relations to the wealth of a prospective husband is the attitude of the man and his relations to a poor bride. It is just as shocking for a rich man to marry a poor girl as for a poor girl to refuse a rich husband. General Tilney is the classic example of the outraged father when he turns Catherine neck and crop out of Northanger Abbey as soon as he finds that he was mistaken with regard to the size of the dowry. It is assumed in *Sense and Sensibility* that Mrs. Smith will disinherit Willoughby and Mrs. Ferrars Edward if they do not marry wealth, and when it comes out that Edward is engaged to Lucy, his mother and sister are so ill that the doctor has to be summoned. Lucy's guilt is, of course, double, for she is not only poor, but lower class. For the only social standard in the novels which competes with money is snobbery. It is true that this snobbery is a favourite subject of Jane Austen's satire. but Lady Catherine de Bourgh and Sir Walter Elliot are only ridiculous in being exaggerated. All the characters are fundamentally snobs with regard to class, and their snobbery is the same as that of the Victorian bourgeoisie. Every one of the novels ends happily and the end is happy in four out of the six because the heroine, in spite of difficulties, marries above herself. Emma, it is true, does not marry above herself, but she is the most snobbish of all the heroines. She can tell Harriet that she (Emma) could not have visited her (Harriet) if she had married the yeoman, Robert Martin—"you would have thrown yourself out of all good society". And the reason she gives illuminates the class consciousness of Jane Austen's environment:

The yeomanry are precisely the order of people with whom I feel I can have nothing to do. A degree or two lower, and a creditable appearance might interest me; I might hope to be useful to their families in some way or other. But a farmer can need none of my help, and is, therefore, in one sense, as much above my notice, as in every other he is below it.

It sounds like the Charity Organization Society in the eighteen-nineties.
                                                                    [*1942*]

Arthur Marshall

BOOKS FOR GIRLS

THE Girls of Britain are, thank heaven, themselves again. Last year the stories concerning their adventures contained far too many references to beauty culture: Are Hilda's plaits as glossy as Ada's? Where is Prudence's bejewelled hair-slide? Who has tampered with Eileen's cold cream? This year one sees with relief that authoresses have no time for anything but making their characters scurry from one scrape to the next. The wretched girls whizz from the smugglers' cave to the Head-mistress's study, undergo a terrific wigging, and are back at the haunted ruins in a twinkling. This is as it should be. No sooner has Hermione discovered the missing Scholarship papers in Edna's satchel than she ought to be harrying the Botany mistress and behaving all anyhow in the boot-hole.

But why are there no spies this year? We must, I feel, move with the times and it wouldn't take a second to write in a gripping scene with Cynthia unmasking an old peasant-woman in the market-place and finding the plans of the School drainage system tucked skilfully into a vegetable marrow. She could then be decorated by a Very Important Person with the head-girl clapping her on the back and crying: "Bravo, youngster; I say, care to split a ginger-pop with me some time?"

Not that there is any real cause for complaint for this year there has appeared the most absorbing and astonishing tale of its kind that I have ever read; it is called *Miss Wilmer's Gang*. "Outwardly prim and precise, Miss Wilmer at forty-five was raging and fuming inside." She is also "compound of nervous activity and tremendous energy", and she inherits two uninhabited islands in Patagonia. Accompanied by six girls, she sets out to farm her property. The girls are "just spoiling for action of some sort", and three of them receive proposals of marriage before you can say Ella Wheeler Wilcox; it is all "Life in three-inch capitals".

Miss Wilmer sleeps "with a trusty little automatic under her pillow" and looks "very business-like in khaki tunic and

breeches with a mackintosh over all". Thus equipped she strides
through "dank herbage", twists her ankle, gets rescued from a
"marshy bit", and is subsequently "thatched down with a lot
of dried swamp grass". She then sits too near the fire and her
thatch goes up in flames. She is rolled in the damp grass,
abandoned while help is procured, and sees approaching a
Patagonian Indian with "arms like an orang-outang". What
will Miss Wilmer do? "This was no time to play the weakling...
If she was discovered . . . she would launch herself straight at
him and she would scratch and claw with primitive fury." Instead, however, she "chokes back a rending scream" and "casts
herself away in the bushes anyhow". Her girls eventually rescue
her and put her on a stretcher but she is flung out against a
tree; she manages, however, to tell her stretcher-bearers:
"You're both made of good stuff for sure", to which they reply:
"Don't you fret, chief dear." They then "hoist" her on board
the boat (this operation is described as "fearful work"). Soon
after, Miss Wilmer is throttled by a delirious Portuguese and
emerges from his grasp gasping: "Bah! That was a breathless
bit." Her methods of dealing with the patient are original indeed: "When he fell a little quiet she dozed; when he raved and
yelled she just sat up and took notice", and this process is later
referred to as "Going all out nursing him".

Then the local aborigines have a rising, attack some neighbouring islanders, and Miss Wilmer and her girls hurry to their
aid in the motor-boat. Pris drives too fast and Daphne Frost
(who sometimes uses "four clean hankies" a day for crying into)
is sick. They have their first brush with the enemy. Miss Wilmer
"was clawing and tearing" aborigines who are "almost un-
clothed save for a garment of skin about their middles". Her
girls "surged to and fro, hitting out wildly". There are "thresh-
ing arms". Miss Wilmer "let her fist drive full in the face" of all
and sundry, and Violet Breame, a "deep contralto", "prodded
and punched, raining blows on naked flesh". But the pace is too
hot even for Violet and when she is carried off by an aborigine
"there was no spring in her anywhere and he must have found
her a bit of a lump". All the girls are captured and Miss Wilmer,
"swinging up her arms", "shoots" out of the house in pursuit.
She "hitches her foot in something", falls headlong, is carried
upside down by an aborigine ("Oh, it was awful") and is

described, rightly, as a "corker". Finally Miss Wilmer receives two proposals of marriage and the girls join in "a couple of staves from Rule Britannia". "One might go a long way", says Violet Breame, "before one encountered another Miss Wilmer." Yes indeed.

Miss Angela Brazil's offering for this year is called *The School on the Cliff* and concerns the adventures of "the three R's", Rosamunde Barton, Ruth Davis and Rhoda Fielding. There is much talk of "folk-lore, nature myths, folk-memories, and elfin maidens"; and even the vanishing of Miss Ward's "illuminated ode" is traced to the pixies. There is a "disgruntled senior" called Myfanwy who behaves "in a most unsporting fashion" over tennis. Rosamunde, "just a light-hearted schoolgirl" is a "recorder in the Botany section" and frequently "rambles up the mountains" collecting "butterwort and bog pimpernel", finally achieving "a most important botanical find". There is a splendid outing of The Nature Study Club; "Miss Graham sprang to her feet in excitement. 'An otter! An otter!' she cried. 'Look, girls . . . Oh, it's dived now! You must all enter that in your nature diaries.' " Then Ella falls into a pool and "spoils the ramble". The school amateur theatricals include girls representing "the spirit of summer, the four winds, the sea fairies, and a band of gnomes". Ruth is chosen for "the south wind . . . all gauze . . . with trailing pieces to blow about". Rosamunde is in pale-blue satin: " 'You look no end!' admired Ruth." The orchestra contains "a further touch of Cambrian interest" in the shape of two harpists "dressed as bards". Winefred Wynne is the cynosure of all eyes, singing and acting "with all the Celtic fire infused by her Welsh blood". At the prize-giving the girls are found to be "a healthy bonny set" and Ruth gets a prize entitled, *A Hundred Things a Bright Girl Can Do*. Rosamunde, complete with "album of snaps" and her mother (who has a maid called Blodwen) set out on a cruise to Palestine. On board there is an Amusements Committee and plenty of shuffle board and bucket quoits, and a fancy-dress party with Mrs. Barton in a Japanese kimono. The streets of Palestine are found to be "dirty and malodorous", and there is a know-all called Miss Hirst who translates the word "baksheesh" and advises them not to drink the water. Rosamunde comes across some "borage and speedwell", but "the Arabs

aren't romantic at close quarters", and "after all the noisy
natives it was delightful to be back on board, with British
seamen and stewards and the Union Jack, and the Captain,
and their own cabins and Western ways".

In *Nancy Returns to St. Bride's*, Desdemona Blackett, with a
"brown mane" and an art bursary, and Nancy Caird with an
organ scholarship, arrive at St. Bride's and are put by the
temporary headmistress, Miss Warren, into the Raspberry
room. The real headmistress, Miss Caldwell, who had been
"putting a pretty stiff strain" on herself, "crashed at the end
of last session" with brain fever, and her substitute, who
"absolutely runs amuck" if she is disobeyed, is much disliked.
The head-girl, Laurie Sims, is very "go-ahead" and wants to
keep St. Bride's abreast of the times: she discusses it at tea: "Lax
is all right I agree, but the best game—more toast?—is footer."
Lectures on psychology are started though "this is not a subject for
the lower school to get hold of". " 'No more talking, girls!' broke
in Miss Warren's voice . . . 'Get out your rough note-books. . . .
To-day I am going to tell you something more about complexes.' " Sonia Martin takes to it like a duck to water: "She
loves psychology—laps it up like anything"; however "hygiene
was different; it taught what you needed to know and then
stopped in time". Poor Sonia gets so carried away that she
becomes "a good deal too highly strung" and grows worse after
each lecture. Eventually she goes "absolutely to pieces . . .
nerves, I suppose". There is a characteristic mademoiselle who
appears among a riot of exclamation marks. " 'Mais, comme
vous êtes méchantes!' wailed Mademoiselle, 'It is not possible
that you be permitted to so conduct yourselves! . . . Biddy
Cochrane! Maeve O'Brien! I see you laugh! Je vous donnerai
quelquechose pour rire! I send you all to Miss Warren!' "
Emotionally the girls are active and one of the juniors is
"frightfully keen" on Nancy Caird and is writing her biography,
while Nancy herself is "besotted with Desdemona Blackett".
The latter who has given "extra time to anatomy" wins second
prize at the "Glasgow Galleries" for a pastel portrait of Nancy;
"Nancy, in her school uniform, sat on the organ-stool, one hand
on the keys, and the other reaching back to pick up a sheet of
music, her face turned over her shoulder, across which fell
her long fair plait. Her expression was half laughing, half

serious, and Desda had caught the blend with marvellous skill."

The Oxford Annual for Girls contains a rich variety of stories including "L for Learner", in which a dashing girl called Lesbia foils some thieves and returns Lady Arkwright's jewels to the proper quarter. Lesbia has not obtained her School Certificate, but she had "that instinctive flair for doing things . . . which had made her such a competent leader of her gym team at school". In "Just a Jig-saw Puzzle" things are never dull "when the stalwart games captain breezed into the room. 'Jumping Jupiter! What have we here?' Glen Gordon boomed, striding across to the table. 'Whence this unwonted industry so late in the day? Jig-saws forsooth! . . . Two prefects? Tut!'" In "Freckles' First Term" Freckles has "two ginger plaits" and "seems to have plenty of pep". She plays hockey, "goes down like a nine-pin", dodges round the right-back, scores the winning hit, and is handed a medal by Sir Richard Trevallion. There is also an article on Dalcroze Eurhythmics.

Now, which of these books are you to get for Ruby's stocking? To which shall Irene glue her fascinated gaze the very moment Christmas breakfast is over? It matters little, and luncheon will be congealing on the table with Irene still staring, her eyes popping from her head, trying to discover just who it was who garotted Mademoiselle, set fire to the Chapel and tarred and feathered Miss Parkinson's bust.   [*1938*]

David Gascoyne

ORPHEUS IN THE UNDERWORLD

CURTAINS of rock
And tears of stone,
Wet leaves in a high crevice of the sky:
From side to side the draperies
Drawn back by rigid hands.

And he came carrying the shattered lyre,
And wearing the blue robes of a king,
And looking through eyes like holes torn in a screen;
And the distant sea was faintly heard,
From time to time, in the suddenly rising wind,
Like broken song.

Out of his sleep, from time to time,
From between half-open lips,
Escaped the bewildered words which try to tell
The tale of this bright night
And his wing-shadowed day,
The soaring flights of thought beneath the sun
Above the islands of the seas
And all deserts, all the pastures, all the plains
Of the distracting foreign land.

He sleeps with the broken lyre between his hands,
And round his slumber are drawn back
The rigid draperies, the tears and wet leaves,
Cold curtains of rock concealing the bottomless sky.

[1938]

Roger Fry

MR. EPSTEIN'S SCULPTURE

OF all the forms of boredom which afflict civilized man, there are probably few more acute or more unvarying than that which results from having, on occasions, to contemplate ordinary works of sculpture. Indeed, so evident is this that it would doubtless be universally recognized, and the habit of erecting sculptures would cease altogether were it not that the bulk, durability and expense of sculptured stone and cast bronze make them peculiarly suitable for memorials and monuments. But fortunately these objects perform their function without troubling us much—except just the moment after the Royal person has unveiled the object, we are not called upon to give it much attention. It is safe upon its pedestal for the rest of time, and can only exhale a faint exhortation to conventional public spirit which flatters the good citizen and only slightly aggravates the bad, who looks upon the work as a symbol which he and his fellow revolutionists may look forward to the fun of destroying at some future date.

Such then being the main uses of sculpture, most of us naturally look upon it as entirely remote from any personal emotion or interest other than that general all-pervading feeling of boredom with which it is so thoroughly imbued, we need not be surprised that the exhibition of Mr. Epstein's busts throws the town into a fit of excited enthusiasm. We are brought up to a pious belief that sculpture is an altogether noble and reputable affair. We know the names of the great sculptors of all ages, and yet sculpture has always bored us— till now. And now comes Mr. Epstein, and as we pass round the small gallery each bronze head gives us a new and distinct sensation, a thrill of wonder, surprise, recognition, and, as a result of so pleasant a surprise, admiration and gratitude. What miraculous gift is this which can make bronze reveal to us definite, singular, vivid human beings—human beings more definite, more emphatically personal, more incisive in the accent of their individuality, more invasive, at a first glance, of our own consciousness, than the individuals of actual life?

Mr. Epstein started from the first with remarkable gifts, but in his early work he was an experimentalist in styles. He ingeniously combined a kind of archaistic decorative simplicity with rude accents suggestive of actuality. Then at one moment with his insatiable technical acquisitiveness he learned to treat each sitter according to what he felt to be a style corresponding to his or her character—we had the strangest mixture in one series of Chinese bronzes, early Greek marbles, Aztec and Rodin. Now at last he has found himself, has developed a method and a manner of seeing which look as though they were definitive. One imagines that he can go on indefinitely along these lines, increasing the intimacy of his reading of character, the psychological intensity of the mood, the incisiveness and brio of the execution. He is surely to be congratulated on having found his own indisputably original and unique artistic personality. There is no doubt about it; it sticks out authentically from every work, however varied the subjects are. However completely he seems to abandon himself to the personality which he is interpreting, it is Epstein's personality that really startles, interests, and intrigues us. That is the way of the great masters, or at least of most of them; and indeed, when we realize the astonishing assurance, the indisputable completeness and efficacy of these works, the brilliant resourcefulness and certainty of the technique, we must call Epstein a master.

His technical resourcefulness is extraordinary. By frankly accepting the nature of clay modelling he gets a strangely vivid and exhilarating surface quality. That is to say, he accepts the fact that the head is built up by adding small pellets of clay one after another. He never tries to cover up his traces: one sees how the head has grown centrifugally, how the prominences have gradually pushed outwards to receive the light. Whether we realize this growth from within or not, we feel that the way these pleasingly broken surfaces take the light when once the clay has been translated into bronze is eminently evocative and allows of the utmost accent with the greatest breadth. Were the surfaces which take the light smoothed down, they would lack the glittering variety of light and shade and the sense of mass and resistance that go with that.

Now that he has found his style we can recognize certain definite mannerisms. It would be easy to parody an Epstein. But the mannerisms are not idle or irrelevant affectations; they are the inevitable result of the end he pursues. Since it is the personality presented as drama that he envisages, he seizes on those aspects of the head which reveal it most sharply. Generally the head is tilted back so that the chin protrudes and the planes of the forehead, eyelids, nose and upper lip are turned to receive the fullest light. All these planes are enlarged and their lower limits either deeply undercut or at least marked by a sharp edge. In general the features are amplified so as to occupy the whole of the mask, and the mask in turn is pulled out, as it were, at the edges, receding frequently to an anatomically impossible hollow above the ears so as to give all possible expression to the receding ridge of the cheek bone.

In general Mr. Epstein follows the tradition of dramatic sculpture by working with ridges and bosses rather than by the architecture of planes. For this dramatic sculpture is no new thing, though it has boasted few great masters. Where Mr. Epstein is perhaps peculiar is in the vehement notation of actuality in the individual head, but even here those who knew Guido Mazzoni's Pieta at Modena will recognize that at least one artist of the Renaissance had anticipated a result which seems surprising when we thus meet it afresh and with all the marks of modernity. Indeed, Mr. Epstein's Weeping Woman is singularly like one of the mourners in that group who kneels with hands clasped and mouth awry. Mr. Epstein's distortions then are not caprices; they are not made to show how modern he is; they come inevitably out of his aim; they are necessary to his full expression. Decidedly Mr. Epstein is a master.

But a master of what? murmurs a still small voice within me which all the turbulence and impressiveness of these works does not entirely silence. A master of what? Of the craft of sculpture, undoubtedly; of vigorous characterization, certainly, after a fashion, but even here I should have to make reservations. Even if we are to regard sculpture as a peculiarly effective form of representation—more than making up for the lack of colour by the palpability of its form—even so, one can imagine a finer, more penetrating, less clamant kind of interpretation of character. One might tire, perhaps, of the element not only of caricature—since all interpretation of character partakes of the nature of caricature—but of its direction. One might soon long for something which, even at the cost of being less immediately impressive, wooed one to a gentler, more intimate contemplation—something in which the finer shades were not so immediately blotted out by the big sweep of the most striking, first-seen peculiarities. One would prefer to live with something less vehement in its attack, rather more persuasive.

But this is a question of taste and perhaps of individual temperament, and there can be no doubt that if we are to regard sculpture in this light it is better to have such strong, broad, racy, even brutal, characterization than the merely toned-down, the insipid, the genteel of fashionable portraiture. This at least is alive; it stirs and moves some corresponding fibres in our nature. This has at least a genuine dramatic appeal, even though,

like some greatly admired actors, it seems a little too much pre-
occupied with getting its effects over the footlights and right to
the back of the pit.

But this digression has not stopped the inner voice. It persists:
Is he a master of sculpture? And, alas! I am bound to say to the
best of my belief, No. If I examine my own sensations and emotions I am bound to confess that they seem to be of quite a different nature when I look at good sculpture from those I feel
in front of Mr. Epstein's bronzes. There is an undoubted pleasure
in seeing any work accomplished with such confidence and
assurance, such certainty and precision of touch; there is a
powerful stimulus in the presence of such vividly dramatized
personalities, but the peculiar emotions which great sculpture
gives seem to me quite different. They come from the recognition of inevitable harmonic sequences of planes, of a complete
equilibrium established through the interplay of diverse movements and a perfect subordination of surface and handling to the
full apprehension of these and similar qualities. It may be, of
course, that I am so carried away, so disturbed, if you like, by all
those other qualities of drama and actuality which Mr. Epstein's
work displays, that I cannot feel this purely formal stimulus to
the imagination which is what I seek for in sculpture. But there
is the fact as I see it. These busts are for me brilliant but rather
crude representations in the round. If these are sculpture, then
I want another word for what M. Maillot and Mr. Dobson
practise, let alone Luca della Robbia and the Sumerians.

Fortunately for Mr. Epstein, there are a great many people
whose imaginations are excited by really capable dramatic representation, and there are very few people who happen to like
sculpture in my sense. The majority are quite right to acclaim
him as a master, since the gift necessary for such work is a very
rare one and he has used it and developed it pertinaciously, and
since it does give genuine pleasure. Such work as this is infinitely better than the stylistic, decorative arrangements with
which Mr. Epstein started, and in which some of his most celebrated foreign rivals still persist. It is a triumphant expression
of genuine feelings about people's character as expressed in their
features, and if it does not evince any peculiar and exhilarating
sense of formal harmony, so much the worse for the few people
who happen to have a passion of such an odd kind.   [*1924*]

Louis MacNeice

LES SYLPHIDES

LIFE in a day: he took his girl to the ballet,
Being short-sighted himself he could hardly see it—
    The white skirts in the grey
    Glade and the swell of the music
    Lifting the white sails.

Calyx upon calyx, Canterbury bells in the breeze,
The flowers on the left mirror to the flowers on the right
    And the naked arms above
    The powdered faces moving
    Like seaweed in a pool.

Now, he thought, we are floating—ageless, oarless—
Now there is no separation, from now on
    You will be wearing white
    Satin and a red sash
    Under the waltzing trees.

But the music stopped, the dancers took their curtain,
The river had come to a lock—a shuffle of programmes—
    And we cannot continue down
    Stream unless we are ready
    To enter the lock and drop.

So they were married—to be the more together—
And found they were never again so much together,
    Divided by the morning tea,
    By the evening paper,
    By children and tradesmen's bills.

Waking at times in the night she found assurance
In his regular breathing but wondered whether
    It was really worth it and where
    The river had flowed away
    And where were the white flowers. [*1939*]

Anton Chehov

(*Translated by* HUBERT BUTLER)

A FISHY AFFAIRE

This story of Chehov, though written in his very early manner, was not printed in "Oskolki" (the comic paper in which so many of his early stories were issued) till 1892. He had by then ceased for five years to be a contributor to "Oskolki", was already the author of "Ivanov", "The Wood Demon", "The Steppe", etc., and had taken his journey to Sachalin.

Perhaps it was an old story he had found in his drawer, perhaps he wrote it to please Leykin, the Editor, who had asked him for something in his old manner. He sent it with two other stories all signed by one of his familiar pseudonyms, "The man without spleen".

ODD as you may think it, the solitary carp that lived in the pond near General Pantalikin's villa fell head over heels in love with Sonia Mamochkina, who was there for the holidays. But anyway what is there odd about it? Did not Lermontov's Demon fall in love with Tamara, and the swan with Leda, and do not clerks quite frequently fall in love with the manager's daughter? Every morning Sonia Mamochkina came out and bathed with her aunt. The infatuated carp used to swim right up to the bank and stare at them. Owing to the proximity of Messrs. Krendel and Son's Iron Foundry, the water in the pond had been permanently discoloured, but all the same the carp was able to see everything. He saw how white clouds and birds swept across the azure sky, how the lady visitors undressed and how young persons peeped at them from behind bushes along the bank. He saw how the portly aunt used to sit on a stone for five minutes before venturing into the water and, patting herself complacently, used to say: "What an elephant I've become! I'm a perfect sight!" Throwing off her light clothes, Sonia plunged with a squeal into the water, swam about and squirmed with the cold, while the carp devotedly swam after her and greedily kissed her little legs, her shoulders and her neck.

71

When they had bathed the visitors went off home and had tea and fancy bread, but the carp swam about all alone in the huge pond and reflected.

"Of course I know I haven't an earthly . . . ! How could a fascinating creature like her fall in love with—a carp! It's simply out of the question. Do not deceive yourself with false hopes, miserable fish. For you, there can be only one way out, and that is death. But how can one die? There are no revolvers or match-heads in the pond. For us carp only one death is possible, and that is being eaten by a pike—but where is one to get hold of a pike? There was one pike here in the pond some time ago, but it died of boredom. How dreadful it all is!"

And reflecting on death the young pessimist plunged into the mud and wrote up his diary.

One day in the late afternoon Sonia and her aunt sat down on the bank and began to fish. The carp swam close up to the floats and kept his eyes fixed on the beloved face. Suddenly like lightning an idea flashed into his mind.

"I will die at her hands," he thought, and he gave a merry frisk with his fins. "Oh! That will be an exquisite, a sweet death!"

And steeling his heart and turning slightly pale, he swam up to Sonia's hook and swallowed it.

"Sonia, you've a bite!" shrieked her aunt. "Gracious, pet! you've a bite."

"Oh! Oh!"

Sonia leapt up and tugged as hard as she could. Something golden flashed in the air and flopped into the water, leaving rings behind it.

"It's got away!" wailed both the ladies, turning pale. "It's got away! Oh dear, Oh dear!"

They looked at the hook and saw a fish's lip on it.

"Goodness gracious!" said the aunt. "You oughtn't to have pulled so hard. Now the poor little fish has lost his lip."

When he had torn himself from the hook, our hero was absolutely stunned and for a long time could not realize what was the matter with him; then coming to himself he groaned: "Once more alive! Once more! Ah, the irony of fate!" Then noticing that he had no lower jaw the carp blanched, gave a wild shriek of laughter and went out of his mind.

I am afraid it may seem odd of me to wish to occupy the attention of a serious reader with the fate of an insignificant and uninteresting creature like a carp. But what is there odd about it, after all? Do not lots of ladies write in fat periodicals about gudgeons and snails—and what use are they to anyone . . . ? Well, I'm just imitating the ladies. Perhaps I'm a lady myself, just concealing my identity with a masculine pseudonym.

So the carp went off his head. The poor creature is living to this day, though carp nowadays make nothing of dying. Sonia married the proprietor of a drug-stores and the aunt went to live at Lepetsk with her married sister. There is nothing odd about this, for the married sister has six daughters and they are all very fond of their aunt.

But that is not all. Engineer Krisin has been appointed Director of Krendel and Son's Iron Foundry. He has a nephew, John, who, as everyone knows, writes poems, and has a passion for printing them in newspapers and magazines. One sweltering noon the young poet passed by the pond and took it into his head to have a bathe. He undressed and slipped into the water. The demented carp took him for Sonia Mamochkina, swam up to him and gently kissed his spine. This kiss had the most disastrous results. The carp infected the poet with pessimism. Suspecting nothing the poet climbed out of the water, and with a hollow laugh went home. In a few days he left for St. Petersburg; and there, during his visits to editorial offices, he infected all the poets with pessimism, and from that day to this our poets have been writing gloomy melancholy verses.

[*1935*]

Desmond MacCarthy

CHEHOV

THE spread of a taste for Chehov has been due mainly to two causes, though I think we dramatic critics have helped in a measure: Constance Garnett's translations of his stories, and, above all, the delicate, imaginative expertness of M. Komisarjevsky as a producer. He is a marvellous producer; without him neither *Ivanov*, nor *Uncle Vanya*, nor *The Three Sisters* would have made a deep impression. The attentive would have no doubt perceived that they were the works of a dramatist of genius, but they would have been forced to intensify in their own imaginations what they actually saw and heard on the stage in order to appreciate the intentions of the author. In the case of every Chehov play not produced by M. Komisarjevsky, I have found myself obliged to do this in varying degrees; least in the case of *The Sea-Gull*. The Art Theatre's production of *The Three Sisters*, for instance, some years ago, completely concealed from me the fact that it is the finest play of them all.

Chehov follows in the steps of Turgenev: his favourite theme is disillusionment, and above the kind of beauty he creates might well be written "desolation is a delicate thing". He is fond of the same kind of settings as Turgenev; summer woods, a country house full of cultivated people who talk and talk, in fact *une nichée de gentilhommes*. Here you will find the idealist who melts over his own futility, the girl who clutches daily duties tighter in order to forget that youth is sliding away under her feet, the clever man turned maudlin-cynical after his failure to find a purpose, the old man who feels he has not yet begun to live, and the old woman who only wants things to go on quietly on familiar humdrum lines. The current of their days is slow; the air they breathe is sultry with undischarged energy, and only broken by unrefreshing nerve storms. It is an atmosphere of sighs, yawns, self-reproaches, vodka, day-dreams, endless tea, endless discussion. These people are like those loosely agglutinated sticks and straws which revolve together

74

slowly in a sluggish eddy. They long to be detached, and ride down a rushing stream, which they fancy is sparkling past them. Some day—three hundred, five hundred years hence— perhaps life will be *life*. And those fortunate heirs of the ages who live then, will they be grateful to their poor predecessors who made that glorious life possible? No: they will probably never think of them—another reason for self-pity. Stop! This is ridiculous, they argue. What *are* we doing for them? Nothing. What, indeed, can we do? Nothing, nothing. Such is the atmosphere in which Chehov's characters live and move and have their being. It differs from that of Turgenev's generation in being stuffier, and more discouraging to effort and to hope. There are no Bazarovs to break its spell and bring down the rain of tragedy. Tragedy is there, but it is in the form of a creeping mist which narrows the world to the garden gate. Sometimes the warm, wet mist thins away, but it soon shuts out again the golden vista of race-hope.

This is a generalized picture of Chehov's world. What, you may ask, has it in common with us that it should move us so deeply, we who belong to a race of eupeptic and moderate Crusoes? Well, I am not convinced that many of us have not after all more in common with these characters than at first sight seems probable. We have more self-control and are less hysterical, 'tis true, but when examined closely do not our lives often resemble that of flies in a glue-pot? But it is not only upon this resemblance that the appeal of this drama rests. To watch a Chehov play is to recapture one's youth, that most uncomfortable yet enviable time when there was intensity even in moments of lassitude, when self-torture did not seem vain, when hope alternately lit up and took the shine out of the present, and when time at once seemed endless and yet impossible to fill worthily. "Why, these people", the spectator exclaims to himself, "are suffering from an unduly protracted youth!" In Vanya's elderly passion for the self-centred Elena there is something of the piteousness and the humiliation of young longing that expects everything and does not understand itself. To all of them, except the meaner, harder sort, it seems that life would be beautiful, if, . . . With the three sisters it is "*if* we could get to Moscow", with the baron "*if* I could find my work", with Vanya "*if* Elena loved me",

And to feel like that is to be, as far as it goes, young. It is young to want to prop your ladder against the horn of the moon. It is also young not to know that though we have immortal hungers in us, there are—paradox thanks to which the world goes on —extremely satisfying properties in a little real bread; and Chehov's characters have not learnt that. They have a wail in them responsive not only to their own particular frustrations, but to an inevitable disillusionment. This quality in Chehov's work which, though it is, as commentators point out, the product of a phase, a period in Russian history, must keep it fresh.

"Entbehren sollst du! Sollst entbehren.
Das ist der ewige Gesang"

is a theme which cannot grow out of date.

Chehov is the artist of farewells; farewells to youth, to our past, to hopes, to love. The climax of *The Cherry Orchard* is a farewell to an old home and all that can mean to the middle-aged; at the end of *Uncle Vanya* the words "They've gone", uttered by one character after another as they enter after seeing off the professor and his siren wife are like the tolling of a bell for the burial of passion and excitement. It is then that Sonia, touchingly and admirably played by Miss Forbes-Robertson, comes close to her stricken uncle and makes her dim little speech about the next world where all tears will be wiped away, and whence even the long dingy years that are yet before them both will seem beautiful in retrospect; a speech the pathos of which is increased a hundredfold by our knowledge that for Vanya himself no such comforting faith is possible. He cannot, to use Tom Kettle's phrase, break "the parting word into its two significant halfs, à Dieu". The close of *The Three Sisters* is even more poignant. It is their good-bye to their youth. The military band is playing; the regiment is marching away from that detested provincial town; the girls will never exclaim again, either in hope or misery, "To Moscow! To Moscow!"; Irina's lover, the plain, weak, worthy Baron has been shot by a romantic "superman" whose hands smell; their once promising, brilliant brother Andrey, cuckold now and slave, will go on pushing the pram for his nagging, vulgar wife; Masha has lost her eloquent lover and must live henceforth alone with her incessantly chirpy, methodical husband—kind, yes, touchingly kind—but how devastatingly limited Kuligin is! Masha's fate again reminds me of Tom Kettle's essay in *The Day's Burden* which Chehov would have appreciated, "Life is a cheap table d'hôte in a rather dirty restaurant, with Time changing the plates before you have had enough of anything." Our best courage is needed for adieux.

Yet out of this conception of life which might be labelled "depressing", Chehov makes a work of art which moves us and exalts us like a beautiful piece of music. It is not in a mood of depression one leaves the theatre after seeing *The Three Sisters*. How true it is that a good play should be like a piece of music!

For our reason a play must have logical coherence, but for our emotions the sinuous, unanalysable appeal of music. In and out, in and out, the theme of hope for the race and the theme of personal despair are interwoven one with the other. Each character is like a different instrument which leads, and gives way alternately, sometimes playing alone, sometimes with others, the theme of the miseries of cultivated exiles, or the deeper one of the longing of youth: the dreamy, once gay Irena, the sober and steady Olga, the passionate Masha, half ashamed of her greedy clutch on happiness—vulgarizing herself, she knows, but not caring for that. And what queer harsh notes proceed from that black pit of egotistic megalomania and ferocious diffidence, Solyony (perfectly played by Mr. Seabrooke). Solyony thought himself a romantic Lermontov; nowadays he would pride himself on being a ruthless superman. *Plus ça change, plus c'est la même chose.*

And again with what effect the *leit motif* of "It's all the same" comes from that cracked old fiddle which has long ago lost all resonance of feeling, Chebutykin. (Mr. Dan Roe gave a masterly performance.) In this character and in the drawing of the exasperating Kuligin, Chehov shows his peculiar gift of delaying till precisely the right moment the revelation of character. At first Chebutykin strikes us as an affectionate old man devoted to the three sisters and especially to his pet, the youngest. In the last act we see that his amiability only springs from his having no feelings. It is revealed again in that astonishing moment when the little schoolmaster puts on the false beard he has taken that morning from a boy in class, in order to distract his wife in her misery on parting with her lover. We discover just at the right dramatic moment that there is after all in Kuligin a fund of loyal kindness; inept, uncomforting kindness, but beautiful, inexhaustible, humane. Skilfully managed, too, is the transition from the rosy-posy, diffident Natasha in to the harsh upstart she proves herself to be when once she has caught her man; with her mechanical maternity, her mincing gentility and her rasping, competitive selfishness. One realizes while watching those scenes between her and her sisters-in-law what a handicap magnanimous sensitiveness is in dealing with a sobbing, hectoring, managing vulgarity. There have been dramatists with a wider sweep and a stronger hand than Chehov, but none has brought to the weighing of human character more delicate scales.

I have no space in which to describe the acting or the skill with which the scenes were orchestrated. Miss Margaret Swallow's Masha I must, however, single out; and since to pick little holes in performances which have profoundly delighted one, is a sincere though backhanded compliment from a critic, I will mention some points in the two productions which disappointed or disconcerted me. In *Uncle Vanya*, memorable for Mr. Farquharson's Vanya, as good as any I could imagine, for Miss Forbes-Robertson's Sonya, for Mr. Hewitt's Astrov, and for perfection in the minor parts, I missed a very important something in Elena; while the scene which should hit one exactly between wind and water, between laughter and tears, when the maddened and hysterical Vanya shoots at and misses the professor, struck me as less well stage-managed. It is better that the terrified, open-mouthed, goggle-eyed old Struldbrug should come leaping with flying coat-tails down the centre of the stage and Vanya after him. The timing of the first shot off stage was not quite exact. There should be just time enough for us to think that Vanya has shot *himself*. Astrov, whose acting of drunkenness, though excellent and greatly appreciated, was too prominent a feature in the play, should have looked a more slack, dilapidated person. In *The Three Sisters* Vershinin disappointed me. He did not vary enough. He is a one-speech man, and there should be a difference between the glow of his first performance before a fresh audience which at once captivates the heart of 'Masha, and the gramophone-record effect of his last burst of optimism before leaving "the three sisters". This is most important if the last turn is to be given to the ironic screw. Mr. Gielgud as the baron was too much of a *jeune premier*; one wondered why Irena could not love him. When she said, "I will marry the baron" it should have given us a pang. The baron must be unattractively commonplace. But these are small rebates on my debt of gratitude for two performances which I shall reckon among those that have helped to make my profession of dramatic critic worth following.   [*1926*]

Stephen Spender

WHAT I EXPECTED

WHAT I expected was
Thunder, fighting,
Long struggles with men
And climbing.
After continual straining
I should grow strong;
Then the rocks would shake
And I should rest long.

What I had not foreseen
Was the gradual day
Weakening the will
Leaking the brightness away,
The lack of good to touch
The fading of body and soul
Like smoke before wind
Corrupt, unsubstantial.

The wearing of time,
And the watching of cripples pass
With limbs shaped like questions
In their twist,
The pulverous grief
Melting the bones with pity,
The sick falling from earth—
These, I could not foresee.

For I expected always
Some brightness to hold in trust,
Some final innocence
To save from dust,
That, hanging solid,
Would dangle through all,
Like the created poem
Or the dazzling crystal.   [*1931*]

Kingsley Martin

NOSTALGIE DE LA BOUE

WHEN I began my "cure" at Piestany three weeks ago, I looked forward to its end as a slave might anticipate freedom. Now that it is over, now that I have been baked in my last mud pack and boiled in my last mud bath I am astonished to find myself regretting the interruption of a routine and a discipline which, almost intolerable at first, I have actually learnt to enjoy. It would be easy to pretend that if I return to Piestany it will be for the sake of its beauty, its comfort or its amusements. But it would only be pretence. The gardens are indeed miraculously scented with jasmine and the parks loud with nightingales. I know no place where the birds so emphatically and so continuously give the lie to that odd English myth that

it is only in the British Isles that wild birds sing musically. I
have sat under the trees at night and heard gipsy music
while a dazzling moon rose over the wooded foothills of the
Carpathians. I have listened to the May bugs which tumble
all day from the trees with a sound like October apples falling.
I have wondered at the endless rain of gossamer which the
silver poplars shed; at the prodigious elaboration of the
peasants' Sunday finery; at the tough Slovak women who pull
sufferers to the baths in Sedan chairs, running like coolies
between the shafts; above all I have wondered at the English
visitors, their faces ironed like their shirt fronts, taking their
pleasures exactly as they would at any place which had a golf
links, a dance floor and a good cuisine. But it is not any of
these attractions that I shall miss and it will not be in search
of them that I return to Piestany.

Surely, I said, when I first saw the *Schlammbad*, surely Dante
passed this way? It was here that he conceived the idea of
a burning lake, here where in truth the sulphurous liquid boils
and bubbles while twisted, naked souls, their feet in scalding
mud and their heads enveloped in undying steam, weep out
their sins and their rheumatism. Yes, I cried as I trod the
burning steps and noted that in this cauldron one was forbidden
to swim or to spit or to make a noise, here indeed is the very
prototype of the Inferno.

Nor do our torments end with the *Schlammbad*. Parboiled
already, we are swathed tightly in blankets, helpless as mummies
and left to stew in our own vapours. And on days when the
Higher Powers reprieve us from the *Schlammbad*, the *Schlamm*
itself, black and hot, is brought to us in great buckets from the
depths of the river bed by attendant demons who arrive back-
side first through holes in the ground. We are rolled in the
scalding pitch; it is plastered over us; we are one with it,
ourselves part of the river, part of a volcanic process. We
have returned to a nature more primitive than the apostles
of the simple life ever imagined. Here is a refinement of the
torture of Tantalus. For most of us, if we are honest with ourselves, will admit that there is in us a liking for mud and that
with this mud, thick, malleable, smelly and luscious, the child
in most of us would gladly play. But we cannot play with it;
we are its plaything. The grown-ups with their slaps and

scoldings never invented any deterrent so effective as to bury us alive in the object of our passion. It is as if a hungry man were smothered in caviare or one who dies of thirst drowned in champagne. Tightly packed, our strength and our desires ooze out of us in great drops of sweat. The temperature of the mud is carefully noted. Our skins may not be burned. But no one measures the fantastic temperatures which our blood must reach, as we lie buried. To sweat is our fate and our condemnation. In the pack I have wept from sheer weakness. My tears, mingled with sweat, have flowed unnoticed. To ask what would have happened if I had laughed is to strain fancy. Laughter in hell is as unthinkable as swimming or spitting.

All this was my early impression. And I had my private torment. Fast in my *Pack* the deep fear of the trapped animal arose in me. It was only by summoning all my inner force that I kept from shouting for help and struggling with my tormentors. And then a change. I learnt the tricks of the captive and even something of the virtue of suffering. Like other prisoners I found ways of alleviating my captivity. By a cunning extension of my elbows I was able to prevent the blankets as they were wrapped about me from binding fast, just as a man who is tied with ropes for show swells his muscles so that the bonds which seem to cut into his flesh are really slack. My hands free, I am no longer terrified. If Göring appears I can at least make shift to free myself enough to give him one in the eye with a lump of hot mud. And I can do other things with my hands. My fingers with an inch or two of play explore the mud around them. Unexpectedly they find foreign bodies in the mud, small stones and bits of stick. Of these I made a secret hoard, smuggling out one or two each day with a sense of triumph. Even in the *Schlammbad* itself I dug up stones with my toes. I was after all free; the Powers had not succeeded in preventing me from playing with this lovely mud.

Then the second stage of emancipation. This was not Hell I had reached, but Purgatory. For each bath and each cure had an end. Our sentences were fixed, not eternal. None need abandon hope who enters here. We could watch the clock until the divine moment of purification, when the mud would be washed from us in the cleansing shower. And how good was the clear water of the *Spiegelbad* where they leave one a floating thermometer instead of a celluloid duck to play with! There is not room to swim in the *Spiegelbad* and I did not want to spit, but I dared to sing and whistle and no one said me nay. Even the strain of the mud pack is relieved by attendants, whom I soon ceased to see as demons. Now one and now another comes my way; looks with a pitying smile, and wipes the sweat from my face. Each I found had his own technique with the towel. Some would thoroughly wipe the eyes and forehead, neglecting the agonizing tickle of unseen drops around my nostrils. One boy above all had the vocation. He wiped my nose with the tenderness of St. Veronica, and his *Bitte* in response to my *Danke* had in it the compassion of the angels and the tears of the nightingales. I grew patient waiting for his return and for the moment of purification. I saw that all here had learnt patience, resignation and hope.

At first I thought that some poor souls must give up the unequal struggle with the vapours of the *Schlammbad* to sink perhaps unnoticed to the bottom where they would be quickly assimilated to the mud. Could we perhaps vanish? No, it does not happen. Statistics are against me. The same number emerge each day from the bath as enter it. In this Purgatory none gives up: all live by hope, seeking purification and healing through suffering. They endure not as stoics, but as optimists and penitents. Religiously they pass through the fire, confident of bliss to follow. Year after year they come, these voluntary martyrs, knowing that they may indeed find healing here. They look eagerly at the museum of crutches thrown away by the brave saints of the past. The claims of the Piestany mud are not fraudulent. For many it is indeed the way of salvation. The halt and the maimed who now hobble about the streets in dressing gowns may some day mount up with wings like the eagles; they may run and not be weary; they may walk and not faint.

This is the story that every sufferer will tell you—that they endure in the hope of release from future pain. They do not say—what rational person could?—that they enjoy the Purgatory of the Mud. But if my confession is to be complete I must plead a different and less rational experience. If I return to

Piestany I shall have other reasons in addition to the hope
of release from pain. It will be in part at least because I have
come to love the mud itself, not because of its healing virtues,
not yet because of its perfection as a childish plaything, but
because of the discipline it imposes. Twenty minutes in the
Schlammbad once seemed an eternity. At the end of a quarter
of an hour I wondered how another five minutes could be
endured. And yet by the end of my allotted sentence I was not
always in haste to breathe the free air again. I had endured
twenty minutes; why not thirty? So it was half eagerly and half
reluctantly that I stepped out of the mud. Sweating in the
Pack I would begin desperately to count the seconds. But sometimes my thoughts would have reached a certain tranquillity
before the clock struck the signal to *auspacken*. I should like to
claim more, to range myself with the masters of contemplation.
Spinoza, buried in mud, would have found a new metaphysic,
Boethius rejoiced once more in the consolations of philosophy
and Bunyan experienced another chapter of *The Pilgrim's
Progress*. My own is the more modest achievement of learning
to bear it with some serenity and sometimes to forget it. It was
something to have endured when endurance was difficult. If I
go again next year to Piestany it will be in part at least in the
hope of finding a greater serenity. The monk who finishes his
penance may perhaps feel as I do. He may regret the last
stroke of the scourge on his back. Even so I hanker after the
mud. Even so I know *la nostalgie de la boue*.   [*1935*]

Herbert Palmer

PRINCESS MARY'S WEDDING JEWELS AND THE PIED MINSTREL

(Written April 1st to April 12th, 1922.)

"THERE's a boycott in Fleet Street of Passion and Song."
  Queer men are saying things, "Where are we bound?
Sham and confusion; Right cheapened by Wrong!
  And our sky-cleaving pinions are beating the ground."

I have three pounds ten in the fold of my purse,
  And nothing to come, neither paper nor gold.
I have printed three ballad books wrecked by a curse;
  They lie in the Cork Street shop unsold.

And I'm cornered, and done with—and down in the mire;
  And that seems the sum and the short of the tale,
For my critical prosing has darkened my lyre;
  Oft returned, or gone lost, like a fisherman's sail.

But hark to me, all ye Spectres of Night,
  And every curator of dungeon and jail—
One more try; and I'll set all their windows alight,
  For I'm living in England where Right should not fail.

And you listen, and whisper me, "Why make it worse!
  Creep through a broken pane, smash in a door.
Write prose and more prose, and let Song have the Hearse;
  Someone will raise her ere June twenty-four."

But who can write prose with his heart in a flame,
  And his brain playing hobby-horse over the moon,
And half of his spirit gone twisted and lame,
  And half of it dancing with ghosts, aswoon!

85

And his body oppressed by four low walls—
   A match-box den that is dismal in June,
Where rarely the sunlight of morning falls,
   And never one gleam in the afternoon.

And the whole of him asking in grief and disdain,
   "Who am I? What was I? Where am I bound?"
Left me nought save the wind and the rain,
   Land for me none, save a six-foot of ground.

Yet was I not long ago Solomon the Jew?
   A love lay he carolled—dimly read through a mist;
And Deborah; and David whose touch rang so true—
   All who changed burning Thought into Song's amethyst?

And was I not Omar, the praiser of wine,
   Of dawn-fire, and roses, and lips to be kissed;
And Alfred, whom Vikings thought minstrel divine,
   He, the Spider of Song, weaving webs at her tryst?

And was I not Cynewulf the fire-breathing thane;
   And Blondell, who rescued our Richard when thralled;
And Wolfram, the "Grail" chanter; Olaf the Dane;
   And Widsith; and Caedmon—scop, troubadour, skald?

Think of me—Taillefer, light o' the slain,
   Singing at Senlac a ballad so fair,
First of the Norman knights glory to gain,
   Singing, and whirling his sword in the air.

But now they have clouded the clear ringing lyre,
   And dimmed are the splendours of long, long ago.
Neither England nor Scotland nor Wales show desire,
   Or stoop for the blooms that the dreaming-men throw.

I have died in a thousand garrets of pain
   Since I sang to the brave of the sword and the bow,
Neglected and scorned; or a drunkard—Verlaine.
   Oh, what a tumble to measureless woe!

Pity me, weep for me, proud millionaire,
   Was it not tragical—Mangan and Poe!
Thompson and Thomson, mad Villon and Clare,
   Chatterton, Middleton—tossed like the snow?

Hunger, strange passion, wild rage and despair,
   All have I suffered, and bled to the blow.
But Valour was mine, a fine instinct to dare,
   To lasso the sunlight and burn in Life's glow.

See on my proud head a coronal of thorns;
   Man may not sorrow or sin, but I know;
I am stabbed by a million sharp down-pressing horns,
   I totter and fall, and my strength is laid low.

And I raise me and brood; then I thunder and sing.
   Man's soul in my hands is a rosebud of fire.
I touch Vision and Mystery, Ecstasy's wing.
   I see God; I am rapt; I cleanse all by my lyre.

You may read on its flame-bow the name of a king,
   And o'er it a seer's—so shall Singing aspire.
There are palms in my left hand, round wrist-bone a ring;
   And the Staff of the Ages is knit to the wire.

And I measure Earth's boundaries by radiance of dreams,
   The bright stars and planets seem jewelry of Tyre,
Whirled dewdrops, or spray from our swift flowing streams.
   I draw them all down to my knees at desire.

Round me they heap and fall, emeralds and pearls,
   Sapphires, clear topazes, rubies of rose,
Crystals for queenly heads, gems for dear curls.
   Under my feet deep profundity glows.

East, West, and North and South, all the sky swirls;
   Out of Night's mouth bright Immensity flows;
O'er me and round me a hemisphere whirls;
   Wide through Heaven's windows a singing wind blows.

D

More! how they dazzle, blind, flash on mine eyes!
　　Turquoises, diamonds, and opals dream blue,
Red, green, and pale yellow—every hue, form, and size—
　　Rainbows of radiance and crystalline dew.

"Stay with me, speak to me, Power of the Skies!
　　Hear me, sweet Jesu and seraphin.
What shall I do with the wonderful prize?
　　These are enough all Earth's kingdoms to win."

Into the high vault tremblingly I peer,
　　Heaven's sword is too nigh, and God's soul is so chaste.
Softly a whispering voice steals on my ear,
　　"Give them to Mary, and fear not—but haste."

Marvellous answer! Tears spring to my eyes.
　　"Thy Mary, dear Lord, casts them down from her dress."
Oh, what a ringing laugh sunders the skies!
　　"I mean England's Mary, your gracious princess.

"For now may be proved thou art mightier than scorn,
　　Or than Earth's gleaming merchandise, silver, or gold;
Take her the stars that from Heaven thou hast torn;
　　Bewitch her with Wordcraft and Thought's shining mould;

"Ring on her listening ears a carillon of Morn,
　　Make radiant her mind with the suns here down rolled;
Bind, to gladden her eyes, many gems to Song's Horn,
　　Mary, faithful as Penelope, fine as Isolde,

"And valorous ,a soldier's wife, lovely as morn,
　　Her eyes soft as wind-flowers, her lips brave in speech,
Her tresses like ripe-waving billows of corn,
　　And honourable her deeds, and her hands swift to reach.

"To this land she shall be as a ministering sun—
　　Walk with suns in her hands, and glad stars in her hair,
And thee I will aid—now; and when thou hast won.
　　Thou shalt sing many songs, and the finest deeds dare.

"And run to brave Mary, go steadily and strong
　And softly—creep lightly up terrace and stair.
And fear not her henchmen, their steel nor the thong;
　No harsh hand shall strike thee while I'm watching there.

"And fear not her guests, nor the proud watching throng,
　Nor glittering of raiment, bright riches and power,
Though the stairway be steep and the corridor seem long,
　Thou shalt get there, and rest there, and heap high her dower.

"And tell her I love thee—I, Angel of Song.
　We are wed, for I bought thee, and radiant the price.
Though one thou art many—all have suffered Life's Wrong.
　I will richly reward thee in Paradise.

"And tell her my name; 'tis her right and her due.
　I kiss her; 'tis easy as launching of ships.
I swing like a barque 'neath a wind-shaken blue,
　To poise a brief spell on the wave of her lips.

"O! tell her my name, make it plain, whisper clear,
　Say it—Spirit of Song, Life's one kernel and pole,
All stirring emotion, strong seed in the sear,
　Pure maker, creator, sin's cleanser, Form's Soul.

"And tell her that oft at Collation and Feast,
　By the red wine and white wine and sweet-scented tea,
I shall lurk in her cup like a smouldering yeast,
　And make her heart glow, for I'm Joy and pure Glee.

"And take her these gems, she will use well the gain,
　For there's gloom o'er the Land by the starving's Despair.
There's a Fiend in your Sin, who has poisoned Christ's rain,
　And cryings and wailings are shaking the air,

"And the Soil is dishonoured; but utter this plain
　There is Hope and Salvation by deeds that are Fair,
If only the Mighty will wash out the stain
　That has darkened your Judgment Seats everywhere."

                                            [*1923*]

Elizabeth Bowen

UNWELCOME IDEA

ALONG Dublin Bay, on a sunny July morning, the public gardens along the Dalkey tramline look bright as a series of parasols. Chalk-blue sea appears at the ends of the roads of villas turning downhill—but these are still the suburbs, not the seaside. In the distance, floating across the bay, buildings glitter out of the heat-haze on the neck to Howth, and Howth Head looks higher veiled. After inland Ballsbridge, the tram from Dublin speeds up; it zooms through the residential reaches with the gathering steadiness of a launched ship. Its red velvet seating accommodation is seldom crowded—its rival, the quicker bus, lurches ahead of it down the same road.

After Ballsbridge, the ozone smell of the bay sifts more and more through the smell of chimneys and pollen and the July-darkened garden trees as the bay and line converge. Then at a point you see the whole bay open—there are nothing but flats of grass and the sunk railway between the running tram and the still sea. An immense glaring reflection floods through the tram. When high terraces, backs to the tramline, shut out the view again, even their backs have a salted, marine air; their cotton window-blinds are pulled half down, crooked; here and there an inner door left open lets you see a flash of sea through a house. The weathered lions on gate posts ought to be dolphins. Red low-lying villas have been fitted between earlier terraces, ornate, shabby, glassy hotels, bow-fronted mansions all built in the first place to stand up over spaces of grass. Looks from trams and voices from public gardens invade the old walled lawns with their grottoes and weeping willows. Spit-and-polish alternates with decay. But stucco, slate and slate-fronts, blotched Italian pink-wash, dusty windows, lace curtains and dolphin-lions seem to be the eternity of this tram route. Quite soon the modern will say, chip, fade. Change leaves everything at the same level. Nothing stays bright but mornings.

The tram slides to stops for its not many passengers. The Blackrock bottleneck checks it, then the Dun Laoghaire. These are the shopping centres strung on the line: their animation congests them. Housewives with burnt bare arms out of their cotton dresses mass blinking and talking among the halted traffic, knocking their shopping-bags on each others' thighs. Forgotten Protestant ladies from "rooms" near the esplanade stand squeezed between the kerb and the shops. A file of booted children threads its way through the crush, a nun at the head like a needle. Children by themselves curl their toes in their plimsoles and suck sweets and disregard everything. The goods stacked in the shops look very static and hot. Out from the tops of the shops on brackets stand a number of clocks. As though wrought up by the clocks the tram-driver smites his bell again and again, till the checked tram noses its way through.

By half-past eleven this morning one tram to Dalkey is not far on its way. All the time it approaches the Ballsbridge stop Mrs. Kearney looks undecided, but when it does pull up she steps aboard because she has seen no bus. In a slither of rather ungirt parcels, including a dress box, with a magazine held firmly between her teeth, she clutches her way up the stairs to the top. She settles herself on a velvet seat: she is hot. But the doors at each end and the windows are half open, and as the tram moves air rushes smoothly through. There are only four other people and no man smokes a pipe. Mrs. Kearney has finished wedging her parcels between her hip and the side of the tram and is intending to look at her magazine when she stares hard ahead and shows interest in someone's back. She moves herself and everything three seats up, leans forward and gives a poke at the back. "Isn't that you?" she says.

Miss Kevin jumps round so wholeheartedly that the brims of the two hats almost clash. "Why, for goodness' sake! . . . Are you on the tram?" She settles round in her seat with her elbow hooked over the back—it is bare and sharp, with a rubbed joint: she and Mrs. Kearney are of an age, and the age is about thirty-five. They both wear printed dresses that in this weather stick close to their backs; they are enthusiastic, not close friends, but as close as they are ever likely to be. They both have high, fresh pink colouring; Mrs. Kearney could do with a little less weight and Miss Kevin could do with a little more.

They agree they are out early. Miss Kevin has been in town for the July sales but is now due home to let her mother go out.

She has parcels with her but they are compact and shiny, having been made up at the counters of shops. "They all say, buy now. You never know." She cannot help looking at Mrs. Kearney's parcels, bursting out from their string. "And aren't you very laden, also," she says.

"I tell you what I've been doing," says Mrs. Kearney, "I've been saying good-bye to my sister Maureen in Ballsbridge, and who knows how long it's to be for! My sister's off to County Cavan this morning with the whole of her family and the maid."

"For goodness' sake," says Miss Kevin. "Has she relatives there?"

"She has, but it's not that. She's evacuating. For the holidays they always go to Tramore, but this year she says she should evacuate." This brings Mrs. Kearney's parcels into the picture. "So she asked me to keep a few of her things for her." She does not add that Maureen has given her these old things, including the month-old magazine.

"Isn't it well for her," says Miss Kevin politely. "But won't she find it terribly slow down there?"

"She will, I tell you," says Mrs. Kearney. "However, they're all driving down in the car. She's full of it. She says we should all go somewhere where we don't live. It's nothing to her to shift when she has the motor. But the latest thing I hear they say now in the paper, is that we'll be shot if we don't stay where we are. They say now we're all to keep off the roads—and there's my sister this morning with her car at the door. Do you think they'll halt her, Miss Kevin?"

"They might," says Miss Kevin. "I hear they're very suspicious. I declare, with the instructions changing so quickly it's better to take no notice. You'd be upside down if you tried to follow them all. It's of the first importance to keep calm, they say, and however would we keep calm doing this, then that? Still, we don't get half the instructions they get in England. I should think they'd really pity themselves. . . . Have you earth in your house, Mrs. Kearney? We have, we have three buckets. The warden's delighted with us: he says we're models. We haven't a refuge, though. Have you one?"

"We have a kind of a pump, but I don't know it is much good. And nothing would satisfy Fergus till he turned out the cellar."

"Well, you're very fashionable!"

"The contents are on the lawn, and the lawn's ruined. He's crazy", she says glumly, "with A.R.P."

"Aren't men very thorough," says Miss Kevin with a virgin detachment that is rather annoying. She has kept thumbing her sales parcels, and now she cannot resist undoing one. "Listen," she says, "isn't this a pretty delaine?" She runs the end of a fold between her finger and thumb. "It drapes sweetly. I've enough for a dress and a bolero. It's French: they say we won't get any more now."

"And that Coty scent—isn't that French?"

Their faces flood with the glare struck from the sea as the tram zooms smoothly along the open reach—wall and trees on its inland side, grass and bay on the other. The tips of their shingles and the thoughts in their heads are for the minute blown about and refreshed. Mrs. Kearney flutters in the holiday breeze, but Miss Kevin is looking inside her purse. Mrs. Kearney thinks she will take the kids to the strand. "Are you a great swimmer, Miss Kevin?"

"I don't care for it: I've a bad circulation. It's a fright to see me go blue. They say now the sea's full of mines," she says, with a look at the great innocent bay.

"Ah, they're tethered; they'd never bump you."

"I'm not nervous at any time, but I take a terrible chill."

"My sister Maureen's nervous. At Tramore she'll never approach the water: it's the plage she enjoys. I wonder what will she do if they stop the car—she has all her plate with her in the back with the maid. And her kiddies are very nervous: they'd never stand it. I wish now I'd asked her to send me a telegram. Or should I telegraph her to know did she arrive? . . . Wasn't it you said we had to keep off the roads?"

"That's in the event of invasion, Mrs. Kearney. In the event of not it's correct to evacuate."

"She's correct all right, then," says Mrs. Kearney, with a momentary return to gloom. "And if nothing's up by the finish she'll say she went for the holiday, and I shouldn't wonder if she still went to Tramore. Still, I'm sure I'm greatly relieved to hear what you say. . . . Is that your father's opinion?"

Miss Kevin becomes rather pettish. "Him?" she says, "oh gracious, I'd never ask him. He has a great contempt for the whole war. My mother and I daren't refer to it—isn't it very mean of him? He does nothing but read the papers and roar away to himself. And will he let my mother or me near him when he has the news on? You'd think", Miss Kevin says, with a clear laugh, "that the two of us originated the war to spite him: he doesn't seem to blame Hitler at all. He's really very unreasonable when he's not well. We'd a great fight to get in the buckets of earth, and now he makes out they're only there for the cat. And to hear the warden praising us makes him sour. Isn't it very mean to want us out of it all, when they say the whole of the country is drawn together. He doesn't take any pleasure in A.R.P."

"To tell you the truth I don't either," says Mrs. Kearney. "Isn't it that stopped Horse Show? Wouldn't that take the heart out of you—isn't that a great blow to national life? I never yet missed a Horse Show—Sheila was nearly born there. And isn't that a terrible blow to trade? I haven't the heart to look for a new hat. To my mind this war's getting very monotonous: all the interest of it is confined to a few. . . . Did you go to the Red Cross Fête?"

The tram grinds to a halt in Dun Laoghaire Street. Simultaneously Miss Kevin and Mrs. Kearney move up to the window ends of their seats and look closely down on the shop windows and shoppers. Town heat comes off the street in a quiver and begins to pervade the immobile tram. "I declare to goodness," exclaims Miss Kevin, "there's my same delaine! French, indeed! And watch the figure it's on—it would sicken you."

But with parallel indignation Mrs. Kearney has just noticed a clock. "Will you look at the time!" she says, plaintively. "Isn't this an awfully slow tram! There's my morning gone, and not a thing touched at home, from attending evacuations. It's well for her! She expected me on her step by ten—'It's a terrible parting,' she says on the p.c. But all she does at the last is to chuck the parcels at me, then keep me running to see had they the luncheon basket and what had they done with her fur coat. . . . I'll be off at the next stop, Miss Kevin dear. Will you tell your father and mother I was enquiring for them?" Crimson again at the very notion of moving, she begins to scrape her parcels under her wing. "Well," she says, "I'm off with the *objets d'art.*" The heels of a pair of evening slippers protrude from a gap at

the end of the dress box. The tram-driver, by smiting his bell,
drowns any remark Miss Kevin could put out: the tram clears
the crowd and moves down Dun Laoghaire Street, between
high flights of steps, lace curtains, gardens with round beds.
"Bye-bye, now," says Mrs. Kearney, rising and swaying.

"Bye-bye to you," says Miss Kevin. "Happy days to us all."

Mrs. Kearney, near the top of the stairs, is preparing to bite
on the magazine. "Go on!" she says. "I'll be seeing you before
then."   [*1940*]

Sagittarius

NERVES

I THINK I'll get a paper,
I think I'd better wait.
I'll hear the news at six o'clock,
That's much more up to date.

It's just like last September,
Absurd how time stands still;
They're bound to make a statement.
I don't suppose they will.

I think I'd better stroll around.
Perhaps it's best to stay.
I think I'll have a whisky neat,
I can't this time of day.

I think I'll have another smoke.
I don't know what to do.
I promised to ring someone up,
I can't remember who.

They say it's been averted.
They say we're on the brink.
I'll wait for the *New Statesman*,
I wonder what they think.

They're shouting. It's a Special.
It's not. It's just street cries.
I think the heat is frightful.
God damn these bloody flies.

I see the nation's keeping cool,
The public calm is fine.
This crisis can't shake England's nerves. . . .
It's playing hell with mine.   [*1939*]

Desmond Shawe-Taylor

AN AUSTERE FICTION

MISS COMPTON-BURNETT is one of the very few really original
novelists alive, but her work is known only to a limited public.
Though she could never become a best-seller, there must be
many people (particularly among those who do not much care
for modern novels in general) who, if they knew of her, would
cheerfully undertake the continuous intellectual exercise of
reading her books for the sake of the continuous intellectual
exhilaration—and something more—which is its reward. It is
to them, and not to the convinced Compton-Burnett fans, that
this review is addressed.

Her novels all have the same sort of characters, the same sort
of plot, and the same sort of title: *Men and Wives, Brothers and
Sisters, Pastors and Masters*, and now *Daughters and Sons*. They are
carried on almost entirely in dialogue of extreme formality,
precision and concision, unless one of her bores is speaking (and

a Compton-Burnett bore is something to remember), when we have instead speeches of a measured rotundity and unction. No one is ever guilty of "ums" or "ers", of incomplete or ungrammatical sentences—not even the children; yet so extraordinary is the evocative power of this highly stylised art that the twelve-year-old Muriel is one of the most memorable and defined characters in *Daughters and Sons*. There is generally a group of adolescent brothers and sisters who comment caustically and accurately upon the actions and words of their elders. Inquisitive and peculiar neighbours are invited to dine with the family, usually at some moment of appalling though latent crisis, and utter a fair share of pungent comment themselves. (Miss Compton-Burnett's dinner-parties are indeed grisly affairs; as though Jane Austen should try her hand at the banquet scene of *Macbeth*.) The action is confined to some small English country town or village (unnamed), and the period inclines to be some thirty ot forty years ago. But we are really outside space and time, for we see nothing, nothing is described, there is no scenery, no weather, no props, none of those odds and ends put in by all ordinary novelists for the sake of atmosphere and reality. This is the novel *démeublé* with a vengeance. A picture of the world is conveyed not unlike that which one might attribute to a man born blind, but with his hearing, awareness and nervous sensibility proportionately sharpened.

And what does it all lead to? What is the matter, the action that underlies all this politely impolite conversation and provokes so many acid generalizations? The matter is usually the extreme internal tension of family life, fed by jealousy, nerves, suspicion, the lust to dominate, and the usual discrepancies of age and outlook, and brought at last to such a pitch that the chief characters are scarcely sane. Eventually they reach the limits of endurance, and lose all control, while continuing to talk effortless Compton-Burnett prose. Then there is matricide, suicide, infanticide, incest, horror of the classical order, high tragedy. Nor, after the deed, is the tragic chorus silent. The rain of comment continues, life goes on and not very differently, everyone is aware both of the difference and how slight it is. The family reshuffles itself, a new governess is engaged, the neighbours withdraw, the curtain falls upon a situation not resolved, but merely transposed into another key. For this austere fiction is concerned with the skeleton of humanity, and original sin cannot be banished from bare bones.

In *Daughters and Sons* the horrors are less lavish than usual. The plot centres upon Sabine Ponsonby, a magnificently rude old termagant of eighty-five, her son John (widowed with five children) and her daughter Hetta, an insanely possessive woman who has devoted her life to her brother and consequently cannot endure his second marriage. She pretends (perhaps really attempts—we are never quite sure which) to commit suicide, and, when all have accepted the fact of her death, unexpectedly returns; the shock of all this kills old Mrs. Ponsonby. So at least we should put it in our loose way; but her granddaughters, characteristically discussing the impending event some moments *before* it occurs, are, as usual, more exact:

"Aunt Hetta has killed Grandma."

"It is unfortunate to harm anyone of eighty-five. You are said to have killed her, when it is such a small part of the killing you have done. It is eighty-five years that have killed Grandma."

Conventional ideas and phrases are constantly thus tested and found wanting by these mercilessly logical people. Sometimes it is on their own lips that they detect a vagueness of thought which they hasten to correct, or at any rate to question:

"Miss Blake is not even here; she is showing true dignity; but I always wonder if the true kinds of dignity, the dignity of toil and simplicity and frugal independence, are as good as the other kinds. Edith seems to like the ordinary dignity of being married to John: I have noticed how well ordinary dignity sits on people. Now we turn our eyes on a simple, family scene. I don't know why simple is so often coupled with family. Simple family affection, simple family life; yes, it is wrong. . . ."

It is not surprising that a passion for verbal precision should frequently flower into brilliant wit; and on the rare occasions when the author allows herself a brief narrative paragraph, precision is still the keynote of the style. Take the sentence which introduces the speaker of the passage quoted above, Miss Charity Marcon:

"Miss Charity Marcon walked up her garden path, crossed her hall and entered her plain little drawing-room, her great height almost coinciding with the door, and her long neck bending, lest the experience of years should prove at fault and it should quite coincide with it."

If you relish that faultless sentence it is probable that Miss Compton-Burnett is your author, and that you will come to find in this formal, witty dialectic, quivering with sensibility and insight into the human heart, a rare pleasure like no other. It should be observed, by the way, that people coming into the room in her books invariably overhear the last remark, though it is not often meant for their ears. This has the double result of preserving unchecked the flow of the dialogue, and of emphasizing the interlocking horror of family life, which is her constant theme. There is an interesting passage in *Daughters and Sons* in which the author seems to be defending her obsession with this subject. A new governess named Edith Hallam has just arrived and Sabine starts a family row:

"Miss Hallam is seeing us as we are," said Clare. "Do families often stand revealed as soon as this?"
"Yes, fairly often," said Edith. "You would hardly believe about families. Or many people would not.
"We have to belong to a family to believe it," said France, "But everybody does belong to one. It seems too odd, when you think of what is involved."

Miss Compton-Burnett's range is obviously limited, though the limitations are of her own choosing. Her method cannot, for example, portray people who are both stupid and silent; and in all her books the outside characters are rather shadowy, as is almost inevitable. Deep emotions are implied rather than directly expressed, though the threnody of Sabine over her supposedly dead daughter (too long to quote here) rises to heights of eloquence hardly scaled before by the author. Her strange books have about them the golden touch of perfection: in their own sphere they are flawless works of art, and no one else could conceivably have written a page of them.   [*1937*]

Lytton Strachey

THE PRÉSIDENT DE BROSSES

A CHARMING and sometimes forgotten feature of the world as it used to be before the age of trains and telephones was the provincial capital. When Edinburgh was as far from London as Vienna is to-day, it was natural—it was inevitable—that it should be the centre of a local civilization, which, while it remained politically and linguistically British, developed a colour and character of its own. In France there was the same pleasant phenomenon. Bordeaux, Toulouse, Aix-en-Provence —up to the end of the eighteenth century each of these was in truth a capital where a peculiar culture had grown up that was at once French and idiosyncratic. An impossibility to-day! It is hard to believe, as one whisks through Dijon in a tram, that here, a hundred and fifty years ago, was the centre of a distinct and vigorous civilization—until perhaps, one leaves the tram and turns aside into the Rue de la Préfecture. Ah! One has come upon a vanished age. The houses, so solid and yet so vivacious, with their cobbled courts and coloured tiles, seem to be withdrawn into an aristocratic resignation. Memory and forgetfulness are everywhere. It is the moment to reflect upon the Président de Brosses.

Dijon, the capital of Burgundy, had become, in the eighteenth century, pre-eminently a city of magistrates. There the provincial *parlement* assembled, and the laws were administered by the hereditary judges, the nobility of the long robe, whose rule was more immediate, more impressive, and almost more powerful, than the king's. Charles de Brosses was born into this aristocracy, and grew up to be a perfect representative of its highest traditions. He was extremely intelligent, admirably conscientious, and crammed full of life. He was at once a wit, a scholar, a lawyer, and a man of the world. He resembled the generous wine of the country in his combination of gay vitality with richness and strength. His tiny figure and his satirical face, lost in the forest of a judicial wig, might prompt to laughter—"the corners of one's mouth", said Diderot, "couldn't

help going up when one looked at him"; but he was impressive
on the bench; and, late in life, was to prove his patriotism by
his intrepid resistance when the privileges of his province were
attacked by the royal authority. In his leisure he devoted himself to every kind of literary and scientific work. A tour in Italy
produced a series of amusing letters which, published post-
humously, are still read and remembered; his book on the
newly-discovered Herculaneum (1750) was the first on the
subject; his *Histoire des Navigations des Terres Australes* (1756) was
of use to both Cook and Bougainville; his *Culte des dieux fétiches*
(1760) contained a curious speculation on the origin of the
religion of Egypt; his *Traité de la formation mécanique des langues*
(1765) was the earliest attempt at a science of etymology; and
his labours were concluded with an elaborate edition of Sallust
(1777) upon which he had worked for thirty years. The growth
of knowledge has converted his researches and his speculations
into mere curiosities; but it was natural that the citizens of
Dijon should have honoured him as one of their most splendid
luminaries, and that the Président de Brosses should have been
compared in his day to that other great provincial figure of a
previous generation—the Président de Montesquieu. Of course,
though Dijon was select and Dijon was magnificent, it had to
be admitted that there did exist a higher tribunal, at whose
bar taste, learning and behaviour received their final doom
or their crowning approbation: the drawing-rooms of Paris
reigned supreme. In those drawing-rooms the Président was
well thought of; he had powerful friends at Court; was it not
to be expected that at last, in the fullness of time, his worth
would be completely recognized and receive its due reward
in the highest honour that could fall to a man of his pretensions
—a seat in the Academy? A prize, indeed, that it was impossible
not to hope for! The promises of other worlds had grown dim
and dubious; but here, among the glorious forty, was a definite,
and indisputable immortality—and one, moreover, that possessed the singular advantage of being enjoyable here and now,
while the eighteenth-century sun still shone on the rue de la
Préfecture.

The Président was at the height of his exuberant manhood
—he was not yet fifty—when something occurred which had
a strange and unexpected effect upon his history. Voltaire,

having quarrelled with Frederick the Great and shaken the
dust of Potsdam from his feet, had been wandering for some
years in uncertainty among the minor States that lay between
France and Germany. He had settled for a time at Colmar;
he had moved to Lausanne; then he had gone to Geneva and
taken a country house in its neighbourhood. But the Calvinism
of the townspeople, who frowned at his passion for private
theatricals, annoyed him, and his eye fell on the territory of
Ferney, which was just inside the borders of France, but, lying
on the eastern slopes of the Jura mountains, was so remote
as to be almost independent of French control and within a
drive of the free city of Geneva. This was exactly what he
wanted—a secluded abode, where he would have elbow-room
for his activities, and from which he could bolt at any moment
if things became too hot for him. Accordingly, in 1758, he
bought Ferney, where he lived for the rest of his life; and at the
same time he entered into negotiations for the purchase of a
neighbouring property—that of Tournay—which belonged to
the Président de Brosses. The Président, who already had a
slight acquaintance with the great man—his wife, a Crèvecoeur,
was the daughter of one of Voltaire's oldest friends—declared
that he would be delighted to oblige him. There was some
stiff haggling, for each party prided himself on his business
capacity, but eventually Voltaire, for 35,000 francs, became
possessed of the domain of Tournay—which included the right
to the title of Count—on a life tenancy. The bargain, obviously, was something of a gamble; the new Comte de Tournay
was sixty-four and, so he declared, on the point of death; but
then he had been on the point of death ever since anyone could
remember. When it was all over, the Président had an uneasy
feeling that he had been done. The feeling increased as time
went on, and his agent informed him that the estate was being
allowed to go to rack and ruin. He complained, but the poet
replied with a flat denial, declared—what was quite true—
that he had built a theatre at Tournay, and begged the Président to come and see his latest tragedy performed in it. A little
later a new manœuvre began; Voltaire proposed that he should
buy the property outright. The Président was not altogether
averse, but this time he was far more cautious; as the negotiations proceeded he became privately convinced that an

attempt was being made to cheat him, but he said nothing; and the proposal lapsed. Voltaire, on his side, was none too pleased with his bargain. The land of Tournay was poor, and the countship had brought with it various responsibilities and expenses not at all to his taste. He was vexed; and his vexation took the form of bothering the Président, in letter after letter, with a multitude of legal questions upon points connected with the property. The Président was also vexed, but he answered every letter and every question with extreme civility.

In this way two years passed—two years during which the Président published his *Culte des dieux fétiches* and Voltaire his *Candide*. The old creature at Ferney was at last beginning to settle down to the final and by far the most important period of his immense and extraordinary career. Free, rich, happy, with his colossal reputation and his terrific energy, he was starting on the great adventure of his life—his onslaught upon Christianity. Meanwhile, his vitality and his pugnacity were satisfying themselves in a multitude of minor ways. He was belabouring Rousseau, torturing Fréron, annihilating Le Franc de Pompignan; he was corresponding with all the world, he was composing half a dozen tragedies, he was writing the life of Peter the Great, he was preparing a monumental edition of Corneille. When, in the midst of these and a hundred other activities, he received a bill for 281 francs from a peasant called Charlot Baudy for fourteen loads of wood from Tournay, he brushed the matter on one side. More bother from Tournay! But it was ridiculous. Why should he pay for wood from his own estate? And besides, he remembered quite well that the Président, before the sale was completed, had told him that he could have as much wood as he wanted. He did nothing, and when Charlot Baudy pressed for the money, refused to pay. Then, early in 1761, a letter arrived from the Président. "Agréez, Monsieur," he began, "que je vous demande l'explication d'une chose tout-à-fait singulière." Charlot Baudy, he continued, had, *before the sale of Tournay*, bought from the Président the cut wood on the estate; Baudy had now sent in his account of what he owed the Président, and had subtracted from it the sum of 281 francs for wood supplied to M. de

Voltaire; his reason for this was that M. de Voltaire had told him that the wood was a gift from the Président. "Je vous demande excuse," the letter went on, "si je vous répète un tel propos: car vous sentez bien que je suis fort éloigné de croire que vous l'ayez tenu, et je n'y ajoute pas la moindre foi. Je ne prends ceci que pour le discours d'un homme rustique fait pour ignorer les usages du monde et les convenances; qui ne sait pas qu'on envoie bien à son ami et son voisin un panier de pêches, mais que si on s'avisait de lui faire la galanterie de quatorze moules de bois, il le prendrait pour une absurdité contraire aux bienséances." The sarcasm was clear and cutting, and the Président proceeded to give his own account of what had occurred. He distinctly remembered, he said, that Voltaire, at the time of the negotiations about Tournay, had, in the course of conversation, complained of a lack of firewood, and that he had thereupon recommended Baudy as the man who would supply Voltaire with as much as he wanted. That was all; the offensive notion of a present had never entered his head. "J'espère," he concluded, "que vous voudrez bien faire incontinent payer cette bagatelle à Charlot parce que, comme je me ferai certainement payer de lui, il aurait infailliblement aussi son recours contre vous; ce qui ferait une affaire du genre de celles qu'un homme tel que vous ne veut point avoir."

It was obvious to anyone in his senses that the Président was right; that his account of the matter was the true one, and that, as he had said, the only reasonable thing for Voltaire to do was to pay Baudy the money—the miserable sum of money!—and finish the business. But Voltaire was not in his senses—he never was when even the most miserable sum of money was concerned. He could not bear to think of parting with 281 francs. It was monstrous; the land and everything on it was his; the wood had been given him; he would not be set down; and this wretched man had dared to be ironical! At any rate, he had had the wood and burnt it, and the Président de Brosses might do what he liked. Accordingly, in his next letter, he airily dismissed the subject. "It is no longer a question", he said, "of Charles Baudy and four loads of wood——" and proceeded to discuss an entirely different matter. The Président replied in detail and then reverted for a moment to Baudy. "Four loads—read *fourteen*; you dropped a figure; we call this a *lapsus linguæ*" and he begged Voltaire once more to avoid the painful publicity of a lawsuit. Voltaire made no reply; he hoped the whole thing was over; but he was wrong. In June, the Président sued Baudy for 281 francs, and in July Baudy sued Voltaire for the same sum. The cases came on at the local court, and were adjourned.

II

And now the fury of the frantic old desperado flamed up sky-high. Seizing his pen, he poured out, in letter after letter to all the lawyers in Dijon, his account of what had happened— the swindling to which he had been subjected, the insults to which he had been exposed. To a particular friend, the Président de Ruffey, he sent a long formal statement of his case, followed by a private sheet of enraged argumentation. As for his enemy, he was no longer a président—the little bewigged monster—he was a fetish. He would see to it that the nickname stuck. "Le Fétiche," he shrieked, "demande de l'argent de ses moules et de ses fagots. . . . Le misérable m'accable d'exploits." He had put up Baudy, who was a man of straw, to do his dirty work. "Songez qu'il faisait cette infâmie dans le temps qu'il recevait de moi 47 mille livres! . . . Qu'il tremble! Il ne s'agit pas de le rendre ridicule: il s'agit de le déshonorer. Cela n'afflige. Mais il payera cher la bassesse d'un procédé si coupable et si lâche." Finally, he addressed the Fetish himself in a letter composed in his most magnificent style. "Vous n'êtes donc venu chez moi, Monsieur, vous ne m'avez offert votre amitié, que pour empoisonner par des procès la fin de ma vie." In great detail he went over the whole dispute. With singular violence, and no less singular obtuseness, he asserted the hopelessly contradictory propositions, both that the wood was his by purchase and that the Président had given it him; he hinted that his enemy would make use of his position to pervert the course of justice; and he ended with threats. "S'il faut que M. le Chancelier, et les Ministres, et tout Paris, soient instruits de votre procédé, ils le seront: et, s'il se trouve dans votre Compagnie respectable une personne qui vous approuve, je me condamne."

The Président's moment had come—the testing moment of his life. What was he to do? It was still not too late to withdraw, to pay the money with a shrug of the shoulders and put an end to this fearful hubbub and this terrifying enmity. For a short space he wavered. It was true that Voltaire was the greatest writer of the age, and perhaps he deserved some allowances on that score. In any case, he was an extremely dangerous antagonist—a man who had made mincemeat of all his literary opponents and fought on equal terms with Frederick the Great. But no! It was intolerable! His Burgundian blood boiled, and the proud traditions of aristocracy and the judicial habits of a lifetime asserted themselves. "Là-dessus on dit"— so he explained later to a friend—"c'est un homme dangereux. Et à cause de cela, faut-il donc le laisser être méchant impunément? Ce sont au contraire ces sortes de gens-là qu'il faut châtier. Je ne le crains pas. . . . On l'admire, parce qu'il fait d'excellents vers. Sans doute il les fait excellents. Mais ce sont ses vers qu'il faut admirer." And so, taking Voltaire's letter, he wrote upon the margin of it a reply, in which he not only rebutted his arguments, but told him exactly what he thought of him. Point by point he exposed the futility of Voltaire's contentions. He showed that there was actually a clause in the lease by which the cut wood on the estate was specifically excepted from the sale. He offered to drop the matter if Voltaire would send him a receipt in the following terms: "Je soussigné, François-Marie Arouet de Voltaire, chevalier, seigneur de Ferney, gentilhomme ordinaire de la chambre du Roi, reconnois que M. de Brosses, président du Parlement, m'a fait présent de . . . voies de bois de moule, pour mon chauffage, en valeur de 281 fr., dont je le remercie." He pointed out that otherwise he had nothing to do with the business, that Voltaire owed the money to Charlot Baudy, and that it was indeed extraordinary to see "un homme si riche et si illustre se tourmenter à tel excès pour ne pas payer à un paysan 280 livres pour du bois de chauffage qu'il a fourni". His incidental remarks were nothing if not outspoken. "En vérité", he wrote, "je gémis pour l'humanité de voir un si grand génie avec un coeur si petit sans cesse tiraillé par des misères de jalousie et de lésine. C'est vous-même qui empoisonnez une vie si bien faite d'ailleurs pour être heureuse."

As for the suggestion that he would bring undue influence to
bear upon the case—"il ne convient pas de parler ainsi:
soyez assez sage à l'avenir pour ne rien dire de pareil à un
magistrat". "Tenez-vous pour dit," the letter concluded, "de
ne m'écrire plus ni sur cette matière ni surtout de ce ton. Je
vous fais, Monsieur, le souhait de Perse: *Mens sana in corpore
sano.*"

It is difficult, indeed, to imagine the scene at Ferney while
Voltaire was deciphering, on the edges of his own letter, this
devastating reply. But there was worse to follow. A note came
from the Président de Ruffey, in which, with infinite polite-
ness, he made it clear that, in his opinion, Voltaire had no
case, and that he had better pay. At the same time Ruffey
wrote to Madame Denis, Voltaire's niece, advising her to
give the money privately to Baudy. Madame Denis had not
the courage to do so; she showed the letter to her uncle who,
in a dictated reply, still tried to keep up an appearance of
self-confidence. "Je ne crains point les Fétiches," he added in
his own hand, "et les Fétiches doivent me craindre." And
again, at the bottom of the paper, he scribbled: "N.B.—Il n'y
a qu'une voix sur le Fétiche." But such screams were useless;
the game was up. The President's letter remained unanswered;
Voltaire swallowed in silence the incredible affront; and when,
a little later, the Président, feeling that he could afford to be
magnanimous, informed a common friend that he would
cancel his account with Baudy if Voltaire gave 281 francs to
the poor of Tournay, the great man was glad enough to fall
in with the suggestion.

The Président had triumphed; but could he really have
supposed that he would escape from such an antagonist un-
scathed? The sequel came ten years later, when the Président
Hénault died and left a seat vacant at the Academy. There
was a strong movement in favour of electing the Président
de Brosses. There appeared to be no other very suitable
candidate; his friends rallied round him, and D'Alembert,
writing to Voltaire from Paris, assured him that there was
every likelihood that "ce plat Président" would be chosen
for the vacant place. The serious feature of the case was that
the old Maréchal de Richelieu who, after a lifetime of fighting
and gallantry, amused his decrepitude by making his influence

felt in affairs of this kind, supported him. What was to be done?
Voltaire was equal to the occasion: his letters flew. At all costs
the Fetish must be kept out. He wrote repeatedly to Richelieu,
in that tone of delicate cajolery of which he was a master,
touching upon their ancient friendship, and spinning a strange
tale of the perfidies committed by "ce petit persécuteur
nasilloneur", until the Maréchal melted, and promised to withdraw his support. Finally Voltaire despatched to D'Alembert a
signed declaration to the effect that he would himself resign
from the Academy if Brosses was elected. This settled the
matter, and no more was heard of the candidature of the
Président. It seems likely that he never knew what it was
that had baulked him of the ambition of his life. For 281
francs he had lost the immortality of the Academy. A bad
bargain, no doubt; and yet, after all, the transaction had
gained him another, and in fact a unique, distinction; he
would go down to history as the man who had got the better
of Voltaire.   [*1931*]

Walter de la Mare

MAKING A FIRE

Scatter a few cold cinders into the grate;
On these lay paper puffed into airy balloon,
Then kindling wood, parched by the suns of summer, drowsy
    and sweet;
Then coal. A flare: a flame: and a fire will be burning soon—

Antler-tongued and impetuous. But unless you pay heed,
It will fall, fade, and grow heatless and ash away out.
So is it with anger in heart and in brain: the insensate seed
Of fiery enkindling leaps into horror and rout;

But remaining untended, it dies, and the soul within
Is refreshed by the dews of sweet amity, compassion's cool rain.
Not so with the flames Hell has kindled for unassoiled sin,
As soon as God's mercy would quench them, love, weeping,
    lights them again.   [*1931*]

Jean de Néveur

THE SARDINE

THE sea was transparent.

In the boat the young man bent over the girl, whispering to her, softly. Their faces were radiant as the gulls skimmed the foam.

The sardine dived under the hull of the boat and came to the surface again. She was deaf, and could not hear what they were saying, but she knew the secrets of the seaweed and the coloured depths.

The sardine could see the little wrinkles at the corners of the lovers' mouths. She sailed round the fragile barque, darted off to a distance, then peeped in over the side. The sunlight caught one of her scales, and shining up through the waves, alighted gently on the young man's eyelid. As he blinked, the sardine, swept away by the current, joined a passing shoal of herrings.

The bells rang out till the church roof swayed. The young couple were married in the scent of lilies. Their white-gloved hands were like fluttering doves.

The fisherman was spreading his nets. Bitter tears seared his cheeks, for he could not turn away from the horizon.

The sardine was a prisoner.

Time dripped slowly from the myriad parasite clocks and the young people settled down in a tidy house.

In the canning factory the sardine passed hundreds of dirty finger-nails before falling asleep in her tin bed. She slept soundly on the grocery shelves. She did not hear the door creaking, nor count the thousand footsteps alighting to soar again.

One autumn evening, the sardine awoke on a white field between an artichoke and a team of radishes. About to signal the kick-off, she suddenly recognized two distorted faces, angry teeth—a quarrel. She slithered quickly into her shallow oil.

A bright glint caught from the garish lamp slipped beneath the young man's eyelids. He saw the wide ocean, their kisses, the sunshine, and their love.

He touched the woman's hand, and his anger dropped away. With his free hand he impaled the sardine on a fork.   [*1939*]

G. W. Stonier

GOD'S GARGOYLES

COME, take my arm, Chris Smart, and we'll depart
On a visit after your own heart.
Here in stained windows all things praise
God giver of ways and days.
Here animal, insect, bird
Unite to magnify the Word
Divine. The elephants parade,
The spotted deer walks unafraid
Of tiger staring into night,
The owl, the eagle and the kite
Rule each his cage of wire and scorn
Those to the common aviary born.
The blushing fox eludes his stink
On legs that delicately slink;
The parrots curse, the monkeys run
Over a rockery in the sun.
The darting mongoose leaves his bed,
The lovely circus overhead
Delves deep in the mesmeric lake
Where demoiselle crane and drake
Stir ringlets; on the high trapeze
Concolor gibbons take their ease.
Anteater sniffs opossum;
The mandrill airs his bum,
Affrights a visitor. The Diana monkey,
Pretty and bowlegged as a flunkey,
With Confucius' face,
Beard and tufts of yellowy lace,
Stoops to drink or turn a somersault.
While marmosets and capuchins vault,
The lion dreams in his own likeness, and
Cowering on scorched sand
The peahen tries
To forget a thousand eyes.

Sex opens avenues, in Eden barred,
To the bear, the emu and the leopard.
No apple-tree of life
Tempts to centuries of strife,
Among the tortoises no fable
Tells of Cain killing Abel,
And the Esau of the apes
Valiantly escapes
With meat and inheritance, too.
Then, on a visit to the Zoo,
Besides God, the thing is you.
What woe is in this camel's scars.
The ape behind bars
Answers an ape within.
When the parrot speaks
It is a little of yourself that leaks.
Peacocks enjoy in innocence
The vanity that blunts our sense.
You may tickle squirrels' necks
Without encouraging their sex,
You may feel your passion go
Out to the panther, black and slow;
He doesn't know it,
Or that you, a poet,
Are racked by his image forever after.
The bat clings to the rafter
Blind to your curiosities,
The baboon nimbly tries
In public, unashamed,
Vices best not named,
And looks you in the eye. You only stare
At Nature following nature everywhere.
And you, Chris Smart, poor Bedlamite,
Were there beasts tempting to the sight
Among your fellow-sufferers,
Did your verse
Find out an innocence in those
Who escaped sin and guilt in throes
Of mental illness? Or was all black,
All lost, all darkened, all thrust back?

Here is the scene. I set up an easel in the mind,
Brushes, canvas are to hand,
And while I wait the memory stirs
Beyond big beasts to lesser furs:
Jerboa, jumping mouse of the desert,
Mud-skipper, moon-fish, wart-
Hog self-transfixed, the seahorse lonely
A chessman undersea,
The false water-boatman furiously
Paddling along a pool,
The sad, the cruel
Lives of snakes,
Eremites of the desert, for whose sakes
Vermin go on pilgrimages
To worship, to be devoured by stages:
All in a vision kept
By the brain catalept
Of the fury of the earth's plenty,
Of creation's mastery,
A cathedral born and built
Of divine innocence and human guilt.   [*1939*]

Cyril Connolly

PART OF THE PATTERN

I READ this book[1] in an aeroplane. Is that a fair test? When one soars in the sunshine for three hours over a white tablecloth of cloud, with one's ears inflated, does every book appear niggling and terrestrial? Probably a little—and yet, resumed on earth, the general impression remains that this is something that is almost always shallow and often dull. Between pages 1–82 which give a sympathetic account of his childhood, and pages 215 onwards, where *The Vortex* comes out, and he is a success, there lie a hundred and fifty pages of doldrums: a long dull chronicle of dead plays and bad parts from which nothing of importance emerges except the feeling that the author is refusing us his confidence. Of course this whole autobiography is built round old theatre programmes—when one knows the play they have sometimes a sentimental interest, but their cumulative effect is appalling. The hungry sheep cry out and are not fed. Mr. Coward continues to play easily, agreeably, and cagily upon his scrannel pipe and all one can wonder is what lies behind this elaborate by-play. "I firmly resisted the temptation to work during those weeks. This was difficult. A tune certainly did slip through the barricade one day while I was on the beach and, between waking and dozing in the sun, I lazily fitted words to it. It lay forgotten at the back of my mind for many months until it emerged, nearly a year later, as a 'Room with a View'." We learn more about his methods of composition from Miss Ethel Mannin, who describes him as interrupting an epigram to say "that would make a wonderful lyric", and then dancing about the room singing:

> Loose about the hips
> Loose about the lips.

And if you are interested in the genesis of *Room with a View*, you will want to know all about the vicissitudes of *Poor Little Rich Girl*, and the two English and two American performances

[1] *Present Indicative*, by Noel Coward.

of *The Vortex*, and how he got the idea of *Bitter Sweet* and wrote
Private Lives in four days—and that is about all he wants you to
know. The lives of actors are notoriously dull; their emotional
life is vitiated by their performances on the stage; they are an
envious, gossiping, sentimental, generous, reminiscent Thamesy
lot of people, psychologically under-sexed, mentally under-
aged, dreaming of press cuttings, green lawns and coronets and
with the political ideology of a beefeater—any book about them
unless written by Ellen Terry or Mrs. Patrick Campbell, is apt
to be dull. But a playwright's life is different—we should not
expect a dull autobiography from Somerset Maugham. So I
think Noel Coward is deliberately dull, dull because he knows
his minute details of minor performances will satisfy the fans,
and above all dull because he has so much to conceal behind
the smoke screen. Let us try and guess what he is concealing.
First his childhood. There is Mr. Coward's account—wistful,
detached and slightly astringent—of an affectionate middle-
class family meagrely existing in suburbs and taking in lodgers.

The family name was Veitch and there is a genealogical tree and
a crest and engravings of the house in Scotland which my mother
and her sisters never saw, as it passed into alien hands before they
were born.

In fact Noel Coward's Teddington is very like the Dublin of
Stephen Dedalus. I suggest it was really a kind of agony for the
stage-struck little boy, clever as a mongoose, who tasted success
as a page in the comedies of Charles Hawtrey, and that it
generated in him a passionate hatred of failure, an intense
craving for luxury and fame. Poverty and dinginess were the
stick of the rocket, to be dropped only when his talent was well
away and exploding into its shower of stars. I think, too, in his
love for his mother and his early stage appearances we can see
the origins of an obvious narcissism in his temperament.
There are hints of breakdowns. There was a boy who died, a
girl called Stoj, now a Christian Scientist, and two happy
friendships with people suitably unlike him. But one feels all
the same that his emotional formula is unresolved. Simi-
larly of the development of his intellect there is nothing to say.
He read *The Gem*, *The Magnet* and *The Boys' Own Paper* with
sentimental delight. I don't think he mentions having read any-

thing else. Why not? Again, because such a topic is serious—he would have to think about what he liked, and be compelled to realize that his education has never gone forward, never moved in the coils and recoils, the obsessions and indifferences, the deep rhythms of the artistic life. Who can detect the slightest evolution except in technique in the matter of his plays?

From childhood to *The Vortex* his volubility about trivialities is at its noisiest. Beneath that I believe were real privations and humiliations, things that would have made a greater writer, in him only to be buried guiltily by the subconscious, ignored in the fierce struggle for success. With *The Vortex* he obtained it; from then on his career touches all of us, and the book closes with *Cavalcade*. One real emotion appears for a moment, anger —in his rage with the public on the first night of *Sirocco* we see him behave like a free and mature personality. The author who took the curtain call against police advice to show his disdain for his public glows in the recollection of it with a flash of liberated feeling. Then the sleek announcer takes his place again, the chronicle of ovations continues, "I loved noting that fleeting look of pleased surprise in people's eyes when it was suddenly brought to their attention that, in spite of theatrical success and excessive publicity, I was really quite pleasant and unaffected." For the rest of the book he is consistently disarming. I do not grudge the absence in this book of any reference to those moral, social or political issues which everyone looks for to-day—it is absence of all aesthetic criticism that I find so appalling—not one word about schools of acting, styles of writing, creative methods, ideas of any kind whatsoever— nothing but success modestly and crisply described in a kind of protracted scrap-book of lunches and green-rooms. He quotes only twice from his own work—once an early lyric which is as good and as bad as anything he has composed since, and once, at the end, the toast from *Cavalcade*, which, I feel, he thinks the best thing he has written.

Let's couple the Future of England with the Past of England. The glories and victories and triumphs that are over, and the sorrows that are over, too. Let's drink to our sons who made part of the pattern and to our hearts that died with them. Let's drink to the spirit of gallantry and courage that made a strange Heaven out of unbelievable Hell, and let's drink to the hope that one day this country of ours, which we love so much, will find dignity and greatness and peace again.

Mr. Coward found them, afterwards—in the Royal Box; but that does not prevent a complete unreality from degaging itself from the lines. What Englishman would talk like that? Notice the mock biblical prose, and that phrase which positively hangs him, "part of the pattern".

What sort of pattern do you make, reader? "Virtue is a pretty pattern. Vice I think makes rather an ugly pattern." "I am glad they have married. They should make rather a good pattern." "Our hearts that died with them" is from the psalter again, and then comes a touch of the old Oscar in "strange Heaven out of unbelievable Hell", a touch that is swamped in a finale of Rupert Brooke.

What are we left with? The picture, carefully incomplete, of a success; probably of one of the most talented and prodigiously successful people the world has ever known—a person of infinite charm and adaptability whose very adaptability however makes him inferior to a more compact and worldly competitor in his own sphere, like Cole Porter; and an essentially unhappy man, a man who gives one the impression of having seldom really thought or really lived and who is intelligent enough to know it. But what can he do about it? He is not religious, politics bore him, art means facility or else brickbats, love wild excitement and the nervous breakdown. There is only success, more and more of it, till from his pinnacle he can look down to where Ivor Novello and Beverley Nichols gather samphire on a ledge, and to where, a pin-point on the sands below, Mr. Godfrey Winn is counting pebbles. But success is all there is, and that even is temporary. For one can't read any of Noel Coward's plays now —except the newest one. They are written in the most topical and perishable way imaginable, the cream in them turns sour overnight—they are even dead before they are turned into talkies, however engaging they may seem at the time. This book reveals a terrible predicament, that of a young man with the Midas touch, with a gift that does not creep and branch and flower, but which turns everything it touches into immediate gold. And the gold melts, too.   [1937]

T. W. Earp

MONTPARNASSE

AMADEO MODIGLIANI, who died at the age of thirty-five from starvation and consumption, complicated by drink and drugs, was the founder of one of the most prosperous business concerns in post-war Europe. The quarter of Montparnasse in Paris exists upon his legend. The youth of all nations who, by some accident of adolescence, adopt the apparatus and accoutrements of art, instead of those of what happens to be their national sport, are lured thither by his sorry phantom. A few, perhaps, paint or dream of being about to paint. Many, and particularly those who have emerged from the grip of prohibition, find in the story of Modigliani's habits, rather than his work, a preferable example. For their facility the present-day Montparnasse has been created. Three of the most uncomfortable cafés in Paris, without counting the bars, have sprung up where Modigliani used to drink, and "cocktail-dancings" where he used to dance. Their proprietors would probably not have given him credit, but it is to be hoped that they sometimes lay a flower upon his grave, for that is the only relic of him in the quarter now.

It would be a fascinating task to trace the history of those localities which have acquired their fame by their association with the arts, especially in Paris. In the days of the romantics, writers and painters seem appropriately enough to have shared the neighbourhood of Notre-Dame and the Ile St. Louis. With naturalism and impressionism, they migrated to Montmartre; and then, with post-impressionism, changed over to Montparnasse. Montmartre was left, as Montparnasse is now, a prey to those who hope to lead the artist's life without being artists, which leads to curious misinterpretations and large bills for bad champagne.

Where the next genuine quarter will be, nobody yet knows. Except with misanthropes, the desire to talk shop and to amuse oneself without having one's customers about is occasionally irresistible to the creative artist in the period of development, and there are rumours that he is seeking the Montsouris district.

And there, too, the uprising of a new genius may direct the *chasse aux artistes* to the destruction of their peace and the destruction of their haunts. But whatever his manner of life may be, and however lurid a legend he may leave, upon which the business-organizers of human folly will batten, his work and what is important about him will have nothing in common with Modigliani's in Montparnasse.

For Modigliani's work is essentially the product of his time. He adapted marvellously; all the movements then in the air were filtered by his instinct. He discovered nothing, for which reason his imitators are engaged on a barren task; he is worth while forging, but not following. With the prehensile genius of his race he took all that was worth taking and used it exquisitely. Picasso's cubism, negro sculpture, and Brancusi's sculpture—all these he adapted to his own purpose. And the contribution of the art of sculpture and his own practice of it should not be ignored in the consideration of his painting. From them he got that wonderful sense of contour which gives the impression of palpability to his figures, where his imitators attain only flat caricatures. His is sculpturesque painting. For all its delicacy, it is perfectly logical building-up, from a basis which exactly supports the structure superimposed. In spite of their fragility, these attenuated men and women give no sense of collapsing to the ground; their pictorial organization is throughout coherent. Never has structure been so consummately disguised, though at first sight it seems so rudimentarily revealed. Occasionally, too, Modigliani inverted his paradox, transmuting the most squat and solid figures into diaphanous architecture.

In his own way he was an enchanter. "Les Yeux Bleus" is a deliberate essay in painting, satisfying from sheer technique; "Elvira" shows him at his most elusive; "Madame Helmterne" and the "Portrait de Hubert" are subtle characterizations as well as fine paintings. One feels that Modigliani, knowing all about his art, knew exactly how much he ought to know. He is a minor artist, but minor in the best sense of the word. Conscious of his limitations, and always controlling them, he has given permanence to what is evanescent and informed fragility with enduring life.   [*1929*]

Stevie Smith

PRIVATE VIEWS

THE summer show of the Royal Academy is a beautiful
national institution, very tough and bouncing, weird you
know, too, in a way, and sad with the perfume of lavender
water and the lighter toilet scents, fleeting, wistful, nostalgic
and robust. It is a flower that bloomed to perfection in the
Edwardian era, but that is a little remote now, and ever since
then it has been dying off, and the fact that it is not even yet
quite dead, goes to show you how robust it is. All the people
have their friends from the country to come along with them,
and the whole opening vista of any private view day from 1906
to 1938 is very full indeed of this light, warm current of friendship between the friends and the friends of the friends, for they
are all there, and there is this very strong feeling, too, in the
part of the room where I now am, that the friends from the
country are outnumbering their hosts and hostesses who,
maybe, have a town address. That is perhaps why there is this
wistful and robust feeling, for nothing is more wistful than the
scent of lilac, nor more robust than its woody stalk, for we must
remember that it is a tree as well as a flower, we must try not
to forget this, and there is, of course, about these friends
this suspicion of a lilac *motiv* for memory and kindest messages.

So that, sitting on this elegantly buttoned leather sofa in
Room III, we know again the soft moment of excitement when
the rather queer dress was taken from the wardrobe, and the
queer hat was placed at an incorrect angle to the face, that is
for to-day slightly made-up (this is delicious, this quite wrong,
distressing, funny maquillage that makes the women look a
little too bold for their candid eyes). There is one lady who
has a white lace arrangement that cascades from the crown
of her hat across and beyond the wide brim, falling in a soft
movement of a very good lace over her left eye, so that the
remaining one eye, forced into contrasting prominence to do
the work for two, holds and repels enquiry from anxious friends

The men are very staunch and loyal to their ladies at any time during the period under retrospect, they have been brought here a little perhaps noli-voli, but they are splendid, such sports, really you know it is ripping of them to be so kind and docile, not to fall over the trains that some of the ladies wear, and even every now and then to make the right remark, to glance here and there, observe and comment; for they, too, have their part in the merry game of chat and smile, and well they bear it. The fashionable town patrons of our academy artists are without the bouquet of their country cousins, ordinary enough in every way, they are ordinarily fashionable, hardened and regimented in their emotional arteries; but these country others, they are quite extraordinary, and never anywhere else at all ever except at Burlington House on private view day might you see them all together, excited a little, happy and unique. "Tom is back," the merry news bell-tones a country voice. "Did you know? Nell gave a party for him. Tom's back. Harry came. Bob's through and Mary's coming." The country narrative runs on and eddies round. "Can't hear a word," cries Lady Nod, who will not let us forget that this remark, current on every public occasion for many years past, has won her a reputation for wit; clever Lady Nod. The queer white faces of the country cousins, far too whitely powdered, smile and beck. "I come," they say, and the words of this poet are most appropriate to the moment, "I come from haunts of coot and hern, I make a sudden sally. . . ." So they do, but Lady Nod got in first, it is a pity. Over there, in the populous far corner, is another of this poet's fancies, a town friend, I am sure. "The slight Sir Robert with a watery smile, and educated whisker." Perhaps we might write "whisper" for "whisker" in deference to the calendar, and indeed there is nothing so educated as some of the whispers on private view day.

In physique the people who throng the galleries are all rather tall, except for some of the ladies who are rather thin, but still tall, so that for all this it is a little difficult to come near to the pictures on the wall. But these people are happy, oh happy band, how happy they all are, and the pictures, for one must come to the pictures, they are so happy, too, smug in a mediocrity that is sometimes quite excruciating, entirely so pleased with themselves, and happy on this day to receive their dear friends the spectators. "Our Academy", "Our dear pictures", like children the spectators have this possessive feeling; they are very worked up, too, you know, very apt to be provoked; but always, of course, a dignified control operates, loosed only for a toss of the incorrectly poised hat brim, or a muffled howl within a masculine throat.

The portraits of these happy people, for they are hung in oils upon the walls as well as pressed in flesh upon each other, have nothing of their delicate peculiar spirit, are nothing but bright masks, coloured competently to last a year or two, cheer none, appal but artists, woo oblivion. When these people have so much in their faces that one may look upon them for a long time and then not reach the end of it, be held and fascinated in conjecture and pursuit, why is it that the painter, catching nothing of it, must be so tired, abandoned to disinterest before the first sitting is at end? It is certainly the painter's fault, and not the fault of the enthralling ladies and gentlemen who sit for him; the soldier, the public house keeper, the simpering débutante, her older sister, the alderman, the admiral and all the people of the cherry stones. If Goya could paint his revealing Isabella and not have the canvas torn by outraged lady so for all posterity betrayed, might not our artists venture something in pursuit of revelation; no human being is so empty of all virtue and all vice as these poor dummies; so it must be that the artist cannot, and not dare not. Not cowardice but lack of skill restrains, and he, in colouring so often excellent, technique so facile, only dummy-paints; ah, so to paint so well, and yet paint nothing; this is where the sadness lies, too deep to run beneath Edwardian fancies. How deeply sad, with only slight exception, the show of all these pictures is; so many miles of competently covered canvases, and hardly ever at all anything to excuse the paint, the canvas and time spent.

The landscapes in the Academy are mostly representational; one thinks not: "This is a lovely painting," but: "This must be a lovely field, a hedge, a roadway; why, it is for a memory of a dear countryside, this happy England." There is a picture of sea breaking upon a Cornish coast—"Ah, that is the sea." But with a great sea painter, one thinks at once: "That sea is special to him," to the artist, it may be Van de Velde. And

later, if you are on the seashore and the lighting of the sea-
scape is in such a manner, you think: "the sea is Van de Velde".
This ruthlessness of a great artist who takes what he did not
make and makes of it something that only he can make, is
absent from many of our academy canvases.

Of the conversation pieces, Mr. Robey might say that he was
not able to follow the conversation. The nudes are very lean
and hungry looking; haughty, refined, they are the sum of
their separate parts and without sensuality. They sometimes
have a highly polished shrimp surface. There is a young girl
who has this idiosyncrasy, she is resting upon a small bath
towel upon a green bank, she looks rather absurd, you know.
Some of the nudes, even the quite young ones, have an odd
look about the eyes, haughty and vulgar. "You need not think
that because I took my clothes off I am not as good as you."
There is this undertoning the slant of their eyes. It is depressing,
and when the body itself is so sentimentalized as to be not
sensual at all (these unfleshed ladies especially of the symbolic
pieces) it becomes quite horrible.

In the Academy, this pretended home of traditional painting,
our comparisons may be traditional, we have no special quarrel
that Matisse, Picasso, Dali, are not here; but how disappointed
we may feel that among the fine soldiers on the wall there is
no hint of Goya's Wellington, among the grey landscapes no
thought for Corot, and among the genre pictures no rhinoceros
watched by Venetian ladies. *Des fesses et des tétons*? Among
the nudes there is absolutely no sense of this, therefore no sense
at all.

But if the ladies and gentlemen of the private view were
confronted with a work of art that was a great work of art and
in this way a special creation, would they not be very creaturely
sad, and creaturely hostile, too? No, I do not think they would
notice it; or they would notice it; it would not matter; it
might as well not be there, and also it might as well be there.
If they noticed it and were hostile, that would be an unfocused
instinctive hostility, because of the privilege and power of that
canvas—"it isn't fair"—but they would lose this hostility in
restlessness, hurry on, there is so much to see, an excusing
restlessness.

For clean, happy fun there are: horrible ladies, *passim*;

horrible little girl looking at horrible squirrel; horrible short-
horn up to no good with horrible lady; silly lady on silly plank
(by silly artist?) above silly tank; flying moment, monarchical,
nastily stayed, for multiple reproduction; lots of nasty gentlemen. God rest 'em all.   [*1938*]

Clive Bell

Πάντων γλυκύτατον μεταβολή

FRANKLY, I do not greatly care
    Always to be my best;
I like sometimes to take the air,
    Sometimes to take a rest.

Sometimes, austere philosopher,
    I seek what thought reveals:
At other times I much prefer
    Silk stockings and high heels.

And sometimes Beauty moves me much,
    And sometimes Pleasure more;
Great art seems sometimes double Dutch
    And Amabel a bore.

Is God's clock always just at noon?
    Is Heaven always fair?
May angels not adore the moon?
    Is there no tea-time there?

Why, then, how blest are we on earth,
    Who know an ampler range,
With blondes and browns and grief and mirth
    And, above all things, Change.   [*1921*]

William Plomer

EVER SUCH A NICE BOY

You want to know how I first met Freddy? Oh, it's quite a long story. No, we don't come from the same place at all. You see my home's near Gloucester. I was in service there with Major and Mrs. Trumbull-Dykes. Mrs. Dykes was ever such a nice lady, she was just like a mother to me and writes to me every Christmas, not that I haven't got a real mother, because of course I have, and she's always been good to me, too, I couldn't wish for a better. Well, the Major used to suffer from rheumatism something terrible, he was always carrying on and saying the house was damp, though it was as dry as a biscuit. He wouldn't rest but they must move to Devonshire, nagging away all the time.

Well of course Mrs. Dykes wanted me to go with them, but I didn't like the idea seeing that I hadn't never been more than a few miles away from home. It was Mum that persuaded me. "You've got a good home with them," she said, "you'd better go with them." Of course, most of the things was sent off by train, and we was to follow by car, but there was a lot of luggage all the same, just like gipsies we were, all packed in with a kettle and I don't know what else. Of course, I hadn't never driven so far before and the Major drove ever so fast and it quite turned me up, what with the bumps in the road. "Stop, Gilbert," said Mrs. Dykes, "Edith wants to be sick." "I don't *want* to be," I said, "I've *got* to be." Oh, I *was* ashamed. "Never mind, Edith," said Mrs. Dykes, "you'll feel better now." "You'll never make a sailor, Edith," said the Major. Oh, if I was on the sea I think I'd die.

Of course, it was ever such a nice house that they had, just outside Paignton, everything easy to keep clean and the kitchen all white. The reason I didn't want to go away was I was afraid I would be homesick. It's funny, isn't it, when you get homesick? You see, I was only a kid and me never having been away from home before I just cried and cried. "Why, Edith," said Mrs. Dykes, "whatever's the matter? You're not homesick, are you? Aren't you happy with us?" And, of course, when she spoke to me so gentle that just made me cry all the more. "If you're so unhappy," she said, "maybe it would be better for you to go home at the end of the month."

Mind you, the Major was always a worry to her, you never knew what he'd be getting up to. I don't believe there was nothing between them and hadn't been for a long time, though I dare say the Major wished there was, so of course they always had separate bedrooms. Well, one afternoon about tea-time, yes, it must have been about tea-time because I was making the toast, the Major must always have his hot buttered toast for tea, there I was making the toast and the Major come into the kitchen. Of course, I didn't take no notice until he came up and caught hold of me. I asked him to let go and stop his games, but he wouldn't, so I hit at his hands with the toasting-fork to make him leave go of me. He had ever such big veins in his hands, they stood right out. "Oh, you little vixen! You little Spitfire!" he said. "Well, you had no call to lay hands on me," I said, "whatever would Mrs. Dykes say?" And as he wouldn't stop his tricks I said, "Give over, will you!" and hit him again over the knuckles with the toasting-fork. "Damn it, damn it," he said, and then he run out. Just as I was getting tea ready to take into the drawing-room Mrs. Dykes come in, she'd been out shopping, and "Oh, Edith," she said, "I'll just take the Major's tea up to him. He's ever so upset," she said, "he's hurt his hands something dreadful, he's resting in his room. He caught them in the mowing machine and they're all swollen up." Of course I didn't say anything, but you should have seen the state his hands were in. Of course, I didn't mean to hurt him like that, but it was his own fault in a way, wasn't it?

My homesickness didn't get any better. I seemed to be always moping, so Mrs. Dykes said I'd better go home at the end of the month. Well, only a couple of days before the end of the month I was cleaning the windows. It was a lovely morning and when I was doing the window of the spare room I couldn't help noticing that there was a boy painting the roof of a shed in the garden next door, and when I was looking at him he looked up and saw me and he grinned and waved his hand. That's ever such a nice boy, I thought. Of course it was Freddy, though I didn't know at the time. I was ever so pleased. I didn't like to be too forward, but I waved back at him. Then I run downstairs to Mrs. Dykes and I asked her if I could stay with her instead of going home at the end of the month. "Why, Edith, of course we should be very pleased," she said, "but whatever's made you change your mind so sudden?" Well, I knew I could tell her everything, so I said, "I've just seen ever such a nice boy painting the roof of the shed next door, and he waved to me while I was doing the spare room window." With that she run upstairs with me and looked out and when Freddy saw two of us he didn't know what to think. "Yes, Edith," said Mrs. Dykes, "you're quite right, he *is* a nice boy." So I didn't go away at the end of the month, and I just waited, hoping I'd see him again. I'd forgotten all about being homesick.

Next thing a note come to the house, addressed to "Miss Edith". Just like that, "Miss Edith". Of course it was from Freddy, asking me if I would meet him at the corner on my evening out so that we could go to the pictures. Oh, I *was* excited. I run and showed it to Mrs. Dykes and "Of course, Edith," she said, "you'll have to go, but I wish we knew something about him. Isn't there anybody we could ask?" Well, next time the butcher's boy come round I said, "Do you know anything about a fellow round here called Fred Carter?" "Fred Carter?" he said. "No, I can't say I do. What sort of work does he do?" "I believe he's something in the building line," I said. "The only Fred I can think of," he said, "who's in the building line is Fred Baines, him that was painting that shed next door." "And what sort of a fellow is he?" I said. "Oh, he's all right," he said, "but what do *you* want to know for? Has he been round here after you?" "Don't be so nosy," I said, but what I couldn't make out was if his name was Baines why did he call himself Carter, but it turned out that his stepfather's name was Baines so everybody used to call him Baines's boy though his name was really Carter.

So off I went to meet him, and "Do be careful, Edith," said Mrs. Dykes, "don't let him take no liberties," she said, "until you're sure of him." Oh, and do you know, he was *late*. Oh, I was that worried I could have cried, I thought he was just making a game of me. Oh, I *was* upset, I thought I'd

have done better to go back home after all. But just then he
come up, all smiles, and we went off to the pictures, and we
did have a lovely time. Of course after that everything was all
right, but Mrs. Dykes said he must come to the house so she
could see him for herself, and of course everybody liked him,
you know how it is, people always do seem to take to Freddy,
and after that he was always coming round, every night he
used to come round, Mrs. Dykes was ever so kind, and the
Major liked him, too.

Then one evening, late it was, Mrs. Dykes come running
down to the kitchen, screaming blue murder, "Edith! Edith!
Freddy! ! Freddy! ! Come quick, there's a man in my room!"
Well of course we run upstairs and Freddy grabbed the poker
and when we got up to her room there was nobody there but
the Major. Do you know he'd got in through the window,
thinking to surprise her, she wouldn't let him set foot in her
room at all in the ordinary way. "What on earth's all this?"
he said when he see us. "Why, Gilbert, it's only *you*!" said Mrs.
Dykes. "What do you mean by giving us all such a fright,
creeping in at my window like that? Why, I thought it was
a man!" At that Freddy and me couldn't help giving a laugh.
Soon after that I left to get married, and I was sorry to leave
in some ways, Mrs. Dykes cried when I went away, ever so good
she was. Poor soul, I can't help thinking of her sometimes, with
that Major of hers.   [*1937*]

Alex Comfort

A LEGEND OF UNO
(Attributed to Thomas Ingoldsby)

Praesens nominanti Diabolus

THE President sat in the President's Chair—
Playboy and Commissar, all were there:
Every Statesman, every Tycoon,
And Britain's Upholder, Sir Peto Colquhoun,

Mr. Muddington Maughan, which the toffs pronounce Moon,
Together with every type of buffoon
Everyone bad And everyone mad
Who'd foregathered to see what there was to be had,
Cheered like the Devil, and joined in the revel
(Except, of course, Franco, since he was in Seville,
But he dropped them a card, as he used to on Neville
That he could not take part in the business afoot,
But he'd take the occasion to send them some fruit).

The President sat in the President's Chair—
Sir Peto was making a very long speech
And the Delegate Members, all and each
Drew on their blotters and twiddled their hair,
Thought about whiskys they just couldn't reach
Hung out their tongues And expanded their lungs
While their minds ran on glasses and corkscrews and bungs—
And dreamed of a winner
And what was for dinner
And wished he'd sit down, the long-winded old sinner.
Muddington Moon In a species of swoon
Was hoping the speech would be finishing soon
But Sir Peto was doing his damndest to prove
That anything slightly resembling a move
Would certainly queer The whole pitch, far and near,
If Franco were made to go out on his ear
And they'd better put off the whole show for a year—
The Commissar growls And the Commissar scowls
And prays from the depths of his Socialist bowels
That Sound Dialectics, Karl Marx, or Old Nick
Would fly off with Sir Peto uncommonly quick—
And quite unawares, as he eyes the conventicle,
He draws on his blotter a thing called a PENTACLE
When Hark! there's a bang on the door of the Chamber
The delegates jump It's a Hell of a thump—
The President, up on the President's stump
Stops reading "*Forever* (I think it was) *Amber*"
And in walks the most diabolical Stranger.
He's tall as a pole: from his head to his sole
He's as black as the best kind of Graded Steam Coal—

The President stares, for he's covered with hairs,
And you wouldn't receive as a personal friend
A type with a tail, and a fork at the end

But the Stranger comes in, seems at home, slaps the back
Of Sir Peto, who chokes at the terrible whack,
Bows to the chair With the confident stare
Of a pedlar who hopes to dispose of some ware:
While in the offing Sir Peto keeps coughing
At the dense cloud of Brimstone that's filling the air
And the delegates mutter and edge for the door
And begin to look green For they seem to have seen
The stranger himself, or his photo, before
In a "regime whose nature they deeply deplore".
But the Stranger seems bent upon taking the floor,
And as ugly as sin, he begins with a grin
"Don't disturb yourselves, comrades: I want to come in.
I've a very good right to be heard in debate
As the Sovereign State
Which I have the honour to represent here
Has been growing of late At a singular rate
And its right to a Delegate's perfectly clear—
I've attended such gatherings year after year
And I think I may say that it gives me great plesure
To confer with so many old colleagues at leisure:
We'll be too pressed in Hell,
And then there's the smell:
No time like the present—you do yourselves well.
There's a question or two That I'm putting to you—
May I ask why you've taken the title "United"
And why the—Blue Legion—was I not invited?"
And then to the Chair: "As is honest and fair,
I demand for the Mephistophelian Mission
De facto, de jure, your full recognition."
Mr. M. became blue Pursed his lips and said "Whew!"
And the President murmured "The Devil you do!"
"And what's more" said the fiend, turning round on Sir Peto
"To end this abuse I intend to make use
If need be, of my Mephistophelian Veto."
Sir Peto Colquhoun Hummed a short tune

In fact, he recovered remarkably soon
While the delegates stuttered And scowled and muttered
But Sir Peto knew which side his omelette was buttered
And as Satan sat down With a horrible frown
And a thunderclap like to wake up the town,
And the delegates edged for the door labelled FIRE
And the boys from the Press made a rush for the wire
And the President muttered what sounded like "Cheek!"
Sir Peto was up, and had started to speak.
"Mr. Chairman, I move that the Stranger be heard—
He's a singular bird, but ! think, in a word
That General Franco, to whom I've referred,
And the rest of the issues we've met to decide
Could be much clarified
If we let Mr. Satan explain the affair—
After all, he should know, because *he put them there*:
He's experienced, able— There's even a fable
That he was the first to Place Cards on the Table
He's a wizard at Scenes And Spilling the Beans
And an expert of note on Infernal Machines—
Inventor of Treaties, Banks, Profit and Barter,
And I heard someone say At the club yesterday
That the Devil knows what has become of our Charter
He might as well come, since he's calling the tune—
I call on my friend Mr. Muddington Moon . . ."
Mr. Moon said a word Which nobody heard
What it was I won't swear Since I wasn't there
But it certainly wasn't a psalm or a prayer:
Sir Peto went on, and the stooges came back
From the bar where they'd bunked at that last Thunder-crack
And the short and the long of the Plenary Session
Was to end by creating H.E. Mr. Satan
The President, Treasurer, Plenipotentiary
Everything, barring Chief of the State Penitentiary—
Curator of Treaties, Trieste, Iron Curtains—
And the Delegates, thinking of Basses and Burtons
Wasted no time in debate or division
But at once went on And made him, *nem. con.*,
Sole Delegate to the Atomic Commission.
They were heard to remark in the Lobby, as well,

That the Permanent Seat will be moving to Hell,
For it somehow appears since old Nick was invited
That they all, for the first time, are really United.
Sir Peto and Moon Still humming a tune
Went off to wire Franco: "O.K.—See you soon."
Moral. If ever you're met to concoct a new Peace
Experience teaches Don't make windy speeches
And see all the doors are kept shut by Police:
Don't damn people's eyes, or a horrid surprise
May appear in the form of the Father of Lies:
Don't accept gifts of fruit, if the postmark is Seville.
Don't doodle, don't cant, and *don't speak of the Devil!*

[*1946*]

R. H. S. Crossman

THE PROPHECIES OF JACK LONDON

I HAVE been reading again Jack London's *The Iron Heel.* Jack
London was a far more successful proletarian novelist than our
near-communist young writers who are read mainly by University students and connoisseurs of realistic literature. In spite
of the introduction by Anatole France, which is included in my
edition, he wrote not for the critics but for the people of all
nations, and he was read by uneducated people because he
could tell an exciting story with immense gusto and no respect
for the conventions of good literature. He also happened to be
a passionate revolutionary Socialist when the I.W.W. was
spreading fear and hope throughout America. But he never let
his Socialism squeeze out the love-interest, and *The Iron Heel* is a
unique mixture of Wild-West thriller and Marxian sociology,
which must have had more influence than all the contributors
to *New Verse* put together. By the conventional canons, it is
worthless literature and crude sociology. But it has one advantage over its modern counterparts; it is the sort of book which
the non-reader reads, which means that it is as genuine proletarian literature as *Merrie England.*

The Iron Heel, first published in 1907, tells the story of a self-educated American worker who woos and wins the daughter of a rich Californian professor and then leads the revolutionary Socialist movement to glorious defeat by the Fascist oligarchy. Ernest Everhard (surely a romanticized self-portrait) first confutes the academics, bishops and business men in argument and then, as the inevitable crisis of Capitalism develops, warns the working-classes of the impossibility of an early victory and is executed after an unsuccessful rising. The story is told by his wife, and breaks off quite suddenly at the moment of the workers' worst defeat. It is only through the annotations of an imaginary historian of the millennial future that we learn of the ultimate victory of World Socialism.

A profound pessimism is the most striking feature of *The Iron Heel*. Unlike William Morris and Blatchford, Jack London seems to have been filled with a melancholic certainty that Socialism could not come for at least three centuries, and would be preceded by the epoch of the Servile State, in which a new dynamic capitalism, led by men with a religious certainty of their mission, would seduce the skilled workers, suppress the proletarian revolution and rule by means of a paramilitary army of Scarlet Mercenaries. The material achievements of this new despotic capitalism would be immense, matched only by its "high ethical righteousness".

> Out of the ethical incoherency and inconsistency of capitalism, the Oligarchs emerged with a new ethic, coherent and definite, sharp and severe as steel, the most absurd and unscientific and at the same time the most potent possessed by any tyrant class. The Oligarchs believed their ethics, in spite of the fact that biology and evolution gave them the lie; and because of their faith, for three centuries they were able to hold back the mighty tide of human progress—a spectacle profound, tremendous, puzzling to the metaphysical moralist, and one that to the materialist is the cause of many doubts and reconsiderations. . . . There were no more idle-rich young men. Their strength was used to give united strength to the Oligarchy. . . . They went into the multudinous divisions of the Government, took service in the colonial possessions and by tens of thousands went into the various secret services. In every function, they performed the important service of moulding the thought-processes of the nation in the direction of the perpetuity of the Oligarchy.

This is surely one of the most astounding prophecies in history. Jack London believed that when war came in 1913 a strike in Socialist Germany would stop it, and he was convinced that it was America which would go Fascist and claim the world as its *Lebensraum*. But these mistakes are trivial compared with the immense achievement of predicting the shape of things to come after Liberal capitalism was finished, and incidentally spotting that Japan would produce the most savage Fascist movement and try to capture "the whole Asiatic portion of the world market except India".

But even Jack London could not foresee the whole horror of our age. He assumed that war would be chiefly civil war and so argued that the main problem of his Oligarchs would be to split the working-classes by concessions to the Unions, and to provide employment for the masses and an outlet for surplus profits. So he pictures his Fascist State at peace with the world and throwing its whole energy into colossal public works.

> Magnificent roads will be built. There will be great achievements in science, and especially in art. When the Oligarchs have completely mastered the people, they will have time to spare for other things. Under their direction and generously rewarded will toil the artisans. The result will be great art; for no longer as up to yesterday will the artists pander to the bourgeois tastes of the middle-classes. It will be great art, I tell you, and wonder cities will arise. . . .
>
> Thus will the surplus be constantly expended while labour does the work. The building of these great works will give a starvation ration to millions of common workers, for the enormous bulk of the surplus will compel an enormous expenditure. . . . These things will the Oligarchs do because they cannot help doing them . . . and beneath will be the Abyss, which will fester and rot and ever renew itself, the common people, the great bulk of the population.

There is Hitler's vision of Fascism, but not the reality. For even Jack London could not foresee that, instead of the great public works of peace the totalitarian rulers would spend their millions upon the instruments of war, or that the artists among them would be constantly thwarted by military exigencies from fulfilling their dreams.

Stranger even than the accuracy of its prophecies is the fact that *The Iron Heel* enjoyed such an immense popularity among working-class thinkers. Contemptuous of the Trade Unions, hating the subservience of the common people, Jack London put his trust in the revolutionary violence of a tiny élite. Not for him the comforting faith of Reformist Democracy or the illusion that the proletariat was in itself a revolutionary power. The Socialist he conceived was a member of a church as select and secret as that of the primitive Christians: like them, he lived in catacombs and holes in the ground or permeated the Oligarchy itself. Like them, he had no faith in unregenerate man, far less in a particular class, though he believed that the redeemers would come from among the poor and dispossessed. Probably it was this profound kinship between the faith of revolutionary Christianity and Jack London's myth of violence which made *The Iron Heel*, in spite of its pessimism, so popular among simple people, who still believe that it is only through the suffering of the elect that the Kingdom of Heaven can come.

It is impossible to pretend that *The Iron Heel* is either good literature or among the best of Jack London's stories. There is too much argument and the action consists too exclusively of murder and rapine, culminating in a description of the Chicago Commune, in which the corpses are piled so high that interest slackens. Re-reading it now, over thirty years after it was written, I was struck by its childish ecstasy in carnage and secret conspiracy. Jack London, like many working-class revolutionaries of all parties, experienced the existing misery and the fantasies of destruction so violently that he was content to leave all serious thought of "work, wealth and happiness" to his successors in a distant Millennium. He expressed not the will to power of a rising class but the escape into violence, whether real or imaginary, of those who could not conceive that they would be called to sit in the seats of the mighty. That is why he could never quite suppress his admiration for the Fascists, whose coming he prophesied with such apparent pessimism. They were the Spartan bosses of his dreams who would give the "helot" workers what they deserved. This philosophy is a far more geniune expression of proletarian self-consciousness than Marxism or Social Democracy; it was also one of the causes of Hitler's success. I wonder if *The Iron Heel* was banned in Germany.   [*1940*]

Robert Lynd

LIGHT ON THE BOURGEOISIE

I HAVE been reading the translation of the official verbatim report of the Moscow trial, and I confess that, as a member of the
bourgeoisie, I read certain passages in the speeches of the lawyers with a sense of shame. The exposure of the rottenness of our
class is, of course, an old story; but never is it repeated authori-
tatively in public without causing a fresh twinge. In England it
has hitherto been regarded as a compliment, or at least not as
an insult, if you call a man a gentleman: in Russia, where they
know better, it is as dangerous to call a man a gentleman as to
call him a liar or any other sort of blackguard. There, indeed, it
is realized that nearly everybody belonging to the classes once
called respectable is hopelessly corrupt. There is always the
money taint. Even if the respectable man has no money himself
he is probably related to somebody who once had some. In this
way corruption gets into the blood. Take Lobanov, one of the
Moscow prisoners, for example. This is what the Public Prosecu-
tor said of him: "Of course he is a corrupt type. . . . It seems to
me that he is the embodiment of all the peculiar features of the
class of which he is a representative, of the class that is already
morally corrupt, that has morally exhausted itself. His father
was a factory owner, his brother rented a flour-mill; that is his
genealogy, which defines his moral fulcrum. We know these fulcrums, we know these morals. They are embodied in Lobanov."

It is no wonder that an eminent English K.C. recently expressed the opinion that Russian justice is on the whole the best
in the world. It is the best largely because the Russians are the
first nation to realize the importance of family history in estimating the guilt of accused persons. Even the Russians have not yet
gone quite far enough in applying their great discovery. They
still occupy the time of the court with a great deal of what seems
to me irrelevant evidence.

In the courts of the future, I hope, when a man is accused of
a crime, it will be enough for the prosecuting counsel to point
out that his brother rented a flour-mill in order to obtain a

conviction. How much time English juries would have been saved if evidence of this kind had been accepted as proof of guilt. On several occasions in recent years we have seen old public schoolboys in the dock, and, instead of pointing out that they were old public schoolboys and therefore guilty, the prosecution has called all manner of tedious evidence to prove the obvious. For my part, I should like in such cases to see the counsel for the prosecution calling no evidence at all apart from the school and university career of the accused. What speech for the prosecution could be more damning than a speech consisting of the single sentence: "Gentlemen of the jury, the prisoner is an old Etonian"? This would at once define the moral fulcrum of the prisoner; and the jury, knowing these fulcrums, knowing these morals, would convict without leaving the box. They would know that the prisoner belonged to a class that had morally exhausted itself and that, even if he had not a brother who rented a flour-mill, he was one of nature's criminals.

In England it used to be the custom to describe certain people as having been born of "poor but honest parents". Even in England, however, no one ever dared seriously to speak of a man as having been born of "rich but honest parents". Riches and honesty do not go together; the most brazen-bred nineteenth-century capitalist never pretended that they did. The truth is, in capitalist countries it is only the poor who are expected to be honest. One of the lawyers in the Moscow trial aptly quoted Lenin on this point. "When a worker steals a loaf of bread in a bourgeois country," said Lenin, "he is sent to prison for it; but when a rich man steals a railway he is appointed to the Senate." The young of the present generation may find it difficult to realize that railway-stealing was once almost as common a crime among the rich as bag-snatching is among the petty bourgeois to-day. A railway does not look an easy thing to steal: the ordinary safecracker's tools are useless for such an operation as this. The old-fashioned capitalist, however, whatever else he may be accused of cannot be accused of lack of brains. The more difficult a job was, the more he was keyed up to it. He tackled almost impossible tasks in the conviction that love of money will find out the way. Consequently he stole territories, mines, and all sorts of things on the same scale more easily than you or I would steal a motor-car. Railway-stealing, however, was regarded as the rich man's supreme achievement. The man who could steal a railway was naturally considered so clever that he was called in to the service of the State. Those who are obsessed by ethical considerations may condemn the nineteenth century for this. But what have ethics to do with business or politics? The nineteenth century reverenced intellect, and, knowing that a man who stole a railway had done an infinitely cleverer thing than a man who had stolen only a loaf of bread, it quite logically rewarded the railway-stealer and sent the loaf-stealer to gaol for his stupidity.

I hope no one will think that I am defending the immorality of the rich. I am merely doing my best to point out that from the Machiavellian point of view there is something to be said for them. And in estimating their guilt it should always be remembered that many of them had not the advantage of having been brought up in an atmosphere of proletarian morality. Even one of the lawyers at the Moscow trial recognized the fact that a man who had not been brought up in true proletarian surroundings could not be expected to behave perfectly. Mac-Donald's counsel put forward the extenuating plea that the prisoner's lameness as a boy had prevented him from walking into working-class districts and so getting into touch with proletarian opinion. "Had his legs been sound," he declared, "then perhaps they would have taken him into a working-class district where he would have met with some other William of a more common type, he would have seen a corner of life different from his petty-bourgeois, middle-class, intellectual British family, an idea of which I believe you will get from Dickens's old novels, or from some other novels which depict the environment." Certainly those middle-class intellectual families which Dickens depicts—the Wellers, the Gargerys, the Sikeses, or even the Pecksniffs, the Nicklebys, or the Squeerses—were curiously walled in from proletarian truth and morality. Little fruit could be expected from soil so unsunned. It is all the more surprising, however, that MacDonald's counsel, while realizing that much should be forgiven to anyone born in a middle-class intellectual English family, refused to extend a similar compassion to men who had been educated at Oxford or Cambridge. He even mentioned it as a point in MacDonald's favour that "he was not a representative of those families, members of which get their education at Oxford or Cambridge". Surely, in this terribly mixed world, pardon's the word for all. The old Oxford man may justly plead that it was not his fault that he went to Oxford, that he was brought up in a home that did not contain a copy of Karl Marx, that his mother was honestly convinced that the Ten Commandments were valid, and that it was his environment, not his will, that made him what he is.

It may be argued that, in looking for potential enemies of Communism, the Soviet lawyers are perfectly right to consider a man's social origins very seriously. I agree, but the Russian lawyers went beyond this. They spoke of corruption and immorality as though they were the marks of men such as had brothers who rented flour-mills. I am a firm believer in the immorality of men whose brothers rent flour-mills, but I am also a firm believer in the immorality of men whose brothers do not rent flour-mills. It is easy to be wicked on ten thousand a year; it is equally easy to be wicked on two pounds a week. Crimes are committed by men who have never been at Eton or Winchester. The last time I attended assizes, indeed, I do not think there was a single public schoolboy in the dock. I would like to be able to believe that we could get completely rid of crime by rounding up all the ex-public schoolboys and university men and putting them into concentration camps for life. But I am too profoundly convinced a Calvinist to believe in the sinlessness of everybody who has never been at a public school or a university. I hope I am wrong, but was it an Oxford man who borrowed my car from a parking-place and left it in a side street in Whitechapel? As I have said, I hope so, but I doubt it.

[*1933*]

Harry Roberts

THE EAST END

MEMBERS of the cultivated classes are accustomed to measure
the condition of working people—when they bother their heads
about it at all—by a standard very different from that which
they apply to their own. The people of the East End are no
longer prepared to discuss their problems on this basis. It is the
culture and the luxuries of civilization, of their right to a share
in which they are becoming increasingly conscious. Moreover,
they have had a brief taste of a somewhat fuller life, and it is in
relation to that that they measure their present state. Whilst,
therefore, there is to-day much less crude poverty of the "fod-
der" sort than existed at the beginning of the century, I believe
that there has never—certainly not within my experience—been
so much misery as there is in East London at the present time.
This distinction between misery and crude poverty is well
brought out in the third volume of *The New Survey of London
Life and Labour*, which has just been published. No one should
venture to form, still less to offer, an opinion on the social conditions that prevail among our working population until he has
read this informing, impartial, understanding and altogether
admirable work. It is impossible too highly to praise, or too
gratefully to thank, Sir Hubert Llewellyn Smith and the col-
laborators whose aid he has obtained in its preparation. The
Director of the Survey refers more than once to the tragedy
introduced into many lives by the growth of what he calls the
dynamical element in poverty. "The lives of the poor who have
always been poor are", he says, "hard, narrow, and often
stunted, but they are not necessarily unhappy, for poverty so
extreme as to cause actual physical distress is rare." On the other
hand, there is little doubt that the process of economic degrada-
tion by which those who have known better things sink into
poverty and suffer deprivation of comforts which they have
hitherto regarded as necessaries is often an acutely painful one."
Every day, I come across middle-aged men, healthy and competent, driven almost crazy by a persistent unemployment of

which they have had no previous experience; a state which they had been taught, and had believed, to be the fruit of sickness, incompetence, idleness, or dishonesty. It is poor compensation to such men to learn that "the average London workman can now buy one-third more of the means of subsistence than he could forty years ago, in return for daily labour of an hour's less duration".

A few years ago, East End poverty, so far as the bare necessities of life are concerned, had—apart from housing—almost disappeared. A new life for the people seemed progressively materializing. This was reflected in the movements and faces of adult men and women as well as of the young. One could not walk the length of a street without noticing the general aspect of hopefulness and cheerfulness. The latter was no novelty in the East End. Even in its days of severest poverty, a spirit of philosophic gaiety and an almost humorous acceptance of Fate's hardest blows were generally manifest. Always, the general misery bore little quantitative relation to the general poverty. What had been, was; what was, must needs be; what couldn't be cured, must be philosophically endured. All very English—or perhaps it would be truer to say, all very Cockney. Then came the war of 1914 destroying the established feeling of continuity, of social immobility. Class and cultural distinctions were no longer accepted as having inherent validity. The comforts and pleasures hitherto confined to a rich and remote minority seemed to be coming—actually as well as rightfully—within the possible reach of all. The crumbs from the table grew larger and larger. A new pride of personal appearance, of dress, of carriage, of cleanliness, of language, and of familiarity with current topics—even those of science and philosophy—sprang up.

Soon followed the debacle. A very few years have sufficed, so far as external manifestations go, to undo all the beneficent work of the first post-war decade. I have lived and worked in one of the poorest districts of East London for more than a quarter of a century. When I first went to live in Stepney, the material conditions in which the bulk of the people lived were far below anything to be found to-day. My work was carried on in circumstances to most of my readers unthinkable. Among other things, I attended every year well over five hundred women in what has been called the most sacred event in human life. Com-

pared with the circumstances surrounding a large proportion of
these births, the manger at Bethlehem might be characterized
as the last thing in aseptic luxury. The obstetric mattress, un-
isolated by sheet or blanket, not infrequently had served many
purposes beyond its normal through several generations of men,
women and ill-trained children. The request for a basin of water,
a piece of soap and a towel, was a signal for the scattering far
and wide of every member of the household. Nevertheless, in
spite of all this Listerian blasphemy, "mother and child" could
nearly always be reported as doing famously; for then, as always,
the maternal mortality rate in the slums was about one-half that
which obtained in such relatively salubrious and hygienic districts as Hampstead and Kensington. Life started like that; and
so it continued. Yet light-heartedness was everywhere. To-day,
as by-products of the war, new standards of cleanliness, of
wholesomeness and of decency prevail; but the light-heartedness
is less noticeable, and everywhere one sees the marks of anxiety,
of disappointment, of fading hope, fading enthusiasm and fading
confidence.

Mr. Thomas Burke has written a book, called *The Real
East End*, which, though full of information not to be found in
any other single volume, is, for me, difficult to read with
patience. It has that "intimate", patronizingly knowing quality
which marks the writings of many of our bird-watching natural-
ists. The reader's attention is constantly called to the keen,
sensitive, aesthetically subtle eyes and mind of the writer,
rather than to the things he observes. Although Mr. Burke
expresses his contempt for those readers of his fiction who mistake his "local colour" for objective fact, his present book is
permeated with a melodramaticism even more likely to deceive,
by reason of its lesser crudity. He tells us that the East End "has
the genuine spirit of Bohemia. It proves what artists have not
yet learned—that one can lead the Bohemian life in strict
decency. It is the East End's natural way of living." My impressions do not coincide with Mr. Burke's—or is it that my conception of the Bohemian life differs from his? In the uncoloured
language of *The New Survey* I read that, even in 1929, "one
in seven of those who live in East London were found to be
subject to conditions which if long continued would deny them
all but the barest necessities". In the same factful volume, we

are told that "one-fifth of the total working-class inhabitants of
Shoreditch are living three or more in a room"—scarcely the
most attractive aspect of the Bohemian life. Even last year, in
spite of the relief afforded by Becontree and Dagenham, and the
various blocks of flats erected by the Borough Council, and in
spite of the diminished birth-rate, one-thirteenth of all the inhabitants of Stepney—the borough which Mr. Burke describes
so picturesquely—were living four or more persons to a room;
whilst 60 per cent of all the children under fourteen years of age
were living in conditions of technical "overcrowding". It seems
to me a poor sort of Bohemia that involves the enforced usage
of a common chamber for the three sacraments of supper,
death and birth—not infrequently partaken of coincidently. *The
Real East End* may serve as a useful corrective to the preconcep-
tions of the small surviving number of people who assume the
East End to be compact of moral, aesthetic and intellectual
decadence; but the impartial reader, not already familiar with
its subject, will be wise to regard it as a record of the impressions
of a sympathetic artist with a turn for the flamboyant. The last
page of the book, however, is so wise and true that I hesitate to
dwell too critically on the pages that irritate me. It may well be,
as Mr. Burke says, that in the East End, "not in Bloomsbury or
Mayfair or Hampstead, the true moderns are being born".

[*1932*]

Roy Campbell

THE ZULU GIRL

When in the sun the red hot acres smoulder,
Down where the sweating gang its labour plies,
A girl throws down her hoe and from her shoulder
Unslings her child tormented by the flies:

She takes him to a ring of shadow pooled
By thorn-trees: purpled with the death of ticks,
While her sharp nails in slow caresses ruled
Prowl through his hair with soft electric clicks,

His sleepy mouth, plugged by the heavy nipple,
Tugs like a puppy, grunting as he feeds:
Through his frail nerves her own deep languors ripple
Like a broad river sighing through its reeds.

Yet in that drowsy stream his flesh imbibes
An old unquenched unsmotherable heat—
The curbed ferocity of beaten tribes
The sullen dignity of their defeat.

Her body looms above him like a hill
Within whose shade a village lies at rest,
Or the first cloud, so terrible and still,
That bears the coming harvest in its breast.   [*1926*]

Henry Reed

NAMING OF PARTS

To-day we have naming of parts. Yesterday,
We had daily cleaning. And to-morrow morning,
We shall have what to do after firing. But to-day,
To-day we have naming of parts. Japonica
Glistens like coral in all of the neighbouring gardens,
And to-day we have naming of parts.

This is the lower sling swivel. And this
Is the upper sling swivel, whose use you will see,
When you are given your slings. And this is the piling swivel,
Which in your case you have not got. The branches
Hold in the gardens their silent, eloquent gestures,
Which in our case we have not got.

This is the safety-catch, which is always released
With a easy flick of the thumb. And please do not let me
See anyone using his finger. You can do it quite easy
If you have any strength in your thumb. The blossoms
Are fragile and motionless, never letting anyone see
Any of them using their finger.

And this you can see is the bolt. The purpose of this
Is to open the breach, as you see. We can slide it
Rapidly backwards and forwards: we call this
Easing the spring. And rapidly backwards and forwards
The early bees are assaulting and fumbling the flowers:
They call it easing the Spring.

They call it easing the spring: it is perfectly easy
If you have any strength in your thumb: like the bolt,
And the breach, and the cocking-piece, and the point of
  balance,
Which in our case we have not got, and the almond-blossom
Silent in all of the gardens, the bees going backwards and
  forwards,
For to-day we have naming of parts.   [*1942*]

V. S. Pritchett

THE INVADER

EVERYTHING has to interest soldiers. Up on the downs in the soundless August evenings they used to light their fire under the trees a mile from us, and when their guards had been fixed they came down in twos and threes to our post to look at our hut. It was a plain, thresher's hut on high iron wheels, with steps up to the door and a tin chimney standing out of the roof. "Beautiful evening," the soldiers said, in voices which were strange to this part of the country; and then stood staring at Sidney Taylor, Woolmer, Jim and me.

"That belongs to you?" they asked, nodding to the hut.

"Ah," said Sidney, who was our leader. He never said "Yes".

He was a small man of thirty-five with rings under his eyes, who lived half his life in his childhood still.

"It's got a stove," the soldiers said.

"Ah," said Sidney, growing larger. "And bunks. Four people can sleep in there."

"Go on," said the soldiers, staring at the hut.

"Ah," said Sidney, very proudly, "you could live in it."

The soldiers looked with wonder.

"No," said Sidney, showing off like a boy and defying anyone to deny what he was going to say. "Same as I was saying to Woolmer here, no one'd think to look at it, I lived for five weeks in that hut when I had chickenpox. When I was eleven."

"In there?" Everything interested the soldiers.

"Ah," almost shouted Sidney. "Didn't I, Woolmer?"

It was 1940.

We were all ready to fight for something and at this height with so much country before us, it seemed to be a lot. But Sidney Taylor would be fighting for the hut and those five weeks, twenty-four years back, when he had had chickenpox in it.

One evening, soon after we had got to the post, we were surprised by the sound of loud singing on the road up from the valley. A man was coming up. He was walking in the middle of the road with two boys dancing round him, shouting and pulling his jacket. Sometimes he put a quart bottle to his lips as he walked and they clung round him jeering, "Give us a drop. Don't finish it." Then he put the bottle back in his pocket and stopped to sing. His black hair was plastered by sweat over his forehead, his shirt was torn open to the waist so that his thin and hairy chest stuck out like a case. One side of his gipsy face was drawn in like a big shrivelled chestnut leaf by a scar from jaw to temple. He was flashing with drink.

"Good evening, gentlemen," he said. We gathered round him.

"Sing. Go on, sing!" shouted the boys. "Look, he's going to sing again." The man's face buckled.

"Hah," screamed the boys. "He's soused. We found him in the ditch."

"Where are you going, pal?" asked one of the soldiers.

"Whe-ah?" said the tramp. He had the high-class accent of the cheapjack. "I left me cah behind me so I'm walking. A bottle of cidah and me petah in me pocket and a clean shirt, that's all I want. I left Marlborough, boys, this morning and I'm heading for Winchester."

"You can't get there to-night," said Jim.

"Where are you going to sleep?" asked the soldiers.

"Ah," said Sid, coming closer. He had seen it: the tramp had an eye on his hut.

"On the road, pal. Anywhere."

"Ah," said Sid Taylor, non-committally.

"None of you gentlemen mind if I slept here?" said the tramp. Sid Taylor's eyes went shrewd.

"Sleep where you like, pal," said a soldier. "It's a free country."

"That's the Army," cried the tramp. "I'm an old soldier, pal. I'm drunk but I know a soldier. Kip down anywhere. That's the style. Heah! Salute! Eh? Smarter theah. That's it. Form fours. Right turn. Eh? Oh, I haven't forgotten it!" He saluted and danced through the movements.

A tall, very young soldier came forward and said in a soft, simple voice:

"What was you in, dad?"

"The Buffs, pal. The Royal West Kents. Steady the Buffs, eh?"

"That's it," said the gentle soldier.

"Mons, retreat from Mons, first battle of Ypres, second battle of Ypres. . . ."

The grins of the soldiers went. The tall, gentle one came forward.

"Then you must be an Old Contemptible, dad," said the tall soldier reverently.

"An Old Contemptible," said the tramp. "Boys, that's what I am. First I was a soldier and now I'm a boozer. But I'm not a liar. You think I'm a liar but I'm not. Here look at that." He pushed forward the lapel of his jacket.

"The crossed swords!" exclaimed the tall soldier.

"The crossed swords!" said the tramp. "That's a badge you can't buy. Here." He pulled dirty papers from his pocket. "Come on," he called hoarsely. "I've got me papahs."

We drew back.

"Oh!" whispered Woolmer. "Fancy that, he's got his papers."

"Too true he has," said Jim.

"That's all right, dad, we believe you," said the soldier, putting his hand on the tramp's shoulder.

"You're telling the truth, dad," he said. "You're an Old Contemptible, that's what it says. And now, tell us, dad," he said, silencing the others, "what you got out of it." He spoke like a saint.

"What did I get!" said the tramp. "I'll show you." He pulled back his shirt and shoved his chest out. There was a five-inch scar on his chest. There was the long scar from the temple to the jaw.

Sid Taylor's eyes watered. He had not been in the last war. Woolmer nodded. But the soldiers were not interested. The scars were the only things about the tramp which did not interest them.

"And what did they give you for that, dad?" the tall soldier asked.

"Give me?" asked the tramp.

"Yes," said the soldier, raising his voice a note to the exalted tone of a preacher, standing above the corn and the grass with his mild head against the sky and his blue eyes bluer than the sky was now.

"I'll show you what they give me. Heah, is me bottle all right? What did they give me, you said? Heah."

He pulled a stamped unemployment card from his pocket.

"The dole," exclaimed all the soldiers.

"Ah!" exclaimed Sid Taylor.

"Stamped up to date," cried the tramp. "See." He put the bottle to his lips again. Then he jumped to attention and saluted.

"Smarter there," he cried. He saluted again. "Over the top they go. The Guards, the Coldstreams second to none, the Black Watch, the Camerons, the Gordons, all the Scotch regiments; the Royal West Kents, the Buffs, the Queens, the King's Own." His voice began to chant like an auctioneer's. ". . . the Lancashire Fusiliers, The Ox and Bucks, the Berks, the Devons and the Royal Fusiliers. . . ."

"Fred Karnos," said a soldier.

"The First and Second Surreys, the Hampshires, the mud and glory boys and all the regiments of the line. . . ."

"Cor," said Jim. "Anyone give me a tanner? Going, going, gone!"

"The flower of England," called the tramp.

"And don't", said a soldier, "forget the weeds."

"And now look at me. I'm drunk. I'm a boozer. But I can work. Don't you believe a man who tells you boozers don't work—feel this."

He bent his arm and two or three of us tried his muscle. "A boozer works harder than other men and I'll tell you why. He wants his pay to get more booze. I was working yesterday and that's God's truth, but they made me go up a ladder and that's a thing a boozer can't stand. He gets giddy. I can nevah go up a height! So I packed it up, I got me petah and me cidah and I'm all right," his voice dropped to a whine, "if I can find a nice place to sleep out of the wind. Down by them bags now," he said suddenly, pointing to the sandbags. "That'd do. You gentlemen wouldn't mind me sleeping there."

"You'll be cold there, dad," said the soldier.

"Ah!" exclaimed Sid anxiously. "They got a fire up at their place."

"No, I'll be all right. I'll stay along of these gentlemen." He looked around and, nodding to the hut, said:

"Is that yours?"

"Ah," said Sid Taylor, daring him.

"Well, I'll be near you. I like to be near someone at night. I won't make a sound."

"You come along of us, dad," said the soldier.

"Ah!" said Sid.

"Would that be far?" said the tramp cautiously.

"They'll take you," said Woolmer.

"It isn't far," said Sid eagerly.

"With these soldiers?" said the tramp suddenly reluctant.

"Here," muttered Sid in panic to Woolmer and me. "You take the guard. Stop anyone who comes. I'll take him along. He's got his eye on the hut."

"Just wait till we're off and the next thing he'd be up the steps and Bob's your uncle," said Jim.

"Ah!" said Sid. It was the most decisive, expressive and voluminous of all his "ahs".

The boys, scared of the growing dusk, ran off. The soldiers stood by indifferent.

"Coming, dad?" they said with detachment. A soldier, after all, has nothing.

"I'll bring him along," said Sid. Then the soldiers went off like sheep, and Sid and the tramp followed them like man and dog.

The day had gone, the moon was hanging like an orange in the haze and sending out the first fine shadows. Woolmer and I stood by the road. "Stand back under the trees," he said. "That's what we always had to do in France. When you reckon it out," he said, "it's history we're fighting for; other people don't seem to have any history, not in the same way. They don't keep it up."

"As you might say," said Woolmer shyly. "The Germans don't seem to have any history."

We talked a long time until the moon was white.

Then Sid and Jim came back. We could hear their boots on the road a long time before they came into sight.

"No," said Sidney Taylor. "They got a fire and they've given him some bags to sleep on."

"An' he ain't half telling them the tale," Jim said.

"Same as I was saying to Jim up the road just now, you could see what he was after—getting into the hut!" said Sidney.

"In one of those bunks," said Woolmer.

"Ah!" said Sidney. "A roadster!"

We had driven our first invader off. [1941]

D. H. Lawrence

LETTER FROM GERMANY

(*This letter, written by D. H. Lawrence in* 1928, *shows a remarkable sensitiveness to the trend of events in Germany at a time when Hitlerism, as we know it now, hardly existed.*)

WE are going back to Paris to-morrow, so this is the last moment to write a letter from Germany. Only from the fringe of Germany, too.

It is a miserable journey from Paris to Nancy, through that Marne country, where the country still seems to have had the soul blasted out of it, though the dreary fields are ploughed and level, and the pale wire trees stand up. But it is all void and null. And in the villages, the smashed houses in the street rows, like rotten teeth between good teeth.

You come to Strasbourg, and the people still talk Alsatian German, as ever, in spite of French shop-signs. The place feels dead. And full of cotton goods, white goods, from Mulhausen, from the factories that once were German. Such cheap white cotton goods, in a glut.

The cathedral front rearing up high and flat and fanciful, a sort of darkness in the dark, with round rose windows and long, long prisons of stone. Queer that men should have ever wanted to put stone upon faithful stone to such a height without having it fall down. The Gothic! I was always glad when my card-castle fell. But these goths and alemans seemed to have a craze for peaky heights.

The Rhine is still the Rhine, the great divider. You feel it as you cross. The flat, frozen watery places. Then the cold and curving river. Then the other side, seeming so cold, so empty, so frozen, so forsaken. The train stands and steams fiercely. Then it draws through the flat Rhine plain, past frozen pools of flood-water, and frozen fields, in the emptiness of this bit of occupied territory.

Immediately you are over the Rhine the spirit of place has changed. There is no more attempt at the bluff of geniality.

The marshy places are frozen. The fields are vacant. There seems nobody in the world.

It is as if the life had retreated eastwards. As if the Germanic life were slowly ebbing away from contact with western Europe, ebbing to the deserts of the east. And there stand the heavy, ponderous round hills of the Black Forest, black with an inky blackness of Germanic trees, and patched with a whiteness of snow. They are like a series of huge, involved black mounds, obstructing the vision eastwards. You look at them from the Rhine plain, and know that you stand on an actual border, up against something.

The moment you are in Germany, you know. It feels empty and, somehow, menacing. So must the Roman soldiers have watched those black, massive round hills: with a certain fear, and with the knowledge that they were at their own limit. A fear of the invisible natives. A fear of the invisible life lurking among the woods. A fear of their own opposite.

So it is with the French: this almost mystic fear. But one should not insult even one's fears.

Germany, this bit of Germany, is very different from what it was two and a half years ago, when I was here. Then it was still open to Europe. Then it still looked to western Europe for a reunion, for a sort of reconciliation. Now that is over. The inevitable, mysterious barrier has fallen again, and the great leaning of the Germanic spirit is once more eastwards, towards Russia, towards Tartary. The strange vortex of Tartary has become the positive centre again, the positivity of western Europe is broken. The positivity of our civilization has broken. The influences that come, come invisibly out of Tartary. So that all Germany reads *Men, Beasts and Gods* with a kind of fascination. Returning again to the fascination of the destructive East, that produced Attila.

So it is at night. Baden-Baden is a little quiet place, all its guests are gone. No more Turgenevs or Dostoevskis or Grand Dukes or King Edwards coming to drink the waters. All the outward effect of a world-famous watering-place. But empty now, a mere Black Forest village with the wagon-loads of timber going through, to the French.

The Rentenmark, the new gold Mark of Germany, is abominably dear. Prices are high in England, but English money

F

buys less in Baden than it buys in London, by a long chalk.
And there is no work—consequently no money. Nobody buys
anything, except absolute necessities. The shopkeepers are in
despair. And there is less and less work.

Everybody gives up the telephone—can't afford it. The tram-
cars don't run, except about three times a day to the station.
Up to the Annaberg, the suburb, the lines are rusty, no trams
ever go. The people can't afford the ten pfennigs for the fare.
Ten pfennigs is an important sum now: one penny. It is really
a hundred milliards of marks.

Money becomes insane, and people with it.

At night the place is almost dark, economizing light. Economy, economy, economy—that, too, becomes an insanity.
Luckily the Government keeps bread fairly cheap.

But at night you feel strange things stirring in the darkness,
strange feelings stirring out of this still-unconquered Black
Forest. You stiffen your backbone and you listen to the night.
There is a sense of danger. It is not the people. They don't
seem dangerous. Out of the very air comes a sense of danger,
a queer, *bristling* feeling of uncanny danger.

Something has happened. Something has happened which
has not yet eventuated. The old spell of the old world has
broken, and the old, bristling savage spirit has set in. The war
did not break the old peace-and-production hope of the world,
though it gave it a severe wrench. Yet the old peace-and-production hope still governs, at least the consciousness. Even in
Germany it has not quite gone.

But it feels as if, virtually, it were gone. The last two years
have done it. The hope in peace-and-production is broken. The
old flow, the old adherence is ruptured. And a still older flow
has set in. Back, back to the savage polarity of Tartary, and
away from the polarity of civilized Christian Europe. This, it
seems to me, has already happened. And it is a happening of
far more profound import than any actual *event*. It is the father
of the next phase of events.

And the feeling never relaxes. As you travel up the Rhine
valley, still the same latent sense of danger, of silence, of suspen-
sion. Not that the people are actually planning or plotting or
preparing. I don't believe it for a minute. But something has
happened to the human soul, beyond all help. The human soul

recoiling now from unison and making itself strong elsewhere. The ancient spirit of prehistoric Germany coming back, at the end of history.

The same in Heidelberg. Heidelberg full, full, full of people. Students the same, youth with rucksacks the same, boys and maidens in gangs come down from the hills. The same, and not the same. These queer gangs of *Young Socialists*, youths and girls, with their non-materialistic professions, their half-mystic assertions, they strike one as strange. Something primitive, like loose, roving gangs of broken, scattered tribes so they affect one. And the swarms of people somehow produce an impression of silence, of secrecy, of stealth. It is as if everything and everybody recoiled away from the old unison, as barbarians lurking in a wood recoil out of sight. The old habits remain. But the bulk of the people have no money. And the whole stream of feeling is reversed.

So you stand in the woods above the town and see the Neckar flowing green and swift and slippery out of the gulf of Germany, to the Rhine. And the sun sets slow and scarlet into the haze of the Rhine valley. And the old, pinkish stone of the ruined castle across looks sultry, the marshalry is in shadow below, the peaked roofs of old, tight Heidelberg compressed in its river gateway glimmer and glimmer out. There is a blue haze.

And it all looks as if the years were wheeling swiftly backwards, no more onwards. Like a spring that is broken and whirls swiftly back, so time seems to be whirling with mysterious swiftness to a sort of death. Whirling to the ghost of the old Middle Ages of Germany, then to the Roman days, then to the days of the silent forest and the dangerous, lurking barbarians.

Something about the Germanic races is unalterable. White-skinned, elemental, and dangerous. Our civilization has come from the fusion of the dark-eyed with the blue. The meeting and mixing and mingling of the two races has been the joy of our ages. And the Celt has been there, alien, but necessary as some chemical reagent to the fusion. So the civilization of Europe rose up. So these cathedrals and these thoughts. But now the Celt is the disintegrating agent. And the Latin and southern races are falling out of association with the northern races, the northern Germanic impulse is recoiling towards Tartary, the destructive vortex of Tartary.

It is a fate; nobody now can alter it. It is a fate. The very blood changes. Within the last three years, the very constituency of the blood has changed, in European veins. But particularly in Germanic veins.

At the same time, we have brought it about ourselves—by a Ruhr occupation, by an English nullity, and by a German false will. We have done it ourselves. But apparently it was not to be helped.

Quos vult perdere Deus, dementat prius.   [*1934*]

W. R. Rodgers

THE RAIDER

THERE, wrapped in his own roars, the lone airman
Swims like a mote through the thousands of eyes
That look up at him ironing-out the skies,
Frocked and fanged with fire, by nagging fingers
Of guns jagged and jogged, with shell-bursts tasselled.

Does ever the airman's eye, speeding on
To grim conclusion, alight and loiter
Curiously on the country below?
Or does his gaze easily dissolve
Upon the moving surfaces, and flow
Evenly away like rain on rivers?

Or, roaring back over our armoured rims,
Does his view take in only the bloom and boom
Of bomb beneath him, noting how neatly
It mopped up a map-point town or snouted out
This tip or else that tap-root of resistance?

Yet, pity him too, that navigator
Who now in archipelago of steel
Nears that place where hooked upon barbed air he'll
Halt, hang hump-backed, and look into his crater.   [*1940*]

Edward Sackville West

BEETHOVEN AND THE FUTURE

OF all great composers perhaps Beethoven presents the critic with the most prodigious of opportunities to say something true. Like the laws of a country, great works of art are not static objects: they are systems of communication—barographs which draw a different chart according to the mode of sensibility to which they are at any time attuned. It seems highly unlikely that the *Eroica* means to any of us to-day what it meant to Beethoven's contemporaries. The truth of art is creative.

But the man himself must always be our point of departure. What was Beethoven *about*? The progress of this particular pilgrim is mysterious (1) because he was exceptionally reserved and inarticulate, (2) because he chose to express himself in music, a language to which no one has yet succeeded in attaching a definite *verbal* meaning. Huge emotions—passionate yet ambiguous as colour in changing lights—glow out of the stream of sound: anger, exasperation (this very often and definitely), grief, an unsmiling tenderness, a steely joy; and over all these spreads a meditative rapture which is somehow felt as the essence of all music and is perhaps the nearest we ever get to the direct expression of disinterested love. But, whether momentary or of longer duration, the emotions that surge out at us from Beethoven's (or any other man's) music are all vague and generalized; moreover their connexions are hard to perceive, for the human mind works in words and concepts, and any effort to sustain a double form of perception, and to inter-relate the two, is not feasible. Beethoven's music tells no story and paints no picture; all one can say is that somehow we are made powerfully aware of a moral conflict. The rest is music; but when it has ceased to sound we find ourselves thinking again of the cryptic drama at which we have been assisting. For to a far greater extent than that of any other composer, Beethoven's opus is the history of his moral consciousness. Other composers' work (e.g. Schumann's, Brahms's) seems to grow out so to speak at right angles to their lives, whereas Beethoven's grows along with his and is woven round it. The last sonata shows him alone with the Universe: if I hesitate to say "with God" it is because of the vagueness that surrounds Beethoven's religious beliefs. That he possessed some is certain; that they were ortho-dox Christian is more than doubtful. A Radical in politics, he is likely to have been deeply heretical in religious matters. Yet what we can gather of his philosophy has this much in common with Milton's that the grim integrity, the irony and passion of his mind compelled him continually to be remaking his soul on the basis—not of Christian dogma, or of Kantism, or of some bogus political religion—but of the data of his conscience as an individual. Such preoccupations do not make for sociability or perhaps even leave much room for ordinary civility, and it seems clear that Beethoven's contacts with the reality of the out-side world took the form of clashes, more or less violent, between a fairly accommodating environment and the fantastic precon-ceptions born of a hard, unfair childhood in an exceptionally obstinate, intransigent and idealistic heart. The result was what Mr. A. E. F. Dickinson, in his clever monograph, calls "his determination to be himself in the full sense"—a resolve which, it is safe to say, had not presented itself to any earlier composer in quite that form. Monteverde, Byrd, Purcell, Bach, Mozart, Hadyn: all these were professional men who left the problem of their personalities to work itself out as a natural concomitant of their careers. To them, as to the Wyke-hamist, manners made the man. But with Beethoven, at any rate from the *Eroica* onwards, each work marks a step away from musical good manners; a process which culminated in the *Grosse Fuge*. So that if his passionate individualism, as obvious in his conduct as in his music, was Beethoven's strongest link with the Romantic Movement proper, his position in the history of music has another and greater importance: he was creating a new tradition—that of "impolite" music.

How rude to his listeners Beethoven could be, any student of the later works, comparing their aural effects with those of the polite school (from Mozart to Debussy), can testify. Yet an examination of Beethoven's life reveals a deeper truth behind the rebarbative mask that used to glower at the Queen's Hall audience from the Royal Philharmonic Society's unfortunate bust.

A cloudy veil stretches across the abyss of my nature. I have, however, no love of secrecy and darkness. I am glad to think that God sees through my heart, and if any angel has power to penetrate into it, he is welcome to know everything that is there. Yes, and so may any mortal who is capable of full sympathy, and therefore worthy to come into my depths. But he must find his own way there; I can neither guide nor enlighten him.

I think most people would agree that that adequately describes Beethoven's heart; they may, therefore, be surprised to learn that it is in fact Nathaniel Hawthorne's account of himself. Two more arrestingly dissimilar men can scarcely be imagined; but in the balancing the same profound stresses, two natures often achieve surfaces that are poles apart. The resulting difference, in the case of Beethoven and Milton (to whom that paragraph also applies), is far less great. Both men looked politically forwards; both were deeply committed to a revaluation of religious belief; in one blindness, in the other deafness did more than merely shut them into towers of rebellious egotism. These capital afflictions had, by the law of compensation, the effect not only of reinforcing the image-creating faculty but also of slowing down the tempo of experience, until each facet of the spinning jewel was clearly perceived; so that, by the total erasure of one sense, their minds evolved a technique of getting immediately to the roots of any personal incident—a system not so easily acquired by those whose organs all function normally. It should not then strike anyone as paradoxical if I point out how much there is of Milton's Satan in the *Grosse Fuge*, in the *Hammerclavier*—that monument to Pride, the Finale of which is, as Mr. Dickinson says, "the work of one whose passion for the accurate expression of his mind was tireless to the end"; and for the same reason I suggest that Tolstoy was justified in his fear of the Kreutzer Sonata. On the other hand, the strange, cool lyricism of *Comus* has its counterpart in the Violin Sonata in G, op. 96, while—to reverse the analogy—the Rasoumovsky Quartets and the middle period piano sonatas (the C sharp minor, the Waldstein, the Appassionata) translate *L'Allegro*, *Il Penseroso* and *Lycidas* into an even more purely musical form.

> Paradise, and groves
> Elysian, Fortunate Fields—why should they be
> A history only of departed things,

Or a mere fiction of what never was?
For the discerning intellect of Man,
When wedded to this goodly universe
In love and holy passion, shall find these
A simple produce of the common day . . .

Thus spake Wordsworth, purposely borrowing Milton's diction. The contemporaneity of Wordsworth and Beethoven, considered together with the former's avowed descent from Milton, may help to make my paradox more acceptable. Do not look, however, for the "groves Elysian" in the most obvious place— i.e., the Pastoral Symphony, for this is one of the composer's most impersonal works—an exercise in eighteenth-century landscape painting in the style of Thomson's *Seasons*, the German translation of which (done for Hadyn by the Freiherr Van Swieten) Beethoven is sure to have known. Beethoven's very own Paradise is lost in the first movement of the Ninth Symphony and regained in the two last string quartets: in all these the "produce of the common day"—the sights and sounds of Nature—unite with "love and holy passion" to form a synthesis which in seminal power enormously increased the vocabulary of musical expression. To have done this implies, for the first time in history, an interest in orchestration for its own sake—i.e. as in itself a means of expression and not as a more or less conventional method of "laying out" music for an ensemble of instruments. It was part and parcel of Beethoven's view of art gradually to achieve the individualization of each separate instrument; a process which has gone on ever since, until *Le Sacre du Printemps* started an attempt (pursued by the French post-war school and by the earlier Hindemith) to put the clock back.

Beethoven's treatment of any combination of instruments was no less revolutionary than his use of the orchestra: in all cases the experiments were dictated by the composer's perpetual search for what Mr. Dickinson calls "a compelling communication"; but, more than all this, a glance at the genres in which he chose to cast his musical ideas prompts the conclusion that, as in the case of Milton, it was the conflict between Good and Evil that underlay all his work and that gives it so specifically *human* a significance. For, with the exception of one opera, two masses, the songs, a few sets of variations, and single pieces of an occasional character, Beethoven's entire output is in sonata form;

and that form, by virtue of the perfect malleability it eventually achieved at his hands, the alternation and interaction and working-out—so essentially dramatic—of themes, the combinatory possibilities of the movements, was and still is the finest medium yet devised for expressing the intrinsic situation of man.

Genius of so ponderous and brooding a quality must have its drawbacks, of which unrelenting seriousness is the most obvious. Others lurk in Beethoven's method of composition. It must not be forgotten that he was famous in his day for improvisation at the piano, and it seems probable that the seeds of his works were born in some such manner and that the composer's procedure (as shown in his notebooks) was to formalize this extempore material, gradually hammering his themes into usable shape and nearly always compressing them in the process. All this *Bearbeitung* resulted in a certain lack of spontaneity—of "vocality"—which I think places him below Bach, Mozart, and Schubert on the purely melodic plane. With Beethoven, as with much lesser artists like Mérimée, excessive simplicity becomes indistinguishable from obviousness, as can be seen in the Violin Concerto or the Andante of the Fifth Symphony. Mr. Dickinson suggests that Beethoven "did not aspire to the fascinating rhetoric of artfully changing octave and rhythmic detail which Bach had anticipated and Chopin was to perfect". If this is so —and I think the point is both true and important—the reason is perhaps partly to be sought in Beethoven's growing deafness, which may have made for the wood-cut themes and the violent chiaroscuro of his harmony, but chiefly in the fact that his spirit inhabited an essentially different poetic world from that which was natural to composers like Mozart and Chopin. His search for truth was directed to ends remote from theirs. So that I can see no sense in Mr. Dickinson's remark that Mozart's music is addressed to "a level of aural understanding which has since been superseded". This is robbing Peter to pay Paul, and it only confuses the entire issue to imply—as that sentence does —that, say, the Eighth Symphony has rendered Mozart's in G minor (K 550) out of date. The world will never be so rich in masterpieces that it can afford to regard Mozart as "superseded".

If art is to survive and evolve modern man must learn to live in more than one emotional climate. With Beethoven music entered on its most tremendous phase of development, one which now (*pace* Mr. Dickinson) seems to be drawing to a close —at all events from the point of view of form. The modern symphony, the tone-poem, the rhetorical fantasia, Wagnerian opera, are all results of following up suggestions contained in Beethoven's work, just as his harmonic experiments led to conventional "romantic" harmony as typified by Mendelssohn, Schumann and Brahms. Again, though Bach is the putative, Beethoven is the real father of Schönberg and of all those who have recently engaged in the foolish attempt to rid music of its sensuous elements—as if that were desirable!

The cause of strict, Schönbergian Atonalism may be considered lost; on the other hand, I see no reason to expect a rapid change in the near future from the rather deliquescent chromaticism which has become the homogeneous medium of all modern music—partly because dance-music, which may be expected to remain on the whole the most popular genre, makes use of this harmonic system, in its most degenerate Scriabinesque form, and is therefore bound to exert a normative influence on the uninstructed ear. Only when this chromatic influence is finally exhausted is a simpler diatonic or modal system likely to return to general favour. But apart from the important question of harmony it is doubtful whether the new world, the rather horrifyingly arid outlines of which are already beginning to appear through the social disintegration set up (or accelerated) by the war, will have much use for the forms which music has evolved in the last hundred and twenty years, under the paramount influence of Beethoven. To see in the Finale of the Ninth Symphony the forerunner of the music of an egalitarian society seems to me excessively superficial. Music is the most ambiguous of the arts and it is safe to say that in no other medium would an artist like Miaskovsky have passed as the mouthpiece of Communist Revolution, since he expresses himself in music of a decadent, hysterically Tchaikovskian individualism more esoteric even than that of Rachmaninoff, who was deemed unworthy to represent the "new" Russia. Absurd misconceptions of this kind are often the best indications of the spirit of an age, and this one shows how far music may yet have to go in order to catch up with this century's headlong pace. True art will always take its own way, but it does not

seem unduly arbitrary to expect the music of the future to comment more closely and continuously on everyday life than it
has done up to the present. The immense, lonely symphony,
whether on the Sibelius or on the Bruckner model, will be out
of place, and sonata form, which Beethoven erected into a
tyranny, must become a constitutional monarchy if it is to survive at all. Having created the fantasia as a by-product of first-
movement form, the symphony proper might lapse back into
the Suite from which it originally arose.

Forms, then, will become shorter, less expensive of time and
means, but perhaps more various, abundant and rich in occasional appeal. We are, in fact, probably in process of return to
the pre-Beethoven era, when composers were expected to
turn out immense quantities of music at the behest of a
patron; but in this case the patron will be, not an aristocrat, but
the public. No considerable composer before Beethoven would
have thought two hundred and fifty-six works enough for a lifetime; excused by his precept few composers have since produced
more than half that number. The youngest English school, however, is showing a tendency to abundance and a desire to be
continually on the spot which relates them to Haydn and may
lead them to share that exemplary composer's happy ability to
let his genius look after itself.

There are other finger-posts about. The film, with its scrappy,
rhetorical outbursts, may result in a general telescoping of
symphonic thought into concise fantasias of an aphoristic, sentimental or ironic persuasion, orchestrated for small ensembles.
The piano may become popular again for its *cantabile* rather
than for its percussive qualities. Opera will probably be far too
expensive, as a result of which there might be a revival of the
madrigal, as well as of long strophic ballads, telling a comic or
pathetic story, to words by poets like MacNeice and Betjeman
and Plomer. The effect of broadcasting on music in the long run
remains difficult to gauge; but I should not be surprised if the
ironed-out texture which it is apt to produce may end by discouraging elaborate or subtle orchestration; and that would be
yet another step away from Beethoven.

There is no point in bemoaning these perhaps at first sight
unattractive probabilities. The history of music in the last
twenty years has not been so very brilliant after all: what a num-

ber of false starts, of culs-de-sac, of flashes in the pan, of misguided eccentricities, of outworn conventions obstinately persisted in! The composers of the future will not have been living
in jealously guarded individual isolation, cultivating their feelings; they will have been serving with the Forces and have
acquired a thorough knowledge of all sorts of people. This is
bound to affect their music—possibly in the directions I have
mentioned. Of course there will also, one hopes, be exceptions
—men whom ill health or other extraordinary circumstances
have kept apart from the unified stream of contemporary life;
and these will be the Chopins and Debussys of the future. And
the others too will surely have their unsociable periods when,
suddenly reawakened by some chance incident to the immensi-
ties and immutabilities that underpin all existence, or even to
the essential loneliness of man's condition, they will produce
some counterpart of Beethoven's Cello Sonata in C, op. 102,
or of Busoni's Sonatina Secunda.   [*1941*]

Sidney Keyes

ACTAEON'S LAMENT

I HAVE beaten the drum and danced. I have seen
Incredible faces peering through the green
Leaves of the sycamore, yet did not lack
Company while the hounds were at my back.

Now hounds cry in my bones as once they cried—
Their eyes turned wise and savage—when I died.
For I was torn to shreds as well you know
And in my mouth the blue-tongued lichens grow.

Never a girl—it was the greyhound grace
And rhythm of her limbs, that questing face—
Has torn my heart or laid me down so low
Among the fern as she has laid me now.

Jays flirt and haver in the early year.
Heavy upon my unforgetful ear
The hunter's tread resounds, and far away
My crowned hounds celebrate Diana's day.   [*1944*]

Derek Verschoyle

DUTY RUN

(Articles about operational flying in the R.A.F. generally and understandably deal with occasions marked by the dramatic or the heroic. This article attempts to describe a routine night in June 1942, when absolutely nothing eventful happened. Major censorial excisions, affecting the continuity of the article are marked by asterisks.)

THE Dutch coast came up almost dead on E.T.A.[1] We had been able to deduce its whereabouts for about ten minutes before we crossed it from the tracer aimed at aircraft in front by four or five light guns on the coast. There were layers of broken cloud with tops at about seven thousand feet; the path of the tracer was only visible from the point where it emerged above the cloud. We could see not the positions of the guns, or the coast, until we were almost dead above and a break in the cloud revealed the familiar contours of Walcheren Island.

Above the cloud it was almost as bright as day. On our starboard there was a full moon sixty degrees above the horizon; to our port was the glowing semi-circle of the Northern Lights. All the illumination in the air seemed to be caught and reflected upwards by the carpet of white cloud beneath us.

Flying across the North Sea we had been chattering intermittently on the intercomm.:

"This is too bloody light for my liking."

"It certainly is. You can see anything miles off."

"There's a couple of aircraft astern right now. One's a Stirling, the other looks like another Wimpey, but I couldn't be certain."

"Keep an eye on them in case they belong to the other side."

Once a Manchester came up from astern and passed over us, five hundred feet above, moving about forty miles an hour faster than we were. It was a Manchester Mark I, with triple fins on the tail-unit, and therefore now something of a rarity. It occurred simultaneously to at least three members of the crew that it might be piloted by a friend from another station who was liable to take the air in an aircraft of that type.

[1] Estimated time of arrival.

"My God, I wonder whether that's Prissy in A for Apple."

"You might creep up on him and see."

"It would scare hell out of him if he found himself passed by a Wimpey."

"We'll let him go on and get shot at first. We can call him up to-morrow and ask him if it was him."

A quarter of an hour later we saw the first gunfire.

"Light flak on the starboard bow, some way off."

"O.K. When's our E.T.A. at the Dutch coast up?"

"In about ten minutes."

"Keep an eye on the flak and let me know if we look like passing slap over it."

"It may be one of those bloody flakships and not the coast at all."

Ten minutes later there was a break in the cloud. We were over a wide estuary, with a long flat island a few miles away to our starboard. The tide was low, and we could see the surf where the sea met the beach. The tracer from two light guns came up about a quarter of a mile to our starboard, and the bursts from a heavy gun a little nearer.

"Coastline more or less underneath us. I think it's the north shore of Walcheren."

"It had bloody well better be."

"I suppose those silly saps down below don't imagine they're shooting at us."

"Pilot, will you alter course to 070?"

"070. O.K."

The break in the cloud ended half-way along Walcheren, and the ground was obscured. But it was no longer necessary to see earth to know that we were over enemy-occupied territory. In front, through an arc of ninety degrees, we could see the heads of about sixty searchlights blunted against the clouds; a small circle of illumination, like a phosphorus penny, moved along the top of the cloudbank as each light searched below. From about as many points light flak coiled up into the air above the cloud, and here and there one could see flashes from heavy guns. Another Stirling and two Lancasters passed over us, several thousand feet above, the Stirling weaving in enormous sweeps from side to side of our track, the Lancasters being lost to sight within a few minutes of coming in range of our vision.

Then suddenly there was another lucky break in the cloud, this time a large one. The navigator emerged from his compartment and pin-pointed us over the Maas, ten miles north-east of Breda. Through the gap in the cloud we had a bird's-eye view of the enemy's defences coming into action over an area of about four hundred square miles. In the semi-circle of country before us, clusters of searchlights reached up from about thirty localities. The clusters groped round the sky and periodically flak was fired up at the apex of the cone. This was still mostly light stuff, with tracer, but the proportion of heavy flak increased as we moved inland. Flying over Holland or Belgium has an oddness all its own. Underneath you is the country of an ally-in-arms; in each of the quiet villages over which you pass there are men and women whose dislike of the German race is probably sharper and more bitter than your own, because kindled by the horror of daily contact. Their resistance to the aggressor is a process of personal, deliberate planning; while your role, however much as an individual you may enjoy or dislike night-bombing, is a mere matter of obedience to orders. Warfare abounds in paradoxes, but few odder complexes of emotion can be experienced by anyone than those induced by the fact of living in a flak-defended area in Holland or Belgium —hearing the bombers of your ally pass over you on their way to objectives across the frontier, feeling your house shudder from the guns which attempt to shoot them down, and knowing that an aircraft *in extremis* may be compelled to jettison its load on the defences assaulting it from below, and that if it is shot down its bombs are going to come down with it.

Below us we could see the flarepaths of four aerodromes. One was an obvious dummy; it flicked its lights on and off coquettishly as we passed over, ineffectually soliciting a bomb. The positions of the other three corresponded roughly to the locations of aerodromes where we knew night-fighters were liable to be based.

*   *   *

As we passed over, one of them burst into life. Tracer poured at a low elevation from some fifteen guns sited around the aerodrome perimeter and within the field. There was an explosion in the air and something crashed in flames at the far end of the flarepath.

"Looks as if an intruder had bought it down there."

"Poor sap walked right into it."

"Looked as though he pranged on the flarepath, though. They won't get many more aircraft off there to-night."

Shortly after passing Arnhem, the gap in the cloud ended. An expanse of white cumulus stretched away in front, like a vast semi-circular plateau of snow and ice, its surface flecked by the red flashes of heavy guns and yellow searchlights beating against the cloud-base.

"There's a bit of a party going on over there to the port."

"How far away?"

"About sixty miles, I suppose."

"Emden, I should think."

"Looks like it. Is there anything laid on there to-night?"

"I don't know, but it looks as if someone has gone there, anyhow."

"Pretty ropy navigation."

"Wait until we find our joint."

Our target was in the dock area of Bremen, still some hundred miles away. No sign of a break appeared in the cloud below. As the moon rose higher in the sky, the brightness of the night was accentuated. More bombers were now visible, proceeding methodically in the same direction as ourselves. One Wellington flying exactly at our height, about a mile to the starboard between us and the moon, kept us company for half an hour, visible whenever we turned to look at it. For the most part, though, despite the brightness of the night, one saw other aircraft only through looking at flak coming up and then recognizing an aircraft somewhere in the sky above it.

* * *

The wave we belonged to was not scheduled to bomb until fifteen minutes after the first arrivals. We got there about seven minutes early.

"I think we had better stick around a bit and see what happens."

"O.K. There are some bloody great fires down there already."

* * *

We flew around for about ten minutes, hoping for a last-minute break in the cloud. None materialized, but we were able

in that period of waiting to satisfy ourselves that we had come
to the right place. Apart from the party which Bremen itself
was putting up, our position was fixed by the outward and
visible signs of life from Oldenburg, Wilhelmshaven, Weser-
munde. The cloud was not thick. The searchlights came up
through it in places, and fires and gunflashes were clearly visible
below. Right down the length of the Weser it seemed half to
break, revealing distinctly the line of the river.

"There's no point in waiting for this bloody cloud to break.
We'd better go in."

"I suppose it would be no good going and seeing whether
it's any better at Wilhelmshaven?"

"I don't think so. You can see this damned stuff stretching
away right over the sea."

The aircraft was turned through ninety degrees, and we flew
in the direction of the farthest fire. The odd thing was that, while
we had been prospecting the town, we had seen no other aircraft. Now we saw them converging upon the target from half
the points of the compass. A Hampden came sailing down the
sky above us, a Manchester flashed—too close for comfort—
across our bows, we got in the slipstreams of three or four unseen aircraft, we saw half a dozen others taking up position for
their run in, and we went in to bomb with a Lancaster and a
Wellington on our port and another Lancaster to our starboard.

We were flying at ten thousand feet. A thousand feet below
streams of multi-coloured tracer, like handfuls of Hundreds
and Thousands off a birthday cake, reached their ceiling; they
came coiling out of the cloud, described a gentle parabola, and
fell—with infinite leisureliness—away. They looked extraordinarily pretty and innocuous. The cones of searchlights
reached their apex three to eight thousand feet above. There
were about a dozen main cones, with fifteen to thirty searchlights in each. Other searchlights swept the sky singly or in
pairs. The heavy flak was bursting from about our height to
eight thousand feet above. Suddenly, about four thousand feet
above us, we saw a bright flash at the point of intersection of a
knot of searchlights. The flash expanded into a compact blob
of flame which fell, with fininite slowness, through the air. At
about our height the blob exploded, divided into two halves,
and fell, apparently accelerating, through the cloud below.

"Some poor sap's bought it."

"Looked like a large aircraft."

And then we flew into a cloud of balloons. Or rather they looked like balloons. They floated past, some thirty feet away, looking like dark gross bats and reeking of cordite. It was flashless-propellant flak. We did a sharp turn, gained and lost height, and resumed our course.

"Nice friendly stuff, that."

"It smells bloody awful, anyhow."

From a few miles away, the air above a heavily defended target always appears impossible to penetrate without catastrophe. There seem to be no gaps between the searchlights, no breaks in the pattern of gunfire. The gaps appear only as one goes into the area which has seemed devoid of them. We threaded our way methodically towards the centre of the target area, changing course and altitude as the occasion demanded. The thin persistent cloud still obscured the earth. It was too thick for the minor phenomena of bewilderment, with which Bremen is richly endowed on a clear night, to be seen. One could see below—apart from the searchlights and the guns—only four great areas of fire and the odd valley in the cloud formation which corresponded with the line of the Weser. Just on the far side of that valley was a long stretch of fire, which all the evidence suggested lay in the dock area of Bremen.

"I think we'll let them go over that fire straight ahead. We're not going to see anything better."

"O.K. I'll open the bomb doors."

"Someone else has just dropped his on that fire."

"Straight and level now for half a minute . . . half a minute more. . . . I am going to let them go now. . . . Bombs gone."

"Take a photograph just for luck. Something might come out."

Getting out of Bremen seemed to take much longer than getting in. We headed for the sea, forty-five miles away. To our port Wilhelmshaven was still putting up a spirited performance; away to the starboard Cuxhaven—which is somewhat *sui generi* in the way of defences—was doing likewise; Heligoland, some sixty-five miles ahead, was permitting itself the luxury of a minor, but vicious, hate. They were invaluable landmarks.

We were flying into a strong headwind now, and it took us

twenty-five minutes to reach the sea. For the first twenty miles we were shot at more or less continuously, if never with any great degree of accuracy. Then the fire became intermittent. One would fly along unmolested for half a minute or so; then, just as one had begun to feel that the sea must be underneath earlier than one had expected, a little snake's tongue of fire would flash through a gap in the cloud. The last stretch over enemy occupied territory is always trying: the coastline takes an unconscionably long time in coming up, one's mood is one of apprehensive anti-climax. On a cloudy night (with the added complication of flakships causing confusion some miles out to sea) one is never quite sure when one has in fact left the land behind. On this occasion we could tell within a few miles when we were out to sea by observing the behaviour of Cuxhaven, Wilhelmshaven, Heligoland and the more demonstrative Frisians and taking bearings.

We went far enough out to sea to keep clear of the Frisians, and then turned on to a westerly course. Almost immediately after doing so we saw a fighter. He was about half a mile away to our starboard, almost exactly at our height, flying very fast in the direction of Heligoland. If we had continued out to sea half a minute or so longer our courses would have converged.

"I think I'd get underneath this cloud if I were you. It's too bloody light up here."

"I think you've got something there."

We descended bumpily through several layers of strato-cumulus. It was like doing down into a very deep and very dark basement in an old-fashioned lift. Eventually we saw the sea, and a few hundred feet lower the contours of Holland some twenty miles away to our port. There was a line of gunfire for fifty miles down the coast, aimed at aircraft returning over-land.

Flying back across the North Sea is always a boring business. The navigator still has some work to do, but the pilot generally hands over to "George", his automatic deputy, and (assuming the aircraft to be undamaged) there is nothing much for him and the rest of the crew to do except eat their rations and chew gum, keeping an eye open for enemy fighters and our own air-craft in distress. We saw nothing across the three hundred miles of sea except one Wellington flying slowly almost at sea level and (when we got near the coast) showers of flame-floats from aircraft taking drifts. Waiting for the English coast to come up is invariably trying. The east coast of Great Britain is remarkably unobtrusive: on a dark night in winter as often as not it is quite invisible; even on a bright short night near midsummer (such as this) it is none too obvious. We did not detect it until it was only about fifteen miles distant. But, thanks to good navigation, when it came it was exactly the bit of coast required.

Across the three hundred miles of sea we had seen precisely two aircraft, one belonging to either side. In the sixty miles between the coast and our base we saw at least twenty—Stirlings, Halifaxes, Lancasters, Wellingtons, Hampdens—making for home. As we passed over, we heard half a dozen aerodromes marshalling their flocks.

"Hello Carol A Apple, Monkey answering. Aerodrome one thousand feet. Over to you."

"Hello Dormouse C Charlie, Rattle calling. Pancake. Over to you."

"Hello Chamber, Plover D Donald calling. Can I pancake?"

As we passed over East Anglia the dawn came up. The sky was red and fiery in the east.

"With that sky, there won't be any Ops to-night."

"That's rather a pity. I wouldn't mind taking another crack at that joint if only one could see it properly."

We passed over canals, villages, towns; they looked dirty and unreal, protruding from underneath a white mist like cotton wool. A few minutes before we got within call of our own base the navigator became aware that he was hungry.

"Mr. P.M.C., what's there for breakfast?"

"Bacon and eggs, I hope."

"There had bloody well better be."

"I told the Mess Sergeant."

"His idea of breakfast after flying is bully beef and salad."

"He'll bloody well get murdered if there aren't bacon and eggs."

We landed just after five o'clock in almost broad daylight. Just before landing the front gunner put his foot through the perspex floor of his turret and blasphemed horribly. In the dispersal we got the news from the ground crew.

"How many are back yet?"

"Twelve down including you, Sir, and V Victor's circling the aerodrome now. There's only F Freddie still to come."

"Do you know how they got on?"

"Flight Sergeant Brown got shot up by a fighter and came back on one engine. No one else had any trouble that I've heard of. They are bombing up all the kites again immediately for to-night."

We had been six hours and fifteen minutes in the air. It had been, on the whole, just about an average night.   [*1942*]

Alun Lewis

THE SENTRY

I HAVE begun to die.
For now at last I know
That there is no escape
From Night. Not any dream
Nor breathless images nor sleep
Touch my bat's-eyes. I hang
Leathery-arid from the hidden roof
Of Night; and sleeplessly
I watch within sleep's province.
I have left
The lovely bodies of the boy and girl
Deep in each other's placid arms,
And I have left
The beautiful lanes of sleep
That barefoot lovers follow to this last
Cold shore of thought I guard.
I have begun to die
And the guns' implacable silence
Is my black interim, my youth and age,
In the flower of Fury, the folded poppy,
Night.
                                        [*1941*]

John Strachey

MISS LEE

WHEN Ford got back to the incident at two in the afternoon he
noticed that the rescue men seemed moody. They were picking
about on the top of the mounds of debris without much apparent purpose. It was raining. One of them came over and
sheltered beside Ford in a doorway. He complained that the
borough did not provide them with adequate mackintoshes or
with a change of overalls.

"No good catching your death for a lot of stiffs," he said,
excusing himself for having knocked off.

Just then Ford noticed a change in the atmosphere of the
incident. The nearest squad of rescue men had become alert
again. Quin, who was again incident officer, came over and
told him that they thought that they had heard tapping.

The whole squad began working strongly and fast. One or
two men would from time to time get excited and begin to grab
at the debris, flinging it aside. But that didn't pay in this case, for
it was evident that tons of stuff would have to be moved before
they had hope of coming on anyone. Ford took off his equip-
ment and began the usual filling of baskets, and the passing
of them back, along a chain of hands to be emptied. Every
fifteen minutes or so one or other of the rescue men would ask
for stillness, would listen for the tapping and would call down.
After two or three times some of the rescue men began saying,
"Cut it out. Get on with it. You're holding up the work. We
haven't much time."

Ford guessed that the rescue men were thinking not only of
getting to the buried person, or persons, as quickly as possible,
but also of getting the job done before the dark and the raiders
came back again. But he couldn't conceive that there would be
any difficulty about that. The idea of another night and another
raid beginning was a remote and repulsive hypothesis—the last
night and the last raid seemed only just over. In any case, it
was a difficult matter to decide how often it was justifiable to
hold up the work in order to get a signal from below. It was

necessary to do so from time to time, because by means of such signals alone could they hope to locate the buried persons. And unless he, she, or they could be located, with gradually increasing exactitude, hours might be wasted in sinking shafts and tunnelling in the wrong places.

The rescue men were attacking this very large, irregularly shaped mound of debris from three different positions. After a bit one of the parties working some way away from the cave from which the tapping had first been heard insisted on silence. He claimed that he could hear a voice as well as tapping. After two or three more bouts of digging this rescue man definitely got into touch with the buried person. A voice responded several times, and they all got a much better idea of where to dig. It became apparent that the original cave, which had been deepened into the beginning of a shaft, was much too high up the mound. With reluctance the rescue men who had been working up there were induced to come down and join those who were cutting into the side of the mound. It was now half-past three. The rescue man who was deepest into the tunnel, near the bottom of the mound, began to shout.

"Who are you?" he called. He listened. "What name?" he repeated. He listened. "Bee, did you say, Bee?" "It's a woman," he said, turning his face upwards. "Bee, or Lee, or Tee, or some such name." Quin consulted his records of who should have been sleeping in the house.

"There should have been a Miss Lee," he said. "That's right," said the rescue man. "That's what she's trying to say."

They worked on, obviously encouraged by knowing now that it was a definite person, whose name they knew, that they were trying to reach.

It was now half-past four. The light was perceptibly weaker. Ford realized that, far from there being plenty of time, it was going to be a race to get her out before the darkness and the fireworks began all over again.

The rescue men said nothing, but they began to get a little short and abrupt with each other, working against time. There was more in it, Ford felt, than the rational fear of working in the difficulties of the darkness and a new raid. There had been reawakened in them all an older fear of the beasts, the spirits, and the dark.

They dug. At six-twenty the sirens went. "He's back," said the man working next to Ford. The guns began. At first they heard the thud of distant batteries, south of the river; then the sharp note of their familiar local guns, and then the rising and falling drone of the bombers' de-synchronized engines. The rescue men took no notice. It was still possible to work fairly effectively without the use of torches. Then they heard a wailing from the mound. It was Miss Lee. She too, imprisoned, had heard the new raid begin. Her nerves gave way. An incoherent, terrified sound, occasionally crystallizing itself into words, came from her. Ford heard, "It's there again. They'll get us all; they'll get me." The rescue men began to shout back to her, "No, they won't; you're all right; stick it now." But the wailing shouts went on. "Can't you save me? Don't be so slow. Why don't you come?"

"Sha'n't be ten minutes now," answered the rescue men.

They dug. The light failed. The fact had to be faced that it would be necessary to work on during another night; and, not for ten minutes, but for several hours, as far as could be judged. Miss Lee kept up an intermittent, usually inarticulate, wail, like an animal.

The squad leader sent for a big tarpaulin from the rescue lorry. This he had stretched, like a sort of rough tent, over the mouth of the tunnel so that torches could be used. . . . Before long George, the rescue man who had forced his way farthest in, called back, "I can touch her hand now." "All right," said one of the stretcher bearers (he was a Corporal, and in charge of the party), "the doctor says she can have this morphia tablet." They passed down the tiny tablet. "Can you take this in your hand, Miss?" George said. Ford could not hear the answer. But George said, "She's got it."

The tarpaulin made a little, private torch-lit world of their own, cut off from the rain-soaked, gun-thudding, bomber-droning, world outside. They felt safer.

They worked on. It was seven o'clock. Miss Lee had been buried just twenty-four hours. "I can see her head now," George said. Then, after a bit, the other rescue man said, "That ain't her head—that's her arse. She's lying this way."

"No, she isn't. She's in an S-curve, this way. Aren't you,

Miss?" said George, appealing to the patient to settle this argument as to her anatomy. Ford couldn't hear the reply. But it was clear that as the rescue men got nearer and nearer, so that she could hear them properly and even probably see them by now, she was getting calmer. She had stopped wailing, and was quiet except for an occasional sob.

They dug. Ford began to hear Miss Lee's voice much more clearly. She was saying something about a dog. "Right across my knees," she said. They had evidently got much closer to her now. After a bit Ford bent forward, craning over the back of the stretcher-bearer Corporal in front of him to have a look down the length of the tunnel. To his astonishment he found that George and his mate had now cut their way right through to her. For there she was.

Miss Lee sat facing him, in a tiny torch-lit cave, clear of the debris from her waist up. But her legs and the lower part of her body were still deeply covered by something. She looked to be a slight woman in her early forties, her face and hair covered with the greyish debris. She was perfectly calm now, comforted by the actual presence of her rescuers. She sat there contentedly and innocently, like a dishevelled child sitting up in bed in its night nursery. George, by lying full length, could get at the debris on her right side; he was slowly filling a basket with it. She went on talking about this dog. "Scratched for me, he did," she said. "As soon as the first lot came down on me, I heard him scratching for me and barking. And then the second lot came down, much more heavy, and killed him, right across my legs."

Ford began to realize that she was explaining that the body of this dog was across her legs now: that its body was part of what was holding her legs down. "Saved your legs, lying soft on 'em like that," George said to her.

"Now let's see if we can shift him." Ford couldn't see what George was doing. But he heard him grunt as he tried to move something heavy. Then Miss Lee cried out, "Oh, my legs!" "All right, Sister, all right. Bound to hurt a bit as we shift him off." But evidently they couldn't get at the dog's body. For in a minute they called for a rope. One was fetched by the unseen hands from outside and passed to Ford under the end of the tarpaulin. They gave it to George. He took some time passing it under the dog's body, as Miss Lee cried out whenever the weight on her legs was shifted.

But she was perfectly calm and rational now. She went on talking to them as they worked. "I know I'll never have the use of my legs again," she said, her voice pleading for reassurance. "Oh yes, you will, Sister," George told her. "In ten minutes" (it was always ten minutes) "when we gets you out you'll find the use of them legs coming back to you prompt. That poor beast's body has saved them legs of yours."

Miss Lee said, "I'm a seamstress. Work for Halliday and Knight. Don't use power machines in our shop. All treadle machines. Wouldn't think a big firm like them would have treadle machines, would you? Old-fashioned."

"You'll be all right," said George. He had got the rope fixed under the dog. "Now, Miss, we're going to lift this dog off of your legs. May hurt a bit as the blood comes back into 'em." He turned to the rest of them—"Now heave." They all pulled on the rope and Ford felt it slowly coming. Gradually a darkness was pulled back through the tunnel; it was deposited on to Ford's knees, as the last man in the line. It was the heavy, soft, black body of a very large Labrador retriever. Ford had considerable difficulty in lifting it and passing it out from under the tarpaulin. But in the end the hands from outside got hold of it, and the body was taken away.

There was now enough space in the actual cave in which Miss Lee sat for George to get down into it beside her. He and she sat there quite peacefully together; she, reassured and happy now that she was in actual physical contact with another human being; he, carefully and gently digging round her legs so as to free them. The conversation went on, Miss Lee talking gently about her life and her job; wondering if she'd be long away from work, and would someone at the hospital tell the firm what had happened? George managed to make a good deal of progress towards freeing her right leg, which was nearest to him, though not without causing her sudden sharp pains at intervals. "That's good, Miss, that is," he kept saying, "shows you've got the feeling down your legs."

But he had great difficulty in getting at the debris over her left leg, since to do so he had to reach right over her body. After several not very successful attempts, he said to her, "Could you shift any of it yourself, Miss?" Miss Lee began picking quite strongly with her right hand (her left was slightly injured) at the debris over this leg. Ford remembered what intolerable stuff it was to handle with one's bare hands. He took off his right glove, and said, "Here's a glove for her; pass it down." They took it, saying, "Glove coming down," and Miss Lee put it on her right hand.

By this time George had got her right leg free and was able to lean over more easily and help her with the left leg. After about another fifteen minutes' work, he announced that this leg, too, was coming free. The corporal of stretcher bearers called out to his men outside the tarpaulin, "Ready for the doctor." "Doctor coming down," they answered, and almost at once the end of the tarpaulin was lifted and the trim, mackintoshed figure of the doctor appeared. "Doctor coming down; all out for the doctor," ordered the corporal. The doctor made his way down, guided by the hands of the men, and, not without difficulty, reached Miss Lee, taking the place George had left. He began speaking gently and firmly to her. She was scared as he began to examine her legs. "They're broken, doctor, I know they're broken," she said. "No, no, I don't think they are at all. Let's just see, let's just see." After carefully feeling each leg, he asked for a splint and two triangular bandages. These were passed down to him, and he bandaged her right leg to the splint. "That's all we need do here, Miss Lee," he said. "Now you're coming out," and he wormed his way back down the tunnel.

Ford did not quite see how she was to be got out, though. It was clearly impossible to get a stretcher down that narrow, irregular length of tunnel, still less into the cave. But the corporal called back to his men, "Fetch the Neal Robertson." In a little while two stretcher bearers appeared with a curious looking white object. They put it down near the entrance to the tunnel. The tarpaulin was now rolled back, and they worked for a time with unscreened torches. Fortunately it didn't sound as if there were any German planes particularly near overhead. The white object was unwrapped; it was like an enormous pair of stays, only this stretched the full length of the body. It was made of white, tough canvas, reinforced with struts which were either light metal or some pliant wood such as ash.

The whole thing bent and rolled up into almost any shape. This ingenious device was passed down the sloping tunnel. George was at his old place beside Miss Lee in the cave. Gently and expertly they slid the Neal Robertson stretcher under her —she was able to help quite considerably herself, by rolling on to it. Once on, they carried straps, with which the sides of the stretcher were fitted, across her body, and strapped her firmly on. Then they began the still by no means easy process of working the laden stretcher back through the tunnel. Miss Lee must have been quite a light woman, but it is amazingly difficult to get enough purchase to lift any inert body when one is working in a confined space. However, little by little, and without, as far as they could judge, hurting her, they got the stretcher backed out of the tunnel. Once it was clear they lifted it and Miss Lee together on to an ordinary stretcher. Meanwhile the waiting ambulance was backed close up to the mound. It was just nine o'clock. Miss Lee had been buried twenty-six hours.

While they were doing this Ford came close to the stretcher, and looked down at Miss Lee. She was lying there very still, but seemed calm and unshocked. He saw that his glove was still on her right hand. He bent down and slipped it off. She took no notice. It was really a perfectly sensible thing to do; the glove could not possibly have been of any further use to her. And yet afterwards Ford couldn't help feeling that he had been mean in taking it back. It was rather too careful a thing to do, in the circumstances. But Ford had always particularly hated losing one glove of a pair, as he not infrequently did. So that even after twenty-six hours of the James Street incident the impulse to prevent that occurring was still strong in him. Of all that happened during this long incident this lending and recovery of his glove struck most obstinately in his mind.

The stretcher party picked Miss Lee up, put her in the ambulance and drove off with her. Ford went up to the doctor and asked him whether she had been badly injured. "Not at all, not at all," he said. "So far as I could ascertain—from the very superficial examination that was all that was possible down there—there is no grave physical injury. No limb is broken and there appears to be nothing else seriously the matter with her." Ford and the other wardens felt elation. There was triumph in the wresting of Miss Lee, without injury, and after twenty-six hours' work, from the chaos of the ton bomb. There was triumph in the stubborn digging of the rescue squads, in the use of such a well-designed device as the Neal Robertson stretcher by the stretcher bearers, and, for that matter, in their own efforts. Ford went off duty and slept.   [*1941*]

Richard Church

SEEKING THE ISLAND

Now my life's journey has passed the high places,
I know, having looked out over the waters,
The ocean where the western island was,
That I shall never see its palaces,
Its golden walls where the wise men sit
Heavy with their memory of race, memory deeper
Than reason, the men who never grow old.

But maybe this certainty of losses,
Of time's treachery in lacking hereafter,
The island, where the fountain of knowledge was,
Sunk in the ordinary waves, the terraces
And serene canals no longer lit
With the world's young light; maybe I, the sleeper,
Have reached there, awakened, and shall never grow old
                                                    [*1937*]

C. E. M. Joad

THE FEAR OF DEATH

IT is natural to fear death. "Men fear death as children fear to
go in the dark," says Bacon. But what a "to do" people have
made about it, especially in antiquity. Look through any anthology of poetry and you will be surprised at the enormous
number of entries which concern themselves either directly or
indirectly with death's terrors. And no doubt death is formidable, especially, perhaps, for those who do not believe in a life
beyond. "Death", says Aristotle, with his usual abruptness, "is
a dreadful thing; it is the end." If, of course, we believe in
immortality the position is different; witness the queries in the
celebrated hymn:

> Where is death's sting? Where grave thy victory?

though, for my part, I agree with Adam in Shaw's *Back to
Methuselah* in regarding the prospect of eternal life with even
greater apprehension than that of death.

If only there may be an end some day, and yet no end. If only I
can be relieved of the horror of having to endure myself for ever! If
only the care of this terrible garden may pass on to some other
gardener . . . If only the rest and sleep that enable me to bear it from
day to day could grow, after many days, into an eternal rest, an
eternal sleep, then I could face my days however long they may last.
Only there must be some end. Some end; I am not strong enough
to bear eternity.

Quite so! But this is not, I think, the light in which most
people view the matter; which is, I suppose, why the fear of
death has been strong in proportion as the belief in immortality
has been weak. And precisely because people have been so
terribly afraid of death, moralists and philosophers have never
tired of telling them not to be afraid of it. Because death is
fearful, they have assured them that it is not; and because it is
not, we must not, they say, be afraid of it. *Timor mortis, morte
pejor*: Burton cites the Latin proverb with approval in *The
Anatomy*, while Montaigne quotes another to the effect that

death has less of fear about it than the expectation of it: *Morsque minus poenae quam mora mortis habet*. Seneca proses on interminably assuring us that just as after death there is nothing, so dying itself is nothing. There is, I cannot help thinking, a touch of disingenuousness about these asseverations. "Sir, all the arguments which are brought to represent poverty as no evil, show it to be evidently a very great evil. You never find people labouring to convince you that you may live very happily upon a plentiful fortune." Dr. Johnson's admirable comment upon arguments relating to poverty might, I think, be applied with equal force to arguments relating to death.

Among the various platitudinous considerations with which I am acquainted, the only one which seems to me tolerably reassuring is that used by Socrates in the *Phaedo*. The *Phaedo*, one of the greatest of Plato's Dialogues, is singularly apposite at the present time, and may be read with great pleasure and profit by those who feel that their prospects of dying are rather greater than they were. Socrates argues more or less as follows: Nobody has ever had any experience of death. Therefore we do not know what being dead is like. Therefore we have no reason to suppose that it is worse than being alive; it might just as well be better. It is, therefore, irrational to dread that which might just as well be a change for the better as for the worse. This is not to say that we should welcome death; merely that our attitude should be non-committal. This seems to me to be reasonable. Everything that we know, we know either because we have experienced it ourselves or because we have heard of it from somebody who has experienced it—this, of course, includes the hearing of it by reading books—and whose testimony we are prepared to trust. Now we have not experienced death ourselves; if we had, we should not be alive to wonder about it, and we have not heard about death from anybody else, because if anybody were in a position to give us information on the subject, the mere fact of his being able to do so would show that he was not dead.

I venture to add one other consideration. There is a general agreement to the effect that we ought to be glad to be alive and do our best to make a good thing of life. That, since we *are* alive, we might as well make the best of it I agree, but I cannot see why it should be assumed that we should necessarily be glad of life and, by consequence, resentful of death. After all, we did not contemplate life in advance, decide on balance that it was a good thing and then deliberately choose it; we were pitchforked into life without so much as a by your leave. Hence, if life turns out badly, the fact is no reflection on our judgment or our choice, and we are, therefore, as I conceive it, under no obligation to pretend to ourselves that it is necessarily a good, or that leaving it is necessarily an evil. If life becomes more of a liability than an asset—and one would think that for some people at least it must be so—one would be well advised to quit it.

I conclude, then, that the fear of death has been exaggerated. It is certainly a fact that those people with whom I have recently discussed the matter seem to feel less of it than, if the poets and philosophers are to be believed, was felt by our ancestors. But what they do fear and what I fear is disablement and pain: the being blinded, burnt, mutilated or infected, the losing of a limb, the being tied for the rest of one's life to a broken and a pain-engendering body. This, I think, is what most of us fear from the bombs, this and the loss of our possessions. In so far as we fear death, it is, I suspect, largely because of the pain which dying involves. Death, as somebody remarked, would be all very well, were it not for the dying.

I suspect that there is a definite change of sentiment and valuation here. The ancients feared death but scarcely mentioned disablement or pain. We are more concerned with pain than with death. William James was, I think, the first to remark the change. "A strange moral transformation", he wrote, "has within the last century swept over our western world. We no longer think that we are called upon to face pain with equanimity. The way in which our ancestors looked upon pain as an eternal ingredient of the world's order, and both caused and suffered it as a matter of course, fills us with amazement." When we consider how much more formidable pain and disablement were to our ancestors than to ourselves, that the hurt man had no anaesthetic to relieve his pain, the disabled man no cars or trains to substitute for his legs, no cranes or lifts to serve as extra arms, no books to take the place of his ears, no wireless of his eyes, the change of sentiment is all the more remarkable.

G

What are the reasons for it? Here are four, none of them, I fear, very convincing. There is, first, the influence of Christianity. People have believed and do believe that to die is to be transferred to a plane of being at once happier and more virtuous than this one. The belief has, of course, been accompanied by the rider that the plane of being to which one was transferred might be more miserable and less virtuous. The hope of heaven, in other words, has in most minds been qualified by the fear of hell. Apart, however, from the fear of hell, it is noticeable that Christians have not ceased to find death terrible. Dr. Johnson was a devout and a good man, yet Boswell speaks continuously of his horror of death. Johnson never, he says, "had a moment in which death was not terrible to him".

Secondly, it may be that the moderns fear injury because they are more familiar with it. Paradoxically, civilization, which was to make the world safe, has made it dangerous. There were never so many ways in which a man can get hurt. Men are caught up in machinery, involved in railway accidents or disabled in mines. Above all, they are injured by cars—in 1938, 226,854 of them in this country alone, and in America over a million. In the same year it is estimated that the number of people permanently mutilated by cars in England, the U.S.A., Germany, France and Italy, was over half a million. Meanwhile, films warning us against reckless driving by vividly picturing its effects have made us all disablement conscious.

Thirdly—and here I think we come to the root of the matter —we demand more of life than did our ancestors. We want life of a higher quality to be lived according to a higher standard, a quality which is incompatible with pain, a standard to which the maimed cannot conform. "It fills us with amazement", as William James says, "that people should ever have put up with pain so readily." One wonders that human beings could have been so callous. And why to us *do* they appear callous? Precisely because what was to them endurable and worth enduring would for us have made life no longer worth living. I suggest, then, that it is because we have come to entertain higher expectations of life that, if we cannot have life at a level at which it comes up to our expectations, we are prepared to do without it altogether. In a word, we are less tolerant of pain and less fearful of death because our standard of living has gone up.

Fourthly, the consciousness of many moderns has been imbued with the doctrines of creative evolution. We are instruments of life created by a purpose which transcends us and are discarded when that purpose is served. If we are broken before our time, that is of little moment; life can create innumerable others to take our place. "The life to which I belong uses me", writes Wells, "and will pass beyond me and I am content." Life, in fact, is the end, individuality the means, and who, after all, are we to make such a fuss about the continuance of our personal selves? This is cold comfort and hard doctrine, but there are so many, and these not the least admirable among our generation, to whom it appeals.   [*1940*]

MILTON'S BLINDNESS

To the Editor of *The New Statesman.*

Sɪʀ,—I do not know how it may strike others, but to me it is a curious thought that Milton, in all human probability, was not entirely blind.

He suffered from what the old physicians called "a gutta serena" (cataract)—which does not affect the vital centres, but only the medium (crystalline lens), of vision, and does not altogether destroy this *as* a medium. Milton, it is almost certain, could at least distinguish light from darkness. I think, on the whole, his own words bear this out, and I take the great liberty of italicizing certain expressions in the immortal invocation to Light.

> —thee I revisit safe,
> And feel thy sov'reign vital lamp; but thou
> Revisit'st not these eyes, that roll in vain
> To find thy *piercing* ray, and find no dawn:
> *So thick a drop serene* hath quenched their orbs,
> *Or dim suffusion veiled.*

("Or" for "Or at least" is quite in the Miltonic strain):

> —but not to me returns
> Day, or the sweet approach of even or morn. . . .
> But *cloud* instead, and ever-during dark
> Surrounds me——

("Dark" may surely mean darkness, as when we speak of a dark night.)

And in the analogy he draws between his own physical state and a corresponding mental state we have:

> So much the rather thou, celestial Light,
> Shine inward, and the mind through her powers
> Irradiate, there plant eyes, *all mist from thence*
> *Purge and disperse*——

"Dim suffusion" veiling the eyes is an exact description of cataract.

In any case another curious speculation arises. If in Milton's time surgical science had been what it is now he might have been cured, wholly or partially, of his blindness. *Paradise Lost* would then have been robbed of one of its very finest passages. Possibly it would not have been written at all: Milton himself seems to attribute its direct inspiration to his loss of sight. This may afford matter for reflection to those who account physical efficiency and health, as Bacon accounted truth, "the sovereign good of human nature". If, indeed, they attach any real value to imaginative creations, or believe that life has been ennobled and enlarged by the greatest sustained poem in our language.

Yours, etc.,

PAUL HOOKHAM

Oxford.

[*1920*]

Virginia Woolf

GAS AT ABBOTSFORD

EITHER Scott the novelist is swallowed whole and becomes part of the body and brain, or he is rejected entirely. There is no middle party in existence—no busybodies run from camp to camp with offers of mediation. For there is no war. The novels of Dickens, Trollope, Henry James, Tolstoy, the Brontës—they are discussed perpetually; the Waverley novels never. There they remain completely accepted, entirely rejected—a queer stage in that ever-changing process which is called immortality. If anything is going to break the deadlock perhaps it is the first volume of Scott's Journal, 1825-1826, which Mr. J. G. Tait has been at immense pains to edit and revise. As Scott's Journals are the best life of Scott in existence, as they contain Scott in his glory and Scott in his gloom, and gossip about Byron, and the famous comment upon Jane Austen, as in a few passages Scott throws more light upon his genius and its limitations than all his critics in their innumerable volumes, this new version may one of these dark nights bring the two non-combatants to blows.

By way of inducing that desirable encounter, let us take the entry for 21st November 1825: "Went to the Oil Gas Committee this morning, of which concern I am President or Chairman." Scott, as Lockhart tells us as we can well believe, had a passion for gas. He loved a bright light, and he did not mind a slight smell. As for the expense of those innumerable pipes, in dining-room, drawing-room, corridors and bedrooms, and the men's wages—he swept all that aside in those glorious days when his imagination was at its height. "The state of an illumination was constantly kept up"; and the gas shone upon a brilliant company. Everyone was flocking to Abbotsford—dukes and duchesses, lion hunters and toadies, the famous and the obscure. "Oh dear", Miss Scott exclaimed. "Will this never end, Papa?" And her father replied, "Let them come, the more the merrier." And someone else walked in.

One night a year or two before the diary begins, the stranger was a young artist. Artists were so common at Abbotsford that Scott's dog, Maida, recognized them at sight and got up

187

and left the room. This time it was William Bewick, obscure, penniless, in pursuit of sitters. Naturally he was a good deal dazzled both by the gas and the company. Kind Mrs. Hughes, therefore, the wife of the deaf Dean of St. Paul's, tried to put him at his ease. She told him how she had often soothed her children's quarrels by showing them Bewick's woodcuts. But William Bewick was no relation of Thomas Bewick. One feels that he had heard the remark before and rather resented it, for was he not a painter himself?

He was a painter himself, and an extremely bad one. Did not Haydon say "Bewick, my pupil, has realized my hopes in his picture of Jacob and Rachel?" Did he not add, some years later, when they had quarrelled about money, "Daniel's left foot and leg would have disgraced Bewick before he ran away from my tuition to the shelter of Academical wings"? But we know without Haydon's testimony that Bewick's portraits were intolerable. We know that from his writing. His friends are always painted in a state of violent physical agitation, but mentally they are stock still, stone dead. There is his picture of Hazlitt playing tennis. "He looked more like a savage animal than anything human . . ." He cast off his shirt; he leapt; he darted; when the game was over he rubbed himself against a post, dripping with sweat. But when he spoke, "His ejaculations were interlarded", Bewick says, "with unintentional and unmeaning oaths." They cannot be repeated; they must be imagined; in other words, Hazlitt was dumb. Or take Bewick's account of an evening party in a small room when the Italian poet Foscolo met Wordsworth. They argued. Foscolo "deliberately doubled his fist and held it in Wordsworth's face close to his nose". Then, suddenly, he began whirling round the room, tossing his quizzing glass, rolling his R's, bawling. The ladies "drew in their feet and costumes". Wordsworth sat "opening his mouth and eyes, gasping for breath". At last he spoke. For page after page he spoke; or rather dead phrases coagulated upon his lips, in frozen and lifeless entanglements. Listen for a moment. "Although I appreciate, and I hope can admire sufficiently the beauties of Raphael's transcendent genius . . . yet we must brace the sinews, so to speak, of our comprehension to grapple with the grandeur and sublimity . . . of Michael Angelo. . . ." It is enough. We see Bewick's pictures; we realize

how intolerable it became to sit any longer under the portraits
of Grandpapa flinging out a bare arm from the toga while the
horse in the background champs his bit, paws the ground and
seems to neigh.

That night at Abbotsford the gas blazed from the three great
chandeliers over the dinner-table; and the dinner, "as my
friend, Thackeray, would have said, was *recherche*". Then
they went into the drawing-room—a vast apartment with its
mirrors, its marble tables, Chantrey's bust, the varnished wood-
work and the crimson tasselled curtains pendant from handsome
brass rods. They went in and Bewick was dazzled—"The
brilliant gaslight, the elegance and taste displayed throughout
this beautiful apartment, the costumes of the ladies, with the
sparkle and glitter of the tea-table"—the scene, as Bewick
describes it, brings back all the worst passages in the Waverley
novels. We can see the jewels sparkling, we can smell the gas
escaping, we can hear the conversation. There is Lady Scott
gossiping with kind Mrs. Hughes; there is Scott himself, prosing
and pompous, grumbling about his son Charles and his passion
for sport. "But I suppose it will have an end at a given time, like
any other hobby of youth." To complete the horror, the
German Baron D'este strums on the guitar. He is showing "how
in Germany they introduced into guitar performances of
martial music the imitation of the beating of drums". Miss
Scott—or is she Miss Wardour or another of the vapid and
vacant Waverley novel heroines?—hangs over him entranced.
Then, suddenly, the whole scene changes. Scott began in a low
mournful voice to recite the ballad of Sir Patrick Spens:

> Oh lang lang may their ladies sit
>   With their fans in their hands
> Or e'er they see Sir Patrick Spens
>   Come sailing to the land.

The guitar stopped; Sir Walter's lips trembled as he came
to an end. So it happens, too, in the novels—the lifeless English
turns to living Scots.

Bewick came again. Again he joined that extraordinary
company, all distinguished either for their genius or for their
rank. Again the tiny red beads of light in the chandeliers
blossomed at the turn of a screw into "a gush of splendour

worthy of the palace of Aladdin". And there they all were, those gas-lit celebrities, dashed in with the usual dabs of bright oily paint: Lord Minto in plain black, wearing a most primitive tie; Lord Minto's chaplain, with his saturnine expression and his hair combed and cut as if by the edge of a barber's basin; Lord Minto's servant, so enthralled by Scott's stories that he forgot to change the plates; Sir John Malcom wearing his star and ribbon; and little Johnny Lockhart gazing at the star. "You must try and get hold of one," said Sir Walter, upon which Lockhart smiled, ". . . the only time I have observed him to relieve his fixed features from that impenetrable reserve, etc., etc." And again they went into that beautiful apartment, and Sir John announced that he was about to tell his famous Persian story. Everybody must be summoned. Summoned they were.

From all quarters of that teeming and hospitable house guests came flocking. "One young lady, I remember, was brought from her sick-bed wrapt in blankets and laid on the sofa." The story began; the story went on. So long was it that it had to be cut into "miles". At the end of one Sir John stopped and asked "Shall I go on?" "Do go on, do go on, Sir John," Lady Scott entreated, and on he went, mile after mile, until—from where?—there appeared Monsieur Alexandre, the French ventriloquist, who at once began to imitate the planing of a french polished dinner-table. "The attitude, the action, the noise, the screeches, and hitches at knots, throwing off the shavings with his left hand, were all so perfect that Lady Scott, in alarm, screamed "Oh! my dining-room table, you are spoiling my dining-room table! It will never be got bright again!" And Sir Walter had to reassure her. "It is only imitation, my dear . . . it is only make believe . . . he will not hurt the table." And the screeching began again, and Lady Scott screamed again, and on it went, the screeching and the screaming, until the sweat poured from the ventriloquist's forehead, and it was time for bed.

Scott took Bewick to his room; on the way he stopped; he spoke. His words were simple—oddly simple, and yet after all that gas and glitter they seem to come from the living lips of an ordinary human being. The muscles are relaxed; the toga slips off him. "You, I suppose, would be of the stock of

Sir Robert Bewick?'' That was all, but it was enough—enough
to make Bewick feel that the great man, for all his greatness,
had noted his discomfiture when Mrs. Hughes was so tactful
and wished to give him his chance. He took it. "I", he exclaimed, "am of a very ancient family, the Bewicks of Annan,
who lost their estates. . . ." Out it all came; on it all went. Then
Scott opened the bedroom door, and showed him the gas—
how you can turn it up, how you can turn it down. And,
expressing the hope that his guest would be comfortable—if
not he was to ring the bell—Scott left him. But Bewick could
not sleep. He tossed and tumbled. He thought, as the people
in his pictures must have thought, about magicians' cells,
alchemists' spells, lions' lairs, the pallet of poverty and the
downy couch of luxury. Then, remembering the great man and
his goodness, he burst into tears, prayed, and fell asleep.

We, however, can follow Scott to his room. By the light
of his journals, the natural and fitful light of happiness and
sorrow, we can see him after the party was over, when poor
Charlotte chattered no more, and Maida had gone where, let
us hope, artists no longer paint the favourite dogs of celebrated
men. But after a party is over some saying, some figure often
remains in the mind. Now it is the ventriloquist, Monsieur
Alexandre. Was Scott himself, we ask, glancing at the long
line of the Waverley novels, merely the greatest of all the
ventriloquist novelists, of all who imitate human speech without hurting the dining-room table—it is all make-believe,
my dear, it is all imitation? Or was he the last of the playwright novelists, who, when the pressure of emotion is strong
enough behind them can leap the bounds of prose and make
real thoughts and real emotions issue in real words from living
lips? So many playwrights did; but of novelists who—except
Sir Walter and, perhaps, Dickens? To write as they did, to
keep so hospitable and teeming a house, where earls and
artists, ventriloquists and barons, dogs and young ladies speak
each in character, must not one be as they were, half-ventrilo-
quist, half-poet? And is it not the combination in the Waverley
novels of gas and daylight, ventriloquy and truth that separates
the two parties, and might they not, using the journals as stepping-
stones, with a glance at these crude illustrations from the brush of
William Bewick, break the deadlock and come to blows? [*1940*]

Harold J. Laski

IN PRAISE OF BOOKSELLERS

It is time that someone paid a tribute to a noble body of men and women whose service to the nation in wartime has been badly overlooked—I mean the men and women who run the bookshops of this country. A good bookshop, after all, is one of the supreme temples of the human spirit; and a good bookseller is one of the finest of human creatures. By and large, I suspect that good bookshops have done more solid work in adult education then all the classes organized since the days of the mechanics' institutes; and I hazard the guess that Blackwell's at Oxford and Heffers' at Cambridge provide as much intellectual stimulus as any of the colleges in either of the ancient universities. It has been one of the many tragedies in the history of London University that its scattered character has failed to make it possessive about a good London bookshop. If I were the Vice-Chancellor I would know no rest until I had made that unique Londoner, Mr. J. G. Wilson, of Messrs. Bumpus'—he is, of course, a Scotsman—move bag and baggage from Oxford Street to Bloomsbury; just as every medieval college had its chapel, so every modern university would have its bookshop if it had that sense of the fitness of things which recognizes that browsing among books is the surest highway to thought.

And the good bookshop has done marvels in this war. Publishers may have been blitzed; printers and binders may be short of paper and staff; Mr. Bevin may be adamant about his claims to that type of assistant whose taste and patience and ingenious dexterity in discovering the unfindable proves that Heaven itself made him a bookseller; despite everything, they have kept open. Despite everything, they are eager to talk about their wares, to urge you to the book you somehow missed, to convince you that there is, after all, a realm where thought is free and reason the master of its fate. No sinkings in the Atlantic will prevent my friend Cooper from producing for me that second volume of a treatise from the University of North Carolina which I had not hoped to see until the days of peace; and his eternal good humour, even in the blackest days of 1940, and after an all-night watch with the Home Guard, will remain one of those memories which glow in reminiscence. I know few Tories more absolute than my good friend Heffer; perhaps that is why he insists that he is a Liberal. But not even his deepest suspicion that Cambridge will never be the same place after its invasion by the University of London has prevented him from continuing to welcome me to his palace, even though, in his heart, he is doubtful whether my wanderings ought not to be limited by a Defence Regulation to Collets' in the Charing Cross Road. And what, after all, could be more delightful than to know that the conviction that his opinions are devastatingly obsolete is only less profound among his assistants than that article of their faith which makes of Trinity a kind of minor annex to Heffer?

The bookshops of Oxford and Cambridge have, no doubt, a unique chance in a unique atmosphere. Old David is dead; but his stall still furnishes its mass of attractive oddities with an alert figure by your side who, if his finger darts unerringly to an antique treasure is as likely as not to be Lord Keynes. Or, if you want to know what the war has done to the taste of students, you cannot do better than talk to O. H. Jermy, who not only knows unerringly whether any given book is in print, but can tell you, quite infallibly, that you should send another volume to this student in the R.A.F. as the one you propose is the one he bought himself when he was in Cambridge on his last leave. Nor can I omit that kindliest of old friends, the head of the great foreign room at Deighton and Bells, to whom I think the fall of France was like a break in an affection which had borne the trials and tribulations of dealing with French publishers without resentment for nearly fifty years; I think his personal pleasure in finding for me, within a week, two copies of Renan's famous letter to D. F. Strauss—which ought to be reprinted— was almost as great as my gratitude to him.

Perhaps, in a sense, the bookshop at its best is seen, in war-time, in London or the provinces. There, the client is more general than particular. It may range from an eminent scholar who wants a book that no one will ever buy again, through the soldier, British, American, more rarely from Canada or Australia, to snatch a hurried hour in his leave mentally to renew

his spirit, on to the old lady whom I swear I saw with my own
eyes ask for two of the novels of Emma Jane Worboise (she must
have lived in Kensington). If the Ministry of Information really
wants to know what the provinces are thinking, I doubt if they
could do better than give an hour of talk to that endless appe-
tite for every sort and condition of bookbuyer, from the young
aircraftman who is firmly told of the virtues of Professor Levy's
Introduction to that eminent policeman turned publicist for
empire to whose groans over my soul he will cheerfully listen
while he digs out for me some Quaker pamphlets of the seven-
teenth century marvellously preserved in some back-street house
in Rochdale. Not, indeed, that Manchester will ever be quite
the same since the blitz destroyed, in Hewkin's shop, a paradise
of treasures in early economic literature before which even
connoisseurs like the late Professor Foxwell and that in exhaust-
ible bibliographical fountain H. L. Beales would stand in
reverent admiration. Or there is Grant of Edinburgh, where the
kindness of the staff almost exceeds the adorable unexpected-
ness of the stock, and Thin, of the same place, who handed me
a collection of the pamphlets of Sir Henry Vane with that casual
air, so carefully assumed, which is the ultimate mark of the
great bookseller by nature. Who cannot meet the test of war's
endurance where the men (and women now) who preside over
these noble habitations face its trials and tribulations with a
confidence at once so serene and so proud?

Nor can I forget to emphasize, what every bookbuyer from
San Francisco to Chungking will want to know, that Mr. J. G.
Wilson remains unchanged. Nothing ruffles his cheery dogma-
tism. He lets Mr. Shaw take the other copy of Professor Sabine's
fine reprint of Gerrard Winstanley in a mood that cunningly
combines his sense of pleasure in the purchaser with a due
knowledge of the obligation conferred. I have seen him morally
compel, by sheer force of character, an eminent peer to buy an
ugly edition of one of Trollope's novels because he knew that
his lordship's niece would like (God help her!) the plates in the
volume. His appreciation of the Holmes-Pollock letters ought to
earn him not only the thanks of the Cambridge syndics, but
endless gratification from those whom his own eye for a real
book has taught that the race of great letter-writers is eternal if
one goes down the side-alleys and does not remain content with

the high-road. It was said, I think by a late Bodley's Librarian, that the librarian who reads is lost; Mr. Wilson embodies the profounder aphorism that the bookseller who reads wisely has won his game. The Hitlers and the Mussolinis come and go; is there a reader who frequents the bookshops unaware that while men like Wilson remain, with their endless cheerfulness, their pawky humour, their conviction that, come what may, no tyrant could ever destroy a great book to which one determined bookseller has found his way, this war is an interruption of civilized living only, not a term to that ultimate source of happiness—the satisfaction of the curiosities of the mind.

This, you may challenge, is one man's form of escapism. In some degree, perhaps; and yet, I venture to believe, not wholly so. A friend of mine, part of whose task is the inspection of interned prisoners of war, left with a young Nazi airman, at his request, a copy of Emerson's *English Traits*. Some months later, he heard from the airman, asking if it were possible for him to have the loan of other works by Emerson. A little later still, revisiting the same camp, he talked again with the airman. "If," said the latter, "we had learned these things at home, we should not have been fooled into this adventure." There is the flush of dawn over one man's darkness. So long as we keep our bookshops stocked with books and full of clients that dawn will break over the darkness of others, too; perhaps even over our own. I know no symbol of freedom more vital than the shop on whose shelves neither Jew nor Greek, neither bond nor free, need fear exclusion. For to insist that exclusion and civilization are antithetic terms is to have the clue to humane living. If I had to put the purpose of this war in a sentence I should say that we fight it that men and women may freely choose themselves the books which give nourishment or pleasure. In Germany they burn the books; in Britain we sell them. So long as we can continue to say that, we can be confident of the outcome of this struggle.   [*1943*]

Ethel Smyth

THE WATERFALL

THE following adventure, easily the most vivid of many childish recollections, does not figure in my autobiography, *Impressions that Remained*, because the author-friend on whom I inflicted the early chapters of MS. inquired if I really imagined any publisher would print such an anecdote?

The scene was Paris, 1917; and as this victim of a budding author's ruthlessness was on three days' leave from the front, at first I believed he must be suffering from shell-shock; and so did two intelligent and literary women of our acquaintance: "Comment!" they cried, "vous voulez qu'elle supprime cette histoire delicieuse! . . . si essentiellement anglaise, si drôle, si innocente! et puis si *jolie*!"

But the face of the Englishman (his name was M—ce B—g) assumed a mulish expression well known to his friends, and he went on quietly repeating, "It must be cut out." And cut out it was.

Last summer I told the story to a group of dashing, up-to-date, equally literary but *English* experts. All scoffed at the idea of its shocking anyone nowadays; such prudery was a thing of the past, they said.

I thought to myself at the time "*I wonder*"? And to-day more than ever do I wonder, remembering the recent case of a Polish Count who gave rein to an apparently irresistible passion for certain monosyllablic words: good strong Anglo-Saxon words which, however, are seldom met with in polite letters. The publisher not only returned his poems with horror, but thought well to communicate with the police; and presently these judges of literature were escorting the poet to prison.

We, of Puritan extraction, are careful to lock up in our bosoms any hair-raising monosyllables that come our way. Yet at this moment the thought of that guileless foreigner haunts and daunts me a little; so does a picture by Gilray—or is it H.B.? —showing a female of unprepossessing appearance seated in the stocks, so ran the legend, for having used language ill becoming

196

a lady. And I do so want to attend a "Court" disguised as a
Doctor of Music. The robes are gorgeous and ritually quite
correct according to the Lord Chamberlain's Office. . . .

It's no use; I simply cannot keep this thing to myself! Risk
or no risk, consequences or no consequences, here's the story.

*   *   *   *   *   *

Like most little girls I envied boys on many counts, but
chiefly for a costume which does away with difficulties and
dangers that embitter the lives of their athletic sisters. How
blessed to climb trees without risk of finding yourself suspended
in mid air by your sash; to jump wheelbarrows and not catch
your toe in a hem; to crawl through hedges and never get
stuck half-way because of your petticoats; to fall head over
heels without the added humiliation of what our French
governesses called making an *exposition* of yourself! Altogether,
how wonderful must be life in which hooks and eyes, strings
and pins play no part: a life solidly based on buttons!

At this point one thought of various matters; of occasions
when, nature being nature, things have to be done secretly and
swiftly; O how simple merely to . . .

Stop; that's not a safe road to travel. Better make a fresh start.

In my memoirs I spoke of our passion for dressing up; also
of our box of *grandeurs* (pronounced *grandjers*), consisting of old
ball dresses, wreaths, and spangles of my mother's, military odd-
ments of my father's—false beards, feathers, and so on. Well;
one cold autumn day in the holidays, looking as like Fenimore
Cooper's Indians as these rather sophisticated "properties"
allowed, out we rushed, war-whooping, into the garden.

Now the fancy dress on which I had set my heart was one of
my brother's suits. He was twelve, I only eight, and the idea
was unfavourably received as derogatory to the dignity of a
male wardrobe. But eventually, tricked out with a gold-braided
Horse Artillery forage cap and a crimson sash, I was graciously
permitted to be a Bush Policeman and told to look alive.

My duties were turn about to hide in the shrubbery and dash
out in pursuit of Indians; but all too soon came the moment
when nice-minded little girls explain they have left their
pocket-handkerchief up at the house and will be back directly.
Not so this Bush Policeman. Here at last was a chance of testing

the greatest of all advantages conferred by male attire; had I not often seen my brother disappear behind a tree . . . to emerge almost immediately, gazing aloft as though looking for birds' nests? . . . The Red Indian game seemed slacking off . . . there was no time to be lost . . . I nipped into the shrubbery. . . .

O horror! Midway in a devastating experience that proved the difference between dreams and realities, came shouts of "Ethel! quick, quick! collect wood! We're going to build a wigwam," and simultaneously the tramp of approaching feet! . . . All but caught in a shocking situation, too flustered to invent an excuse for bolting up the house, condemned to stand in misery for the rest of that icy afternoon handing boughs to my elders, I think the severest moralist will allow that, far from fitting the crime, the punishment was several sizes too large for it.

The deed was never discovered; in such cases the ingenuity of the young is limitless. But, incredible as it seems in a country-bred child, not till some years later did I grasp why this gallant experiment was foredoomed to failure! Children can be very unobservant, and such was the case with me.

*　　*　　*　　*　　*　　*

How dark it has got! Is that you, Polish Count, in the corner? . . . and that odd-looking object near the fire, is it the stocks, or only one of those T-shaped foot-rests beloved of the gouty? . . . And you, dim but resplendent vision in knee-breeches, a queer-shaped peaky hat tucked under your arm? . . . Mercy on us! You must be, *You are*, the Lord Chamberlain! . . .

Avaunt phantoms or rather come out into the open, Polish Count, Lord Chamberlain, and gouty foot-rest! I defy the lot of you. Of course, people can read anything they choose into words, but unless you tamper with mine I defy you to make clear to the jury what, exactly, happened that day in the garden at Sidcup Place, Footscray, Kent. And to avoid possible misapprehensions I will only add what perhaps should have been said sooner, that the spot chosen for our wigwam was just where a little stream runs guggling through the rhododendrons and down the bank into the pond. And that is the reason —the sole reason—why this story is called *The Waterfall*. [*1932*]

E. M. Forster

MRS. GRUNDY AT THE PARKERS'

WHEN Mrs. Grundy called at the Parkers', she was informed by the maid that they were "Not at home".

"Do you mean that your mistress is out or is not out?" she asked. Doris collapsed, and said that Mrs. Parker was in, but had rather a headache, and so was resting.

"Then have the goodness to tell her I am here, without further prevarication," said Mrs. Grundy, and seated herself in the austere drawing-room—such a contrast to her own cosy parlour. The Parkers enjoyed making themselves as well as other people uncomfortable, which she had never been able to understand.

"Ah, Amelia," said her friend, coming in. "Quite a voice from the past!"

"Edith, I called about something or other, but Doris's untruthfulness has put it clean out of my head. Why did she say you were not at home when you are?"

"Well, it is only a form of words; a modern convention. One has to keep pace with the times if one is to guide them and they sorely need our guidance."

"And have you the headache or have you not?" Mrs. Grundy persisted.

"I have. Still I am glad you forced your way in, for I want to talk about our methods of work. You don't interfere with people in quite the right way, you know. You are too desultory and impetuous. That was all right in the nineteenth century, when life was slow, and one could point to one impropriety after another with one's umbrella as they crossed the street— but to-day! Why, you'll get knocked down. You'll be run over by a motor-bicycle, and before you can see whether it was a girl on the pillion she will have disappeared. To-day one must select and one must plan; civilization is so complicated. Think of our triumph the other month—that man who was arrested for bathing at Worthing."

"Ah, don't talk to me about bathing. I often wish there was no such place in these islands as the sea-shore."

"That is shallow of you. If there was no sea-shore, how could we catch people on it? Besides, I approve of bathing, provided it is so regulated that no one can enjoy it. We are working towards that. You were a great pioneer, but you made the mistake of trying to suppress people's pleasure. I try to spoil their pleasure. It's much more effective. I don't say, 'You shan't bathe.' I say, 'You shall bathe in an atmosphere of self-consciousness and fear,' and I think I am succeeding. I certainly have at Worthing."

"I expect I read about Worthing, but where everything is so shameless one gets bewildered."

"Why, the case of the visitor who bathed, properly clad, and then returned to his bathing machine to dry. Thinking no one could see him, since the machine faced the ocean, he left its door open. He had reckoned without my foresight. I had arranged that a policewoman should be swimming out at sea. As soon as she observed him, she signalled to a policeman on shore, who went to the machine and arrested him. Now, Amelia, would you have ever thought of that?"

"I certainly shouldn't have. I don't like the idea of women policeman at all. A woman's proper place is in her home."

"But surely there can't be too many women anywhere."

"I don't know. Anyhow, I am glad the visitor was arrested. It will stop him and others going to English seaside resorts, which is a step in the right direction, and I hope the magistrate convicted."

"Oh, yes. Magistrates nearly always convict. They are afraid of being thought to condone immorality. As my husband points out, that is one of our strong cards. In his private capacity the magistrate was probably not shocked. The average man simply doesn't mind, you see. He doesn't mind about bathing costumes or their absence, or bad language, or indecent literature, or even about sex." At this point she rang the bell. "Doris, bring the smelling salts," she said, for Mrs. Grundy had fainted. When consciousness had been restored, she continued: "No, nor even about sex, and we social workers of the twentieth century cannot ignore sex; what we can do is to make it a burden. And we are faced with the difficulty that the average man, if left to himself, does not brood, and forgets to persecute. He has habits instead of ideals. Isn't that too dreadful! He says in effect, 'I go my way about sex or whatever it is, and I let others go theirs, even if I think it queer. It isn't my funeral.' But it is going to be his funeral—at least I hope so."

"And what of the average woman?"

"She is a little more satisfactory, a little more apt to be scared. Though I have known sad cases of women saying, 'Pore thing, we don't take no notice although she did 'ave a little Unwanted, we treats her like one of ourselves.' You see what we are up against—tolerance, good-temper, and un-suspiciousness. It has been no easy matter to cover England with regulations from end to end."

Mrs. Grundy sighed. "I admit you manage to interfere more than I did," she said. "I expect it is as you say, and I was too impulsive. I hurried too much from vice to vice when I was young. I stood outside the music halls, to stop people going in, and then I heard profanity in the cab-shelter, and went to silence that, and while I was doing so the music hall filled up. I went to Africa to make the cannibals monogamous, and during my absence the Deceased Wife's Sister's Bill became law in England. When it's daylight I can see people, which is scanda-lous, and at night-time I can't see them, which is worse. I simply don't know where to turn, and while I am insisting on ulsters for sunbathing the Deceased Husband's Brother's Bill will probably become law, too. You have a sounder method, Edith. You have brought in education, of which I never dreamt, and I am not surprised that your wonderful work gives you the headache."

"My headache, to which you now refer, has nothing to do with my work," replied her hostess. "It has been caused by a piece of bad news which has just arrived from the Continent. Even my husband is upset by it."

"If I had my way there never would have been any Conti-nent," cried Mrs. Grundy, and proceeded to ask a series of agitated questions, such as had the bad news to do with chocolates being allowed in theatres, were sweepstakes to be legalized, was Sunday cricket spreading, had the King been seen patting a race-horse, and so on.

"No, you are quite off the lines. It has to do with something inside us."

"And pray, what can the Continent have to do with my inside?"

"Amelia, you must make an effort to understand. It concerns you as much as myself. It is a sort of discovery that has been made by a kind of doctor. Just as our work was prospering and we were making people stodgy and self-conscious under the pretence of building better citizens, just as we had bullied the lay authorities and coaxed the clerical into supporting us, just as interference was about to be launched on a colossal scale—— But I despair of explaining what it is. Perhaps my husband will be able to." And she called out, "Nosey!"

Mr. Nosey Parker, who now joined the ladies, was scarcely their equal as a field worker. Where he excelled was on committees. Without being obtrusive, he managed to generate that official uneasiness upon which all their work depended. Let me explain. Each member of any committee has, of course, broken the law at some time or other, and desires to prove to his colleagues that he hasn't; he can do this best by being timid in discussion, and by voting for any measure that deprives the public of enjoyment. Furthermore, each member either has a daughter or feels that he ought to have one, and dares not oppose any censorship of art or literature in consequence. Mr. Parker realized all this. He had only to say, "We must think of our daughters," and everyone thought of their skins. He had only to say "I am not narrow-minded, but . . ." and broadness became impossible. He raised the banner of respectability and called it idealism. *Sauve qui peut* was embroidered in brown on its folds. And under it the municipal councillors or the board of magistrates or the jurymen gathered, all afraid of being found out, and when their duties concluded they had not done at all what they intended (which was, generally speaking, to let their fellow creatures alone), but had stopped one man from doing this and another from doing that, and had sent a third man to prison.

"Nosey, do explain what has happened," his wife said.

"Nothing has happened. It is only an idea."

"Ideas have never troubled me, especially from abroad," said Mrs. Grundy.

"You are fortunate. I own myself worried by this one. The

idea is that we, who have helped others, ought now to be helped, and it is proposed to help us by pulling us to pieces." He shuddered. "To you that means little. But I have always had doubts of my own solidity. How can I bring it home to you? They desire to examine your intimate fabric, Mrs. Grundy: they suspect it of being diseased. My wife's and my own they assert to be even fouler than yours. They believe that we all three try to improve people because we envy their happiness and had bad luck ourselves when we were young. What so alarms me is that there is no bitterness in the new attack. We are actually objects of pity."

"And, pray, is that all?" said Mrs. Grundy, with her dry little laugh. "You may have given Edith a headache over this, but you have no such effect on me. I am quite accustomed to pity. I got a lot as a girl. It is merely a term of abuse, and I shall castigate it in due season. Good-bye, my dear sir, and take an old woman's advice: keep away from foreign newspapers in the future." And, gathering up her skirts, she left their house—perhaps for her doom.

"Poor thing, she doesn't know the danger," said Mrs. Parker, looking after their friend anxiously, and observing how she first scowled at Doris and then lectured some navvies for using a word which had been devitalized twenty years previously by Mr. Bernard Shaw. "She is brave because she is out of date. But we—oh, Nosey, Nosey! Fancy, if it gets known that interference is a disease which ought to be interfered with. Men and women will live as they like, they will be natural and decent about one another, and we shall boss and nag at them no more."

"Too true, too true," said her husband, "and yet I see a ray of hope. Our enemies cannot interfere with us unless they organize. As individuals they are helpless. They will have to form Freedom Leagues, or Anti-Fuss Societies or sign Beach Pyjama Covenants, and they cannot do so without constituting themselves into committees. And as soon as they meet on committees . . . yes, I think we shall survive after all."

Will they survive? Only Doris, who is the future, can tell.

[*1932*]

Harold Nicolson

D. H. LAWRENCE

Books which one has eagerly awaited are apt to disappoint.
No such deception is provided by the *Letters of D. H. Lawrence*.
These Letters, as Mr. Aldous Huxley says in his Introduction.
are "beautiful and absorbingly interesting in themselves".
Apart from this, they provide an explanation of Lawrence's
life and character such as exceeds the most exacting requirements. Not only do they fortify admiration and illumine
understanding: they create a mark upon the mind. Lawrence
always leaves a scar—a scar upon our human complacency.
Mr. Huxley, in his Introduction, explains the essentials. He
states the character of Lawrence's genius, and how that genius
impelled him to lead the life he did. He describes Lawrence in
terms of the normal, almost of the ordinary: that is the correct
approach. Other and less fastidious hands have fingered the
soul of D. H. Lawrence, splitting it into psychological fibres,
disintegrating a man whose whole purpose was integration. Mr.
Huxley has made no such mistake. In his Introduction, as in
Catherine Carswell's passionate monograph (withdrawn, alas,
from circulation), we get nearer to Lawrence than we have ever
been admitted before. We realize that he can be approached
only with diffidence and with respect. We see that he was
"different and superior in kind". We absorb his integrity. We
echo his own complaint: "They do not *want* to understand."

The main barrier between Lawrence and the reading public
is his constant preoccupation with sexual experience. This preoccupation, at moments, took extreme forms. It will be many
years before the average reader is able to approach that side of
Lawrence's work with the simplicity, the *innocence*, with which
he approached it himself. "My great religion", he wrote, "is a
belief in the blood, the flesh, as being wiser than the intellect."
That is a hard doctrine, and those of us who have few mystical
tendencies are disconcerted by the incessant intrusion of his
birds, beasts and flowers. We see that he rejected the intelligence as he rejected the emotions, falling back on those ele-

ments in human nature which are most akin to the darkness of plant growth. Yet whereas it is not wholly stupid to be puzzled by his methods, it is ignorant and unfair to attribute them either to morbidity or to prurience. I recommend all those who hesitate to credit Lawrence with a highly spiritual intention, to read his admirable letter to Willard Johnson on page 556, as also his indignant disgust with Casanova on page 523. These are indeed important documents. Even more significant is his antipathy to the emotional lasciviousness of *Wilhelm Meister*. We may not possess sufficient sexual simplicity to approach such matters with Lawrence's own absence of sophistication. But the first lesson that these Letters teach us is that our hesitations, our "censor-moron", as he would say, are not necessarily more respectable than his own directness. We abide in rooms. He, with his pride and clearness of soul, lived in the open air. The first step towards understanding his attitude is to acquire complete confidence in his intention. The Letters give us that confidence. If only in this, they serve their purpose.

What was his intention? "There is a *principle*", he writes, "in the universe, towards which man turns religiously—a *life* of the universe itself. And the hero is he who touches and transmits the life of the universe." His deepest desire, therefore, was "pure unadulterated relationship with the universe, for truth in being". Here, again, is a hard yet evanescent doctrine, which we can scarcely hope to render vivid or permanent to ourselves. Yet that is not the point. The point is that for twenty years and more of adult life D. H. Lawrence kept his aim, this mission, this quest, constantly before himself. This is the second revelation given us by the Letters. A revelation of the amazing *continuity* of Lawrence's own theory. Much has been written about his "duality", about his "inner conflict". The Letters disclose that such discussions are concerned with means, not ends. There was certainly a conflict between his social and his associal self. Towards the end of his life a further conflict appears to have developed between his consciousness and his instincts. The doctrine of "spontaneity" by then was wearing thin. He came to loathe personality, above all his own. But his search for "truth in being" continued unabated through those twenty years. He sought it in social activity, and that failed him. He sought it among a few fortuitously chosen friends, and they, with few exceptions, failed him also. He sought it in remote civilizations and obscure rites. They also provided no answer. His journeys to Ceylon, to Australia, to New Mexico were, as Mr. Huxley said, both "a search and an escape". And finally he sought it in his own instincts. Here again the answer was uncertain and blurred. Yet the point is that he never wavered in his search and never compromised. "Primarily", he wrote to Edward Garnett, "I am a passionately religious man." No one can read the Letters without being overwhelmingly convinced of the truth of that assertion.

Then there is his sanity, his poise. There is a tendency among certain critics, especially in Germany, to regard D. H. Lawrence as a neurotic. That foolish legend will, we trust, be killed by this publication. The whole correspondence of D. H. Lawrence pulsates with sanity, even in little things. "Don't you", he writes, "think it's nonsense when M. says that my world is not the ordinary man's world, and that I am a sort of animal with a sixth sense? . . . They all seem determined to make a freak of me—to save their own short-failings, and make them 'normal' " Lawrence was obviously exceptional, even eccentric, but he was not a neurotic. There is about him a sane, if mobile, seriousness, a "nimble earnestness". "And don't", he wrote to Rolf Gardiner, "be too earnest, not over-burdened with a mission; neither too self-willed. One must be simple and direct and a bit free from oneself above all." Read also his advice to Katherine Mansfield on Jung, and his advice to Willard Johnson on intellectual pornography. Read also his invectives against "clever" conversation: "Never for one second an outgoing of feeling, and no reverence, not a crumb or grain of reverence. I cannot stand it. It is the horror of little swarming selves that I can't stand."

From this continuity of purpose, this balanced outlook, comes also his magnificent assurance. Naturally, Lawrence had many bees in his bonnet and they sometimes buzz. Yet he was able always to refer his moods to his own central *daimon*, he was always, even at moments when the superficial fluidity of his nature played him false, to find firm footing upon the consciousness of his own inherent integrity. "I *know*", he writes to Edward Garnett, "that I can write bigger stuff than any man in England. And I have to write what I can write. And I write for men like D. and H.—they will read me soon. My stuff is

what they want when they know what they want. You wait."
"I shall", he writes again, "get my reception, if not now, then
before long." Such assurance has been more than justified.
D. H. Lawrence was fortunate, perhaps, in not having sur-
vived his disciples. Only by the most sensitive can his refinement be understood. Yet in these simple unemphatic Letters
even the most bourgeois among us can catch a gleam of something segregated, passionate, and tender. One cannot read this
book and remain thereafter just the same.   [*1932*]

John Betjeman

POT POURRI FROM A SURREY
GARDEN

MILES of pram in the wind and Pam in the gorse track
  Coconut smell of the broom and a packet of "Weights"
Press'd in the turf; the thud of a hoof on a horse track
    A horse-riding horse for a horse track
    Conifer county of Surrey approach'd
Through remarkable wrought-iron gates.

Over your boundary now, I wash my face in a bird bath
  Then which path shall I take? That, over there by the pram?
Down by the pond? or else, shall I take the slippery third path
    Trodden away with gym-shoes
    Beautiful fir-dry alley that leads
To the bountiful body of Pam?

Pam I adore you, Pam, you great big mountainous sports girl
  Swishing them over the net, full of the strength of five
That old Malvernian brother, although he's playing for Woking
    Can't stand up
    To your wonderful back-hand drive.

See the strength of her arm, as firm and hairy as Hendren's
  See the size of her thighs, the pout of her lips, as cross
And full of a pent-up strength, she swipes at the rhododendrons
  Lucky the rhododendrons
  And flings her arrogant love lock
Back with a petulant toss.

Over the redolent pinewoods, in at the bathroom casement
  One fine Saturday, Windlesham bells will call
Up the Butterfield aisle, red with Gothic enlacement
  Licensed now for embracement
  Pam and I as the organ
Thunders over you all.   [*1938*]

Clive Bell

MATISSE AND PICASSO

To extol the art of Matisse is, by implication, to raise the Picasso question; and to appreciate Picasso is in the opinion of many foolish people and some others to depreciate Matisse. Of course, the opposition is of a Plutarchian obviousness. The painting of Matisse is a pure and simple delight: to get the best out of Picasso's pictures—out of most of them, I should say—requires some intellectual effort. The one thing common to both is that both are painters born. With Matisse all is plain sailing. Here is the best painter alive, and one who takes his place neatly in the French tradition. That his pictures shocked at first is but one more example of the public's traditional stupidity. There is nothing odd about it; it is just the story of the Impressionists, with whom he has so many affinities, over again. What is odd is that he has so little influence on his contemporaries. It was not always so. There was a moment, about 1907, the stirring and scandalous moment of the Fauves, when the mark of Matisse was everywhere. On almost all the promising young painters (Matisse was born on 31st December, 1869, and is therefore a dozen years or so senior to Picasso and the rest), on Derain, Friesz, Vlaminck, the fashionable Van Dongen even, his influence was exactly what you would expect to be the influence of an original, greatly gifted and older artist. It looked then as though we were in for an "Age of Matisse". Instead it has become the age of Picasso. Why?

If Picasso be, as I maintain, essentially but not predominantly a painter, what is he predominantly? It is particularly difficult to say because, whatever it may be, he expresses it, not always in paint to be sure, but always in visual stuff, in forms. Does he, then, sometimes use the painter's medium to say something unpainterlike? Anyhow, it seems to me that the mystery of his intention may have helped to magnify his prestige. Had he expressed himself in words, his "message", as our grandfathers would have called it, might have seemed less thrilling. Picasso, I suspect, is sentimental (you will not ask me in a short article to define the word, pray fill it with your own meaning), anyhow you have only to look first at his early work (of the blue period for instance) and then at almost anything he has ever done to see that it is so. Now in the depths of his heart almost everyone is sentimental, and almost everyone likes sentimentality. But crude and obvious sentimentality we of the better sort, we who read poetry and go to exhibitions and talk about books and pictures, do not like: at all events, we are ashamed of liking it. Is it possible that Picasso's abstract art is a way of being sentimental in secret?

Be that as it may, I feel pretty sure that Picasso is always interested in humanity as Zola and Dostoievski were interested, as Poussin and Cézanne were not; as Matisse is not. Also, his work is full of it. Possibly therein lies his strength. Possibly, also, we ask more of a picture than of a textile or a pot. Anyhow, those abstract artists who have severely excluded all such content from their pictures—and I am thinking of artists as admirable as Braque, Gris, Léger, Marcoussis—seem to differ chiefly from Picasso in a comparative lack of importance and a lack of surprise. Picasso is the only one of them who has made out of Cubism something as significant and purposeful as "l'art des musées".

A painter's criticism of other painter's pictures will some-

times help to an understanding of his own. I have often heard
Picasso give his opinion. What I know of Matisse's I know
almost wholly at second-hand. Matisse cares passionately for
his own pictures, and, I surmise, for not many others. No
harm in that: exclusive preoccupation with his own work
becomes a particular kind of artist. It became Wordsworth
who, nevertheless, learnt from Milton, and it becomes Matisse
who can appreciate Renoir and Fragonard. Picasso, too, takes
a rather perfunctory interest in other people's pictures; the
rapidity with which he knocks off an exhibition is sometimes
slightly embarrassing to his companion. But in other more
or less formal manifestations of human restlessness and human
desire for perfection he is interested profoundly. The doings
of a house-painter or a shop-window dresser can hold him
spellbound or move him to enthusiastic comment. He will
bring home odd toys or cheap finery to delight in their clever
contrivance or striking effect. Any manifestation of human
ingenuity pleases him. He likes popular art, not the Maypole
and the Morris, but the popular art of the street and the fair,
in which no one but he would, unprompted, have discovered art.
For here he finds common life expressed in some uncommon way.

Let us make no mystery about it, Matisse is interested in
what has interested painters always—his vision of things and
the problem of expressing that vision. Because he is an artist
the expression becomes beauty; because he is original his
beauty was at first mistaken for ugliness. Now that he has
taught the world to see with him, the enjoyment of his pictures
comes as easily as the enjoyment of Renoir's. Matisse looking
out of his window at Nice perceives simple, sensuous loveliness
and renders his peculiar version of it in his own inimitable way.
Picasso, on the beach in Brittany, sees otherwise, sees what is
there and a string of implications as well. A vision of that sort
is not to be expressed simply and sensuously. It might be
expressed coldly and viciously. In fact, the rendering is beautiful and precise: precise with the precision of some deadly
machine the efficiency of which depends on calculations carried
out to the fraction of a millimetre; beautiful because Picasso's
taste is as impeccable as his manipulation is marvellous. What
is rendered, however, is not always the joy of seeing and feeling,
but, as often as not, something flavoured, at times pretty

strongly flavoured; with disgust or despair; that is why the whole, in its wilful cynicism, is what I call sentimental.

Thus it comes about that Picasso, for all his preoccupation with processes, is not predominantly interested in what absorbs craftsmen. A masterly craftsman he is, and he is interested in craftsmanship; but it is the manifestation in craft of odd scraps of individuality, not necessarily profound, but un-expected, scraps which by hook or by crook have escaped industrial regimentation, that catches his eye. The embellish-ment of a match-box, betraying some remnant of artistic feeling, will attract him more than a Chippendale chair. Herein he would seem to discover the authentic aestheticism of our age, the last survival of popular art, an overlooked accident, surprising and pathetic. He goes further, and seems to enjoy the very baseness of the contemporary urban mind once he can find an unmistakable expression of it in some queer place where you would last have looked for expression. A lamp-post, a public urinal, a street-vendor's toy, the lettering on a suburban grocer's shop, all or any of these may become manifestations of the spirit of the age, and as such for Picasso charged with significance. For it is not merely as curious forms that they interest them, as they might interest any modern painter; they move him as symbols, too, as manifestations. He can be cautiously sentimental about them.

I put it forward as a hypothesis, and as nothing more, that what the journeyman, be he tinker, tailor, toy-maker or house-painter, but be he ever so little individual and an artist, is crudely and unconsciously manifesting, Picasso is trying to express deliberately, in full and perfect consciousness, and with exquisite delicacy. It is the complete consciousness that gives the touch of cynicism. He is trying to express his sense of such idiosyncrasy and oddity as has adhered, parasitewise, to our uniform and machine-ridden civilization. Matisse, meanwhile, is painting rapturously, as a bird sings, in the ageless garden of the French tradition. Probably, because he has founded no school, he will be admired by future generations—and he will be admired as long as painting is enjoyed—as the last of the great Im-pressionists. Picasso may be admired as one of the original and inventive minds of a peculiarly inventive and harassed age. But Matisse must be admired: Picasso may.   [*1933*]

Stella Benson

WILD PYGMIES AFLOAT

ON the deck of a ship travelling from England to China I
thought at first that I should find no one to look at and listen
to except "China Hands" (European residents in China)—
who wear always the same set of faces and talk always about
the same set of things. And yet suddenly one day it occurred
to me to look and to listen on a new level, and I found myself
in a new world—a world completely foreign to me—as foreign
as a jungle full of wild pygmies. I mean the world of the
children on board. I am unused to children, and, as a rule,
find them more surprising than charming. They deserve, I
think, the tribute of surprise, and they would repay study
from the *surprised* angle, I suggest, rather than from the maternal or avuncular angle—the point of view of grown-ups who
"understand" children so well that they never look at them or
listen to them. Too often observers in that icy world of the
very young wrap their perceptions in wrappings of patronizing
tolerance—"Dear little mites . . . funny little things . . . quaint
little minds developing. . . ." Too rarely does a dispassionate
and respectful explorer eavesdrop in the jungle thoroughfares
of that far world. There is a crying need for a Baedeker to
supply us with careful notes about landmarks, and industrious
comments on manners and customs—and yet there are points
that a Baedeker might miss. . . .

It seems to me that there is no such thing as youth, except
in comparison with age. Children in the presence of children
are not Little Things at all; they are more appallingly mature
than we, the middle-aged, ever dare to be. Left to themselves,
the children on board played deck games with an austerity
seldom shown by their elders; they were pedantic abiders by
the rules of the games. They were intensely serious in all that
they did when they were alone in their own world; really
"childish" romps and screaming merriments were indulged
in only when grown-ups joined in. The conversations I over-
heard between little girls were always either instructive or

boastful. "There's a place called Siberia, yes—but there's
no place called *Liberia*. . . . My Granny's put her pearls in
the bank. . . . It's the steam that makes the ship go along;
a man called Stephenson saw a tea-kettle. . . . No, silly, the
sea is billions of miles deep. . . . No, of course you couldn't
see Australia unless you had a telescope a mile big. . . . I've
got five pairs of shoes; how many have you got? . . . They
have camels in Africa. . . . Prussia is the capital of Germany."
The conversation of little boys, though equally unsmiling,
was wilder, and made me, as a tourist in this strange region,
feel very ignorant and far from home. Boys' conversation
seemed to be always accompanied by uncomfortable physical
impacts. Two sane and serious little boys, proceeding down
the deck by means of a series of painful collisions, were heard
by me to converse as follows: "Hit you before you can say
Jub. Jub-jub. I hit you first. No you didn't. Yes I did. No you
didn't. Yes I did. No you didn't. Jub. Penny for a Jub. Dirty
liar! Well then, that's sevenpence. Sevenpence halfpenny. Halfpenny, hawpenny, huppenny. Yapenny, yawpenny, yuppenny.
Hit you for a shilling. Can you talk like this: Smile Smit you
for a smilling? (Appreciative laughter.) Smilling. Smilling.
Smelling. You're a smeller. Smeller yourself. Hit you for a
smeller . . ." etc., etc. It was with a kind of awe that I watched
them lurch bumpily away. It did not seem to me that this
kind of talk could be labelled as a rudimentary experiment
in the language that we elders talk—it was surely a fundamentally different language. Not only were the phrases alarmingly
foreign but the mind from which such strange dark utterances
sprang was wholly incalculable. It would be impossible even
for the genius of Mr. Hugo or Mr. Berlitz to reduce the significance of such talk to a system. Yet significance there must be,
for the speakers indubitably understood each other. They did
not feel like budding intelligences—like Dear Little Fellows—
they were, it seemed to me, mature inhabitants of a foreign
land, exchanging ideas.

The children's world was conspicuously homogeneous,
although our ship was a cosmopolitan one. Passengers on
board included English, French, Japanese, Danish, Armenian,
Italian and Eurasian families—to name only those represented
in the pygmy world of my desultory exploration. To each

other, the children of these various races seemed scarcely alien at all. We grown-ups were obviously the aliens—even English grown-ups to English children—Japanese to Japanese. We were left isolated, living in our distant dull bleak world, practising odd dull nagging manners and customs, with the vocabulary of which the children were kind enough to acquire a polite skeleton acquaintance. "Yes, mother . . . non, papa . . . yes, I washed my hands . . . no, I'm not cold . . . oui, maman, tout de suite." The children threw such sops to those large intrusive barbarians, their elders, and then turned with relief one to another, as a tourist relaxes when he may speak his own language.

English was the common language of the children—in so far as the language they spoke could be classified under any known heading at all. Even the French twins, after a week on board, talked English to each other, just as in the talkies Spanish villains, Russian Nihilists, French seducers, hatching their nefarious plots (unaware that the American hero is listening from the cupboard)—the comic French husband and wife pursuing their laughably Latin domesticities in the scullery, far removed from the dignified Nordics in the drawing-room— always address one another in broken American.

Almost all the older children were girls and were also English, so that the tone of the jungle world was pitched on a rather Amazonian, and very British, note. Girls, whether English, Japanese, Danish or French, were the aristocrats and bullies of the world. Large and small, the girls all had readier wits and more stinging tongues than boys; the boys tyrannized only for a moment, usually by forcible means; the girls tyrannized persistently, in speech. There was a little Armenian boy —a courageous and aggressive personality—who was, unfortunately, dressed all wrong. He was too well dressed, really; he wore little shooting stockings, little tan leather Oxford shoes, embroidered braces, a little striped shirt and tie . . . his hair was brushed upwards into an oily crest of curls. All the other children—even the Japanese—wore bathing suits and sand-shoes or almost transparent cotton frocks and shirts. This in itself made an outlaw of the Armenian. To the orthodox inhabitant of that world, the splendid unfortunate clothes were an excuse for unremitting persecution, and though the unlucky child spoke English much better than, for instance, the Japanese children, his clothes brought the deficiencies of his speech into the limelight. "He wants his *deener*—he's hungry for his *deener* —there's the *deener* bell, darling—his *deener*—his *deener*—his *deener* . . ." the pack of the elect would cry—not once—not twice —not fifty times, but hundreds and hundreds of times, following the abashed outlaw about. The sneer never wore thin, nor did its continual application ever rub a callous spot upon the sensibility of the otherwise bold Armenian. As a tactic it succeeded as well on the five-hundredth repetition as it did on the second. It would have been easy (a grown-up might imagine) for the victim to parody with equal venom the scarcely intelligible English of some of his persecutors. But he did not. I think his clothes betrayed him in this war of wits. Instead, he joined a band of brigands (as many broken-hearted outcasts have done before him). The band included only one other member—the French boy twin. The French boy's accent was just as un-English as the Armenian's, but his clothes were perfect in their easy untidiness, so he escaped persecution. He had become a brigand, I suppose, through sheer brigandishness. The activities of this evil pair interested me even more than did the manners and customs of the law-abiding pygmies. They were incurable destroyers; I remember such spoilers of the innocent in my own seaside youth—ranging along the beach kicking down the sand-cities on the making of which we virtuous creators had spent the resources of our souls—running away with the balls of players of stump cricket or rounders—throwing sand at the studious—overthrowing buckets containing priceless accumulations of crabs and shrimps. So that although words could cause the two brigands to slink away, with an expression of impotent and sullen loathing on their faces—although by words they might be undone—by action they could always reinstate their unrighteous self-respect. In the arts of upsetting pedal motor cars— hiding the accessories of deck games—scribbling on the chalked works of art left about by the righteous—tangling the wool of cross-stitch fanatics—bursting balloons—treading on beloved hoards of shells—detaching carefully parked dolls' perambulators from their moorings—raiding unguarded chocolate boxes—they showed a devilish skill. But if they were challengers and rivals to their contemporaries—compatriots

H

in their jungle—they were ruthless tyrants to those negligible aliens, their elders. There was a law in our ship that everyone —grown-ups and children—must sleep, or at least be silent, from half-past one till three in the afternoon. Deck games were swept away, gramophones were gagged, pianos were locked up, small babies were banished to the bowels of the ship. People said "*Ssssh*" if a neighbour so much as hiccoughed. But no law, written or unwritten, could suppress the two young brigands. Every afternoon, as though fulfilling a sacred duty or redeeming a vow, they would make the round of the deck-chairs of unconscious grown-ups—first in front, pulling the toes of male sleepers, and then behind, pulling the back hair of female sleepers. "Wegg up, wegg up," the French boy would say in a most endearing, flutelike voice; his Armenian colleague would accompany him on the mouth organ. When I first watched this fearful deed, my heart stood still; it seemed so inordinately daring and, considering the smallness of the tyrants and the largeness of the victims, so insanely dangerous. But no effective protest was ever made; the brigands were never forced to regret their criminal temerity, or to discontinue their daily round of wickedness. This was partly because both were very agile and very innocent looking, and partly because the repartee of grown-ups is never at its most withering at the instant of awakening. Adult revenge soared no higher than, "Hay—what's that? Get out—shut up—hrrgh, whazza matter . . ." heard by no ear but mine (since the brigands never waited to gloat over the agonies of their victims).

Yes, certainly I was more interested in the brigands than in the elect, during my incursion into that wild world. I suppose this was because their success was the result of immoral ingenuity rather than moral superiority. The brigands were self-made human beings; the elect had inherited their superior rightness from a long line of boys and girls, dating from Abel, the first Good Child. It was the maturity, the assurance, of the elect that frightened me; it made me feel that we grown-ups, all down the ages, had been making an appalling and undignified mistake in trying to interfere in the development of minds that moved on such a remote and lofty plane. We had been missionaries preaching our confused petty gospels to angels—snake-charmers piping our weak tootles to tactfully deaf dragons. I blushed all over to remember complacent grown-up records of, and references to, these proud cool aliens —jokes in *Punch*—(cos Mummy sez so)—stories for Our Toddlers by loving ladies—pictures by Arthur J. Ellersley (I'se bigger'n you, doggie)—some of the juvenile books of Mr. Kipling (Dearly belovedest, teeniest, weeniest . . .). But the brigands comforted me a good deal; the brigands brought my homesick adult self-respect home from the distant and sublime; what were the brigands after all, I thought, but two naughty little boys? No grown-up could possibly be committing an impertinence in smacking their two little heads. And for this reason my heart warmed every time I saw the brigands coming along the deck on some errand of torment, and I was delighted that, almost the last day of the voyage, the junior brigand had a great triumph. It was the French boy-twin who was thus favoured by immoral fortune; he it was who took the responsibility of turning our great ship round upon her tracks —a real achievement for any outlaw of seven years old.

I cannot decide whether the story of this incident is an occult one, or simply the story of a naughty little boy. In any case, here it is.

We had on board our ship a youth who had been giving the ship's doctor cause for anxiety during the whole voyage. The lad had failed in his examinations for the career to which he had dedicated himself, and was being returned to his parents —a failure. He lay brooding in his cabin constantly, he would not eat, he would not read; the doctor was his constant visitor, but suicide was the only theme that interested the despairing youth. On the day I am describing I was sitting on a lonely deck, for once neglecting my scientific eavesdroppings into the affairs of those Wild Pygmies afloat who so interested me. The only person in sight was the suicidal youth, who was leaning on the rail looking ardently at the sea. The sea happened to be so beautiful that evening that even deck golfers could be heard in the distance saying, "Look, isn't the sea topping; come, partner, your shot, one up and two to play." The sea was calm and very highly glazed, those facets of the lazy waves that faced the sunset were wine red; the shadowed surfaces were a brilliant slate blue. Titanic scrawls were scratched upon the huge polished slate of the sea. It occurred to me that the melancholic lad must feel such a sea to be peculiarly tempting, and, indeed, he seemed to fix his eyes with extraordinary intensity upon the disturbed foamy pearl water immediately below him; he had no use for the splendid horizon. All at once there was a general fuss all over the ship; stewards ran here and there; ran to our deck, looked wildly at us and hurried away; there was some shouting; the captain hurried from his golf to the bridge; the ship turned round, flinging the sunset from starboard to port and carving a perfect circle in the sea, and began to return along the groove she had already cut. The doctor appeared, and looked oddly at his suicidal patient. The youth still leaned upon the rail, staring at the sea, ignoring all this pother. From the doctor I learned that the little French boy—the outlaw—had seen a man in the sea; he had screamed loudly, and his mother and a Japanese fellow-passenger, running up, believed that they had seen a hand sticking up out of the sea. The ship, during one hour, fared hither and thither, conscientiously pursuing this tragic will-o'-the-wisp of a story. Passengers and crew were all carefully accounted for; no one was missing. The little French boy, white with excitement, helped in all these activities; to be promoted to the rank of almighty—or at any rate, the almightiest in sight —if only for an hour, is *something*—at seven years' old.

Nobody will ever know if the little brigand deliberately hoaxed his eight hundred victims; if his demoniac enthusiasm imposed an illusion upon his mother and the other woman, or if he really did see a man in the sea. I tried to penetrate the innocent cold mask of his proud face, but nobody can know the secrets of his incredible far world. It is a moon world; no science can account for all its mysteries. The little brigand will never tell the truth about what he saw—*can*, indeed, never tell the truth, for the truth is not cosmopolitan enough to be common both to his world and mine. As for the young melancholic, he can never tell the truth either, perhaps he can never explain what curious power of self-projection his silly young broken heart may have drawn from the sunset invitation of that deadly beautiful sea. Watching the youth's drawn, unreticent face of self-hatred, I thought how much younger we grow as we emerge from that hard chrysalis of maturity we call childhood.   [*1933*]

Peter Quennell

JANUS WEATHERCOCK: OR THE VIRTUOSO'S TRAGEDY

WE have most of us contemplated committing a crime—and
wished that that particular crime could be committed quietly,
impersonally, without involving any danger of detection; but
the darkest intentions are not bad enough, for to commit a crime
one must traverse, or allow oneself very gradually to drift across,
a borderline that separates wishful thinking from desperate acting, his "fashionably dressed" audience from the man in the
dock, ordinary human beings from legendary monsters. The
exact position of this frontier-zone is hard to decide. Where does
it begin? Is there any point in his progress towards criminality
at which the criminal realizes that he has crossed the border and
that wild imaginings have assumed an uncomfortably concrete
shape? Or is the transition quite imperceptible? Many celebrated felons have been habitual day-dreamers. They are also
—most of them—exceedingly conceited persons, either armoured
with an invincible self-righteousness or intoxicated with their
own intelligence and virile bravado. Hauptmann (if we accept
his guilt) was among the former. "I feel I am innocent—I *am*
innocent!" he is reported to have exclaimed during the course
of the long, miserable, disgusting trial that sent him to the electric
chair. Landru was a member of the latter class, a small-time
swindler and petty amorist whose egotism jutted as aggressively
as his famous beard. What pigeon-hole can we find for Thomas
Wainewright? Mr. Jonathan Curling's biography[1] of this
amiable virtuoso and accomplished poisoner is a little too
voluminous and, in parts, rather dully and scrappily written;
but it contains some interesting new material and throws
fascinating sidelights on the criminal temperament.

For example, there are the facts of Wainewright's ancestry.
His maternal grandfather was Dr. Ralph Griffiths; and Dr.
Griffiths, besides being the proprietor of the eminently respect-

[1] *Janus Weathercock. The Life of Thomas Griffiths Wainewright*, by Jonathan
Curling.

able *Monthly Review* (on which he employed Oliver Goldsmith as a sweated assistant), was also the publisher of *Fanny Hill*, that most elegant of English pornographic novels. John Cleland obtained twenty guineas for his manuscript and, disappointed by his ill-success in the field of pornographic literature, turned to the philosophic study of language, producing a book entitled *The Way to Things by Words and to Words by Things*; but the publisher gathered in a handsome profit; and at the time of his death this "free-hearted, lively and intelligent" man, who "abounded beyond most men in literary history and anecdote", had managed to accumulate a fair-sized fortune and had bought himself a large house at Turnham Green. Linden House was strangely connected with Wainewright's destiny. The book-seller and publisher had become a gentleman; and the symbol of his gentility was an impressive building, secluded in its pleasant leafy gardens. Thomas Wainewright was determined to remain a gentleman, and aspired to the combined dignity of artist and author.

By temperament, he was volatile, gay and expansive. "I am certainly an amiable creature" (he admitted in one of his occasional essays). "Every action of my life emanates from a wish to please." His friends, on the whole, agreed with this estimate. He was a "facetious, good-hearted fellow", remarked the rustic poet, John Clare. Barry Cornwall spoke of his "rest-less pleasantry . . . ever veering, catching the sun and shade"; while Charles Lamb referred to him in print as "the light, and warm-as-light hearted Janus of the *London*". And, if he pleased his acquaintances, he pleased himself. Janus Weathercock—such was the pseudonym he had adopted—was the type of essayist who abounds in autobiographical whimsies and in agree-able reflections on his own good taste. He portrays himself in all manner of becoming attitudes. Now he is depicted driving up to London in his smart new gig, whisking "along green lanes, between high hedges of the sweet hawthorn and the elegant wild briar", peeping "betwixt the hazels at the dark blue scenery" or pausing to dabble his face "in a watery bed of cow-slips, wet with May dews"; now he enumerates the graces of his cat and dog and faithful pet robin, his "scarlet-breasted pen-sioner", which "hops fearlessly along the smooth-rolled gravel walk", fixing "the gentle Janus" with its diamond-black eye;

now he appears as a fashionable virtuoso whose "tables groan
with the weight of volumes of Raffaelle, Michael Angelo,
Rubens, Poussin, Parmegiano, Giulio, etc., etc.", whose outer
rooms are embellished with "delicious, melting love-paintings"
by Fuseli and whose inner sanctum is rich with ivories, Renaissance bronzes, blue silk draperies, buhl tables and "sweeping
ottomans", in a Blessingtonian orgy of colours and modes. Amid
these surroundings, Janus Weathercock loved to lie back and
"read a good romance on a shiny day in February" or lapse by
degrees "into that amiable sort of self-satisfaction, so necessary
to the bodying out those deliciously voluptuous ideas perfumed
with languor, which occasionally swim and undulate, like
gauzy clouds, over the brains of the most cold-blooded men".
Wainewright was anything but cold-blooded. "Voluptuous"
and "delicious" were adjectives for which he had a particular
affection; and their demoralizing influence creeps through his
style. In Wainewright's prose, the maidservant who attends him
becomes immediately "a good-natured, Venetian-shaped girl";
the wine he drinks is a "flask of as rich Montepulciano as ever
voyaged from fair Italia"; even the lamp sheds "a Correggio
kind of light" which glows amorously on bibelots and gilt-
tooled bindings.

Equally meretricious—with a hint of lubricity—were his
drawings and water-colours. Wainewright had a lively erotic
inventiveness but an extremely modest share of executive skill,
which he had not improved by studying under Phillips, the
romantic author of several portraits of Lord Byron. Yet one
cannot deny him some scraps of talent. No doubt he could
expand them in conversation till they seemed very much finer
than indeed they were, for it is quite obvious that he imposed
on the contemporary notables whom he assembled round him
at his brilliant dinner-parties in Great Marlborough Street.
These festivities helped to prepare his downfall. Wainewright had
married in 1821—"a sharp-eyed, self-possessed woman dressed in
showy, flimsy finery", who "obeyed his humours" and "assisted
his needs", though "much affection did not apparently exist
between them". Very soon the dashing couple were deep in
debt. Faced with the prospect of being obliged to sell his
grandfather's house (to which he felt a special and symbolic
attachment), curtail his bibelot-buying and give up his luxuries,

Wainewright discovered an ingenious alternative and set to
work with pens and ink and tracing-paper. Five thousand pounds,
left him by a Wainewright grandfather, were deposited in his
name at the Bank of England. The capital, unfortunately, he
could not touch; and Wainewright began by forging powers of
attorney which enabled him to return the money to circulation.
After all (he must have argued) it was *his* money! And what was
a cleverly assumed signature, when executed by a man of
fashion and taste? But his success stimulated Janus's mercurial
brain. Towards the end of 1827 the Wainewrights, again in
difficulties, moved from London to the house at Turnham Green,
accompanied by an uncle who was also a trustee. Six months
later the old gentleman fell suddenly ill, developed convulsive
symptoms and died in the agonies of strychnine poisoning.

He was followed, in 1830, by Wainewright's mother-in-law.
Her agonies were as violent and as inexplicable as those of
George Griffiths; but no inquiries were made into her death and
Wainewright, who had profited by her disappearance to the
extent of a much-needed hundred pounds, was now at liberty
to prepare his final coup. Its instrument and victim was his
wife's half-sister, Helen Abercromby, a dull and unattractive
young woman, who enjoyed bouncing health and had complete
faith in her worldly relatives. By them she was induced to visit
a number of insurance offices, sign false declarations and insure
her life for a period of two years and a total sum of £16,000.
Later she transferred these policies to Wainewright and, later
still, was persuaded by Wainewright, after a visit to the play,
to consume an injudicious midnight meal, which consisted of
oysters and bottled porter. That night she complained of sickness and a "restless headache". The Wainewrights nursed her
devotedly, but Helen died.

So concluded Weathercock's career as a poisoner. Strychnine
and antimony are thought to have been the poisons that he
employed—drugs of which the effects were then but imperfectly
understood; the post-mortem yielded negative results, and, had
it not been for the obstructiveness of the insurance companies,
Wainewright's speculation might have brought in a dividend.
But the companies adopted a truculent attitude. Harassed by
his creditors, unable to collect the profits of Helen's death,
Wainewright was obliged to cross the Channel and vanish into

an indigent and haunted obscurity. What he did—how he lived
—we do not know. It was not till 1837 that he emerged from the
shadows of Continental exile, returned on some unhappy impulse to England and was observed by a policeman "talking to
a female, near a lamp, in Howland Street, Fitzroy Square". He
was clapped into Newgate and committed for trial. Even so, he
was not put on trial for murder—the murders, though strongly
suspected, were never brought home; he was tried for his for-
geries of fifteen years earlier and for them sentenced to trans-
portation to Van Diemen's Land. Of Janus Weathercock's
existence at an Antipodean convict station, during a period
when Australian and Tasmanian prison-settlements rivalled
the worst horrors of French Guiana and the American chain-
gang system, comparatively little can now be gathered. Somehow he struggled through the rigorous probationary stage and,
during later years, was permitted to eke out a livelihood by
doing feeble sketches of the local officials and gentry. But at the
same time, he produced a curious self-portrait, with the cap-
tion: "Head of a *Convict*, very characteristic of low *cunning* and
revenge!"

Neither the face nor the expression is reassuring—a down-at-
heel Mephistopheles, with tilted eyebrows, sharp beady pupils,
foxy moustache and drooping hair. Thus Macready and
Dickens must have seen him when, on a conducted tour
around Newgate with Dickens's illustrator, the other members
of the party were started by a cry from Macready: "My God!
There's Wainewright!" "In the shabby genteel creature, with
sandy distorted hair and dirty moustache, who had turned
quickly round at our entrance, looking at once mean and fierce
. . . Macready had been horrified to recognize a man familiarly
known to him in former days, and at whose table he had dined."
Here Wainewright's defiance is perhaps slightly more engaging
than Macready's ingenuous consternation, Dickens's literary
zest or Forster's moral humbug. Wainewright was a peculiarly
atrocious criminal; but it is interesting to discover once
again how close is the connection between criminality and the
ordinary acquisitive human instincts, and how slight and vague
is the dividing line that appears to separate them. Mr. Curling's
book should abolish the romantic legend that was woven round
Wainewright's name by Oscar Wilde and has since been re-

furbished by Dr. Mario Praz, author of the celebrated *Romantic Agony*. For Wilde, Janus Weathercock was a highly cultured, amusingly perverted aesthete; for Dr. Praz, he is a literary sadist in the grand tradition. Plainly he was neither one thing nor the other, but a sort of Harold Skimpole who resorted to poisoning, as Skimpole himself might have resorted to card-sharping, without the smallest loss of his interior self-esteem. In spite of everything, he was still a gentleman and a man of feeling. It was the custom at Newgate, he remarked, for cell-mates to take turns in sweeping their cell—his companions were a bricklayer and a sweep. "But, by God, they never offer me the broom!" At the same time, it entertained him to shock his visitors; and, interrogated as to how he could have had "the cold-blooded barbarity to kill such a fair, innocent, and trusting creature as Helen", he replied with characteristic jauntiness: "Upon my soul, I don't know, unless it was because she had such thick ankles." Worse reasons have been advanced for killing more attractive and intelligent women; Janus Weathercock offers an impregnable surface to praise or blame. If there was one faculty he lacked, it was that of self-criticism. If there was one weakness that especially distinguished him, it was an unconquerable self-love—a determination that the vulgar world should allow him his due. Poor Janus, why shouldn't he have inherited a fortune? And what a good thing that we are most of us inveterate cowards! [*1938*]

Petronella Elphinstone

TUAN JIM

HE was no water clerk, "racing under steam, sail or oars" against other water clerks, but a prosperous ship chandler, living in great comfort and prosperity above his "vast cavern-like shop, full of things that are eaten and drunk on board ship". It is true that he received his customers in his cool parlour—has he not often, spider-like, inveigled me to drink there in a glass of whisky with him?—whilst the warmth of his welcome certainly "melted the salt of a three months' passage out of a seaman's heart", but his name was Andrews, and, if he had been christened Jim, no one but his far-away godfathers and godmothers were aware of the fact, nor were the Malays in any jungle village given to adding the prefix "Tuan" (which being interpreted is "Lord") to his name. For the simple reason that he had never been farther inland than the suburbs of Singapore, nor had ever fled his memory down any bamboo-filled forest, nor concealed his ample person in a hut. No—his life had been very undramatic and uneventful—ever since an inquiry had been held at Aden on a pilgrim ship bound for Jiddah which had arrived in rather peculiar circumstances.

The result of that inquiry was very much in Andrews's favour. The court complimented him highly on his presence of mind and on his courage and exemplary conduct under difficulties. But that was a long while ago: he was young, then, and had subsequently seen much service in the Indian Ocean. But he left the sea early—forty-five or so, and bought half a ship chandler's business with his savings; when his old partner died he was left alone in his glory. He would often tell of that pilgrim ship—he told me all about it more than once—and one of his many hearers wrote *Lord Jim*. If Andrews ever read that masterpiece he must have smiled; and perhaps, sighed a little—for who would not rather have jumped into the lifeboat and ruled in Patusan, than slept in his bunk and sold "chain hooks for the cable" or "books of gold-leaf for the carvings of the stern" in Singapore?

He was fresh (or very nearly) from his Essex rectory when he signed on as first mate on board the *Patna* (that wasn't her real name, but it has done well enough). She was an old, old ship that had travelled for many years carrying jute between Singapore and Dundee. Her owners were a syndicate of half-caste merchants, who had insured her very heavily from her earliest years. Every year they paid a vast deal of money for her, with never any dividend on her insurance. She never so much as ran aground in a fog, or lost a rudder in a high wind, or collided with a tug in a storm. She was damnably safe. Her log book was duller and more uneventful than Parson Woodforde's diary; she had known rough seas only to weather them in safety, had been afloat more years than anyone except the insurance company liked to count, and had remained everlastingly secure. But she *was* very antiquated, and at last the insurance people got sticky about her long, three-month journeys. So her owners changed her cargo and her port of call, and signed on a new crew (for the old lot couldn't bear the idea of remaining east all the year round, and didn't want to lug a lot of religious-minded natives around, instead of nice, clean jute). Andrews was glad to take the job; he had only been second before, and he still looked (and was) absurdly young and inexperienced. We have read of his "open bronzed forehead" and of "the white line under the roots of clustering fair hair", all of which was true enough. So the crew was made up to include him as first mate, and the eight hundred passengers came on board the ship as she lay at anchor in Singapore harbour. They were all very poor, these pilgrims; men, women, and children of all ages, and of nearly all colours; their clothes varied almost as widely as did their faces. Every shade of cotton and dirty silk seemed to be worn, topped by mushroom-like turbans, or by head veils in colours suggestive of every sort of toadstool. Many brought their own food, rice or fruit or cheeses, and carried gourds of fresh water. They slept all over everything—at night it was impossible to move without stumbling over a soiled heap of rags that resolved itself into a woman sleeping, or a bunch of children, or a whining man.

For the first week the journey was monotonous enough; the sea was like a kingfisher-blue mill pond, and day by day the sun blistered the decks, whilst strange fishes played around the ship. At night the moon waned steadily, from full circle to reversed crescent, quietly, and without haste. Until one night when "Jim" on the bridge was, we are told, "penetrated by the great certitude of unbounded safety and peace that could be read on the silent aspect of nature like the certitude of foster-ing love upon the placid tenderness of a mother's face". It was asking for trouble, of course, to feel so secure, and, sure enough, that very night, for some mysterious reason never ascertained, the whole ship rose a few inches, lifted herself bodily, and went over "something awash, say a water-logged wreck". She went over her jump "as easy as a snake crawling over a stick", then checked herself suddenly. Her engines stopped, and when "Jim" was sent forward to ascertain the damage, he found the forepeak already more than half-full of water, and a big hole in the waterline. The bulkhead, rotten with donkey's years of service, might give way any moment, and then, as the third engineer tersely put it, "the damn thing will go down under us like a lump of lead".

All of which is true, as regards the facts, but not true, as regards "Jim's" alias Andrews's relation to them. For he did not walk the bridge either penetrated by a great certitude or otherwise. Nor did he go forward to ascertain the damage. For the simple reason that, not being his watch, he was asleep in his bunk. He did not make his escape from the doomed ship by jumping into the hurriedly launched lifeboat, instead of George, the acting third engineer. On the contrary. The skipper, no friend of his, left him to sleep and to drown—in his bunk, as callously as he left the eight hundred pilgrims. After all, there were only seven lifeboats and eight hundred passen-gers, and Jim, alias Andrews, even if roused from his slumbers, could hardly be expected to perform a new miracle of loaves and fishes. It must have been George who jumped, after all, for they were five who rowed away across the still sea by the gibbous light of the setting moon, and Jim, alias Andrews, was woke about ten minutes later, by one of the two Malays at the wheel. The noise of the collision, and the greater cessation of noise as the engines stopped, had awakened him, but it was not yet time for his watch so he turned over. When he arrived on deck it was too late to jump. The boat was gone, and it took some seconds for him to realize that it contained his Captain,

Second Mate, and all the ship's three engineers. There was no storm, no squall; across the calm sea Andrews's flow of invective must have reached the little boat, and it is more than likely that they heard, perfectly. The lights of the ship did not suddenly disappear from sight as though engulfed by the hurricane; if they looked back, the five men in the boat could see Andrews and the two Malays standing on the bridge gazing after them.

When he saw the boat row on, out of sight and earshot, Andrews went down the engine-room with his two Malays, found iron and wood, and shored up the bulkhead. It took until dawn, and then was an imperfectly done job, but the eight hundred slept on; trusting, if they awoke and missed the noise of the engines, to the omnipotent white men who do well all things connected with ships.

When the sun rose Andrews, with his two companions, went wearily up on deck and told the pilgrims around him what had happened, explaining that since eight hundred people could by no power, human or divine, be fitted into six lifeboats, their only chance of salvation was to wait quietly, hoping that a passing ship would rescue them before they sank. He had already run up the ensign, union down, at the main gaff; there was nothing more to do but wait. The two Malays translated his speech, and those who heard told those who had not heard, until all the eight hundred knew the peril wherein they lay. They did not stampede, nor rush the lifeboats, nor, in panic, did they attack Andrews and his two companions. The women wailed a little, gathering their children around them; the men looked out across the empty sea, and talked in mournful whispers. Then one or two, followed by two or three, followed by every man, woman and child on that ship, they went down to the hold, where their belongings were stacked. Andrews watched them go, almost unheeding, so tired was he; then he went up on to the bridge. He scanned the horizon for a ship in vain; when he looked downwards on to the deck he saw his passengers reappearing singly, or in twos and threes. Gone were their coloured head-veils, their bright cottons or gay silks— each now wore the simplest of white garments—a shroud. Everyone was in cerecloths; from the oldest gaffer to the smallest baby, all were uniformly clad. They had each one of them brought their grave clothes with them on this their pilgrimage, in case the felicity be theirs to perish on their journey; now that the moment had come to prepare for death, they would meet him simply, already ghostly and unafraid in the pale dawn, wearing their winding sheets. Gone loincloth and turban; to prepare for the sea-change they had cast off all distinctions of age, of colour, or sex. For five hours they waited in the scorching sunlight, for the ship to sink: for five hours Andrews looked in vain for anyone coming; on the horizon was only blue sea and blue sky and no ship's funnels. Not one of the eight hundred pilgrims attempted to escape: the authority of the one white man on the bridge and the fatality of the faith which, faced with dissolution, accepts it uncomplaining, were sufficient deterrents.

At noon Andrews saw a steamer and signalled her: she was a Blue Funnel Line passenger ship, bound for Australia. She put out a boat and when she came up, her crew, after satisfying themselves there was no plague on board, clambered up on the *Patna*, and were gratefully welcomed by Andrews. More men were signalled for, and by nightfall the damage was repaired, the engines were started, and Andrews was provided with five white officers from off the Blue Funnel steamer (which undertook to report the *Patna* safe at Singapore) and with their help Andrews took the *Patna* on to Aden.

Meanwhile the deserting crew in the *Patna's* lifeboat had been picked up by a Marseilles-bound ship and deposited at Aden, where they reported the *Patna* sunk with all passengers, the native sailors and one white officer: they wired the ship's owners (who lost no time in informing the insurance company) and themselves returned to Singapore as passengers, eager to sign off, to draw their wages, and to receive what compensation for their adventures they could extract from the ship's owners.

The sensation in Aden when the *Patna* arrived can well be imagined, and the crowded inquiry has been magnificently described by Conrad. The pilgrims went on in another ship to Jiddah, and Andrews, besides many compliments, was offered a first-rate job by the Blue Funnel Line Company, which he joyfully accepted.

This is the true history of Tuan Jim, as told me by himself.

[*1932*]

Naomi Lewis

CAROL

MARY my wife is a young fair maiden.
I am an old man, with years laden.

I am wed to Mary: she makes no good cheer.
She does not smile to me when I am near.

Mary does not dance for me: she does not sing.
I am an old man, and ask no thing.

Mary has a secret mouth: her eyes look down.
She makes no talk with the women of the town.

By day I toil: by night my couch I seek.
I am an old man—who am I to speak?

Mary would in summer have apricots and cherries;
In autumn I bring her the red hedge berries.

Now in the winter, she would have an ass.
Out of the city by night we pass.

A tale I know, the strangest since the world began.
Why should I marvel, I an old man?   [*1939*]

Hilaire Belloc

ON I KNOW NOT WHAT

When I am dead, I hope it may be said
"His sins were scarlet, but his books were read".

THIS great poem, the noble expression of an exalted but disappointed spirit, was written in the year 1917, and is as true to-day as in that distant epoch when it fell from the pen of genius. For though men are careless of the salvation of their souls (I touch with but the tip of my wing upon *that*) they are all of them anxious, I think, to be remembered after death. And this is particularly true of the writing men, in whom I include the writing women—a far more numerous tribe. For, as the bishop said, or rather wrote, to the parish priest when he put the question about Ash Wednesday: "*Beast that you are! Do you not understand that the term 'man' embraces the term 'woman'?*"

Here you tell me (and how justly!) that you do not understand the allusion. I will explain it.

There was a custom in the old days of superstition, especially in the degraded countries of the Mediterranean, to observe a season called Lent, and this season began upon a Wednesday. It was a season of fasting, mortification, and annoyance, during which the superstitious and misguided herd, turning their eyes from the delicious prospects of this our mortal life, considered the blank horizons of death. They put aside all memory of mortal sweets, of the toothache, of insults, of misunderstandings, of insomnia, of indigestions, of bills, and of all the other things that go with the pride of life. They set themselves to an examination of that which I am told cannot be examined —for did not a certain Frenchman say that one could no more look steadily at death than at the sun? And was he not right?

At any rate they used, I say, to observe this season called Lent which began upon a Wednesday, and on this Wednesday they were accustomed to crowd to the altar, there to receive upon their foreheads from the thumb of a priest the ashen mark of a cross. And as they received it the priest recited the words: *"Remember man thou art but dust, and unto dust thou shalt return."*

Such were their customs. It is related, however, in the chronicles of that time (a little before the taking of Constantinople and a little after the Council of Florence—with which days you are familiar) that a parish priest of the Apennines was in the custom of so marking with ashes upon the forehead the few men that might approach the altar, but not one of the women. For did not the liturgy clearly indicate that it was men only who returned to dust, whereas women, the exemplars of immortal brightness, suffered no such fate? Upon hearing this his bishop (and there is no lack of bishops in Italy) wrote to him that message I have already quoted and set things right.

I have by this time, you will observe, wandered somewhat from my subject. But then, what was my subject? If you know you are wiser than I! What I had intended it to be I know well enough. I had intended it to be a disquisition upon the strange love of posthumous fame which is to be found in all the human race, and particularly in the miserable breed of writers. But really the subject has been done to death. I have myself written upon it recently in at least five places, and for all I know in these very columns. And when you come to think of it there is nothing new to be said about it. You all know the main points; they are obvious enough. We shall not enjoy posthumous fame. It hardly ever lasts. When it does it is usually false. And anyhow, what is fame? You cannot eat it, and under copyright laws your descendants cannot even make money out of it. So much for that.

But though we know all about posthumous fame it is great fun looking at it, turning it over in the hand, examining its flaws, and ridiculing it. It is great fun to do this because we who do it are perfectly safe. Even those of us destined to be famous, through the wrongful acquirement of a vast fortune or in some other fashion, are actually alive, and therefore as yet untouched by it. And as it is not one chance in several hundred thousand that we shall have any posthumous fame we may go to work with a free heart.

The first thing I notice about posthumous fame is that it is not more than a label. Of the ten million families inhabiting

this island, perhaps one million have heard the name of
Milton. And those who have heard of Milton will also have
heard of *Paradise Lost*—though not all of them. And of these
a fraction will tell you *Paradise Lost* was a very fine poem, and
they will praise Milton for having written it.

There they would be wrong, for he did not write it. He
dictated it and this, by the way, is much the easiest form of
getting through one's work. It makes one a little verbose, no
doubt, and it makes one wander from the point—if one has a
point. It dilutes style. It weakens the muscles of the mind.
There is everything to be said against it. Nevertheless, if you
must write, do not write but dictate. I speak from experience.
I know what I am saying. Moreover a great deal of very good
work has been dictated. It would seem that the Romans
dictated. Even their poets did so, and we know that Cicero did.
Of course you may not admire the writings, or rather the
dictations of Cicero. It is much more probable that if you do
admire them you have no acquaintance with them. But I am
not engaged (if I remember right) with the subject of dictation,
but with something else, which I find upon looking back is posthumous fame, or at any rate, the thoughts which it suggests.
And now I remember, I think we were dealing with Milton,
whom some have called unjustly a "crabbed windbag", but
of whom Dryden, a very good judge and a very good writer,
said: "The old man has done better than us all"—or words
to that effect.

I say "words to that effect". There is no more pestilent,
prudish, jejune habit than looking up quotations. It interrupts
the flow, and it is perfectly useless. You know the sense of
what the man said, you even know the rhythm of what he said
more or less (if you have a good ear), and that ought to be
enough for you. Any fool can be accurate with a book of
reference at his elbow, but it takes a scholar to know so many
quotations that he makes mistakes in every one of them—and
I proceed.

Of the remaining fragment, then, that remembers Milton
for his *Paradise Lost* how many have read it? How many have
read even a fraction of it? I have read not only *Paradise Lost*
several times, but, what is more, *Paradise Regained*, and I say
without hesitation that the latter is a bad poem, and the former

an exceedingly good one. But the general fame of Milton is the
fame of a label. It is a repeated fame. It is nothing more.

Then there is also this about posthumous fame: that it is
oddly ill-deserved. A very comic thing it is to notice the difference between the thing praised, as it stands in the mind of
the public praiser, and as it is in itself. I know very well that
there are sundry Germans who will tell me that one never
can see the thing in itself, because the mind does not transcend
phenomena, but I trust that they have learned their lesson.

Also, posthumous fame gets attached to the wrong being.
Who wrote *Vathek*? Beckford, you say. At least you answer
"Beckford" if you are one of the very few people who have
heard of *Vathek*, and at the same time one of the still fewer
people who do remember the name of its reputed author. But
what proof have you that Beckford wrote *Vathek* in its present
form? If I remember rightly it was originally written in French,
and then, if we are to believe him, translated into English by
a clergyman. How much had the clergyman to do with it,
and how much Beckford?

I may be quite wrong in this, and though I have been saying
so braggingly that accuracy in quotation does not matter, I am
all in a tremble and in a sweat lest I should here be talking
nonsense. So I will take another example where I am more sure
of my ground, for I have not read the history of *Vathek* these
ten years though I have re-read the book itself several times
a year for at least fifteen. It is a glory.

I will take, then, the *Itinerary of Robert of Cirencester*. For more
than the lifetime of a man that book was as famous as a book
can be. Gibbon took it for granted, and so did every historian
I can call to mind, except a very few who doubted, but did
not deny. Then came the exposure. It was quite clearly proved
within our own times that the document was false. It was no
more an original list of Roman places and roads in Britain
than I am. It was made up by an Englishman in Denmark,
who successfully palmed it off upon the learned. But there
is more in the matter. One is not even certain that the *Itinerary
of Robert of Cirencester* was a mere forgery. I think, for my part,
that there must have been something behind it. Roads which it
mentioned and which were unknown when it appeared have
been discovered since its appearance. The very misspelling

of names is a powerful argument. I can conceive that the forger, prompted by one of those twisted motives which affect such men, rather than produce genuine fragments which he really had before him, preferred the concocting of a complete piece to the more modest editing of these few realities.

And what else is there about posthumous fame? There is its circumscription in space. Homer is famous enough with us, but not with the Chinese; and, if you will believe me, the French know little of Keats and too much of Byron, and the English are singularly innocent of Lope de Vega. There are even dead men very famous in Wales whom no one has ever heard of in Herefordshire.

On the whole it is better to let it go. It will do us no good anyhow, and hankering after it can do nothing but harm.

After all, the great mass of men whom you may see walking down Piccadilly on a fine day are not concerned with posthumous fame, even that of others, let alone of themselves. And I have noticed this singular and illuminating thing: those who have made great fortunes are very nearly always indifferent to so slight, intangible and airy a thing as renown after death. They also suffer from folly and illusion in the matter of the time that shall succeed their regretted departure. They also passionately desire (as a rule) that their works should remain after them. And they leave fantastic wills, or found a family, or build monuments. But these very rich men (who should be our models in all things) do not as a rule care much for the sort of reputation Catullus still enjoys. And they are right. Cash, says the song, is better than fame or rank.

For that matter I suppose cash can purchase both. And the only reason that a rich man never pays poor poets to write verse for him and to publish it in his name, is, I suppose, that they despise verse as it should be despised.

For what is verse? If it is the verse of antiquity it does not even rhyme. If it is modern verse it is prose. The price paid for it by journals is not only abominably low but haphazard. It is not sold by length, like prose and calico. There is no standard that I know of for the sale of verse.

Many years ago, when I was an editor of sorts, there was a man who used to write to me from America. He used to send me typewritten verse. It was very bad. With each poem, stuck on with a little metal clip, was a slip of paper, also typewritten, announcing the price at which he was willing to sell. It used to have such words on it as: "The price of this poem is ten dollars." I always sent them back because he was careful to put in a stamp—an English stamp. That shows he was an honest man and also a careful man. Had he been a better poet I think he would have been neither.

Reader—it is old-fashioned to say "Reader", but many polite things are old-fashioned nowadays—readerkin, readerlet, do you not think I have kept to my point reasonably well, considering that at the very beginning of this excursion I had already got off the main road, and was diverting through field paths towards the open heaths of nonsense?

Let it be a model to you, if ever you are driven by misfortune to writing. Remember that you can always keep to the point more or less, and that on the whole it is better less than more. For blessedness is in variety of experience, unity of affection. And blessedness is the end of man.   [1920]

V. Sackville West

DECEMBER NIGHT

LISTEN. This winter night when fields are stark,
I lean across the frosty window-sill
   To hear the dog-fox bark
Under the window on his prowl to kill.
Come, join me, friend. The night with frost is shrill,
And fox is rare and secret, seldom seen.
Look from the window with me, on the lean
Low form that slips to coops from sandy hill.
Look from the window: you will seldom see
A wild fox on the errands of his skill.
So, my companion, watch him go, with me.

   Soon, all too soon,
His mouth will run with blood, a frothy frill
Red from some slaughtered fur or tattered quill.
Look from the window: you can see him pass
On slinky pads across the brittle grass.
Each blade stands up to sparkle in the moon,
Hoar with the frost, as bright as splintered glass,
Casting a pencil shadow, tiny mark
Of singularity. The world's a wisp
As fragile as the frozen grass is crisp,
Printed by footsteps that must melt with morn.
Look from the window: all is tranced and still.
The fox goes by, nocturnal visitant.

   Let's follow him by trails forlorn,
To-night, this winter night by pad-prints crossed.
   Let's follow him, that miscreant
Slinking between the garden and the thorn.

   Come, let us follow on his trail.
He'll lead us to the woods, and there be lost.
So let us lose ourselves, and lose the pale

Feathery meadows moonlit in the frost;
Exchange the friendly house for bitter air
And danger of the night with fox to share;
Exchange the radiant meadows for the deep
Silent seclusion of the woods asleep.

Asleep? No, listen, for the wood's awake.
Woods wake while man forgets his ravelled days.
Listen, for woods their midnight secrets keep
And many whispers cross the forest ways
Beneath the beeches, threading through the brake.
Asleep? Oh no, the margin of the lake
Where trees are doubled in a liquid dream
Is animate with restless guests; the stream
Pouring through stone creates its harmony.
The margin of the lake within the reeds
    Is livelier than the meads
Where placid sheep in moonlight rest, and be;
The lake where sometimes, like a myth, the swan
    Descends, and for a day illumes
The water with his Greek voluptuous plumes,
And like a myth by eve again is gone.

The night is neither silent nor asleep.
The night is full of music, rich to creep
Into the hearing heart and pluck a string.
A string of recognition; solitude
Shared with each fearful, woodland, living thing.
    For in the night of terror's reign
When the dread soul's beset by fearful mood,
    And soul or body on a sudden slain,
Our hearts are joint with creatures of the wood.

Listen. Within the night I hear the cry of pain
Well up in darkness in a last appeal.
Some small trapped spirit cries, and cries again,
    Tortured by fang or steel.
The ambushed dangers of the wood are wide;
    Come, friend; let's push aside
The branching chestnut and the silver birch;

Let's go to rescue while our help is near.
    But that shrill voice, our only guide,
Is stilled in greater terror as our stride
      Blunders through undergrowth in search.
    Poor foolish victim, taught by fear
To hush the cry when friendly steps approach,
Does unknown peril greater peril spell?
Would you not risk for present, tasted hell
The unimaginable heaven of release?

(Yet who are we to utter such reproach?
Have we not also shrunk beneath the leaves,
And suffered gins to fasten on our flesh,
Rather than seek an easy proffered peace
Which briefly comforts, tenderly deceives?
Have we not also shrunk from friendship's hand,
    And struggled out, alone, afresh,
By suffering informed and newly manned,
To face another maimed and difficult day?)

    Come, friend; come, let us go,
Since we must leave to anguish and to rain
That small pre-destined body in its pain.
    Come, let's regain the narrow ride
Where overhead the stars in bright array
      Stud a celestial corridor
With golden nails in heaven's blackened floor.
Come, let us wander down the paths we know,
    By pad of foxes trod
And bird-prints crossing on the silver sand,
Towards the riven oak-tree in its pride
    Struck by the wrath of God.
Oh, here did anger fall majestical,
Tremendous, when no man was by to see
The murderous lightning threefold split the tree,
    The stricken oak centennial
Blanched in the after-years to this dead thing
Laid out superb in death, laid out in state,
Sentinel boughs above it, like a king
Lying in state unburied, abnegate.

Or let us turn from this accordant death,
Magnificent in ruin though it be;
        Let us return
Towards the living pines that still draw breath
        And still renew their sap
Each spring untroubled by the thunder's clap;
        Let us, oh friend, return
Towards the pines that on the crest of hill
Rear naked trunks beneath the moonlight still,
        Proud, dark, and taciturn.
The fox is gone to earth with lawless kill;
        What matter? We have seen
        Beauty go by, an outlaw, free;
Beauty and ruin, secrecy and pain;
        This night we both have been
Linked with the heart of night, a certain gain;
Never to lose this freedom or this light
Dawning upon us in the deepest night.

Never to lose, and never to forget
Strength of initiation, gravely won,
But through the day's incertitude and fret
To keep this steadfast secret shared with none;
This transcendental truth of unison
Where we with nature, rarely tuned aright,
        Met more intensely pitched,
Descending changed by that high symphony,
        Changed, different, enriched,
Exalted to a faith in immortality.   [*1936*]

Julia Strachey

COMPLEMENTS OF THE SEASON

A VISIT to my godmother, Miss Jenny Villars, in the country—
"The Manor House, Little Babbiton"—always makes an impression on me. I remember I went down there last on a
Friday night, at the end of the summer, arriving exactly in
the nick of time for dinner.

My godmother met me in the hall, and we embraced fondly
in front of the brass gong on the hall table. "How nice this is!"
we both cried. "How well you're lookin'!" she exclaimed. "I
thought you wouldn't want to bother with changin' all in a
hurry, I thought you'd prefer somethin' to eat straight away.
Come along into the dining-room, dinner is all ready." She took
my arm, leading me into the dining-room.

She herself was already dressed in the familiar black evening
gown, with the black sparks scattered over its folds, and the
little loose white ermine jacket over it. My godmother is about
forty-seven; a thin lady. Her coiffure is in the English style—
that is to say at once vague and neat. Her dress the same. For
example, in the daytime the multiplicity of jackets, short and
long, scarfs, collars, and tying ends, that she wears one on top
of the other, give a very respectable English effect, like the
leaves of a lettuce from the kitchen garden. Her face is a pink
and white full moon, the expression modest and innocent. (At
first sight this pink and white face looks serene; but later one
sees that it is altogether too sensitive, and also too sensible-
looking for that.)

We sat down to table. The aged parlour-maid, Hetty, trot-
ting round with frail humped back, and skinny claws tightly
clutching the various plates and dishes, served us with the first
course—clear lukewarm soup. Next came minced cod in white
sauce served up in cockle shells. Tough meat followed the fish,
in a watery stew. A forest of narrow green paper bags with gold
butterflies painted on the front of each, ranged upon the side
table, caught my eye. "I'm goin' to fill those bags up with
assorted caramels for the village children to take away after

241

their tea in the old coach-house to-morrow. But I do believe I entirely forgot to warn you of to-morrow night's entertainment! The Babbiton Operatic Society (which consists of the tradespeople there, you know) are actin' a 'Phantasia', written by myself and Gwennie Price, at the Babbiton Town Hall. I have promised to take the little Babbiton school children along to it in a charabanc, after the tea. Shall you be able to stay on for it? In any case there is no earthly *need* for you to come."

But my godmother's remarkable productions have been the pride and terror of our family for years—filled to the brim as they are with everything that is grisly. When we were children we acted in scores of them.

"I wouldn't have missed it for the world! and yet, alas! I cannot stay. What is it all about this time?" I answered.

"Oh, it's only just a silly thing," cried my godmother. "Just nonsense—with a chorus of beheaded Royal Potentates, a chorus of Magic Scorpions, and a comic chorus (for the children) of dishes of food—puddin's, joints, custard pies—you know, just a simple thing for the village people to laugh at."

Here old Hetty brought forward a pale chocolate blancmange, with little tinned, halved apricots in a wreath round the base of it. It was standing in a heavy embossed silver dish, which she placed very slowly with trembling hands on the table in front of my godmother. The latter started telling me the gossip.

"I'm obliged to take these wretched daily Roumanian lessons now", she told me, "from the poor unfortunate man who rents our farm from us. He's been with us for ten years, and he can't afford to pay the rent these days; I haven't the heart to turn him away; and if it wasn't for myself and Gwennie Price takin' these Roumanian lessons daily I imagine the poor man would be literally starvin'! Have some more chocolate puddin'? No? However he will keep on spittin' into the fire durin' the lesson. Really a most extraordinarily disquietin' habit. And what with that, and then the fact that I know I can never, under any remotest chance, ever possibly want to speak Roumanian—the lessons do seem somethin' of a weary burden. Shall we move into the drawing-room?"

It was always a pleasant relief to get up and leave the barren Victorian dining-room.

In the chintz-covered drawing-room my godmother showed me her latest watercolour sketches. She handed me, one by one, the stiff, recalcitrant sheets from off her block; each one grained like crocodile skin, bruised, sogged, and indented all over, as if the burly fabric had been fighting with her tooth and nail all the while, defending its virginity from her remorseless paint brushes. Gazing down with me upon the last sketch, my godmother murmured, "Yes . . . I try each year to get there in time for the bluebells. They've always been nearly over before. But this year I think I've really been rather successful." I looked up at her face, pleased and dreamy, contemplating the sketch. It was clear that she was seeing, not the actual paper in her hand—the dark, damp remains of the struggle that had taken place between brushes and paper— but the airy, echoing spaces of the great beech wood in early summer, the hundreds of tiny bluebells shivering and jumping on their wires in the criss-cross currents of the summery breezes, all the spruce animation of a wood in spring-time.

"Do remind me to take you there in the spring-time!" she ejaculated. "It's really the most delightful spectacle!"

We went to bed early that night, having first decorated the coach-house with the flags of all nations for the tea-party.

Next morning after breakfast my godmother took me to see the new cygnets on the lake. Walking down the narrow path that led through the oak copse to the lake beyond, one glance was enough to show that autumn had been some time upon the scene down here in the country. Fallen leaves lay everywhere; and oak trees, silver birches, and the empty fields beyond stood still in a trance, in a species of infinitely wan sunlight that was vaguely suffusing the hazy atmosphere. When we came to the lake, which is quite a large one, we stood upon the bank. There were the four speckled cygnets, sitting quite motionless all together in the centre. I glanced at the rowing-boat lying among the reeds below us, and suggested pushing out into the lake, and trying to get a nearer view of the birds. So in we stepped. I shoved her off out through the rustling reeds, and away we slid into the glassy open water of the lake. The boat slipped forward without a sound. The water being so extremely shallow, and so calm, that the long grey eels and the green blobby water weeds lying on the white sand at the bottom could be

seen as clearly as goods in a shop window. We paddled several
times round the cygnets, who remained, tranquil as the reeds
and trees around them, floating, as if tied all together, in the self-
same spot. Occasionally they turned their heads to the right,
or to the left. Perhaps they were listening to the rushing sound
of the weir which came from the middle of the woods behind
them—certainly there was nothing else to distract them.

The opposite end of the rowboat swung out and glided off
sideways, propelling my godmother, who was knitting away
serenely with pink wool at this time—propelling her at an angle
of forty-five degrees out towards the side of the lake again.
And thus rapidly, silently gliding, off they shot, knitting and
godmother together so to speak, as I neatly twisted my oar
round in the water. The water swirled and gobbled round my
twisted oar-blade, and then as we heeled slowly around silence
again fell on the lake, and only the far-away sound of the weir
in the woods attracted one's attention. The delicate brittleness
of the autumn scenery, of the stubble fields surrounding the
lake, and the bare oak branches, seemed repeated in the frail,
stiffly jointed body opposite me, in the delicate hollowed collar
bones and fine muscles on her middle-aged neck and wrists.
The skin of her throat and hands, satiny white and yet paper-
dry, resembled the gleaming bark of the birch trees on the bank,
in front of which she was now slowly passing. Her eyes, too,
transparent and remote, matched the spring-like blue remote
spaces up above the sunlit oak copse. But what was more
interesting, an identical spirit seemed to inform both landscape
and lady. The stubble and coarsely springing thistles in the
fields, the bracken and brambles covering the low hill-sides,
the distant downs and valleys—all lay tranquilly dreaming,
muffled up in the rich hazy glow of the season. And on my
godmother's innocent face, utterly absorbed above the pink
knitting, sat the very same glowing delicately muted vigour.

"I think I have just time to show you the patent new hen-
houses before my Roumanian lesson," said my godmother,
as she stepped out on to the mooring board. "Hulloa Cork!
What are you doing up here?" Cork was the faded old chestnut
spaniel. His cumbrous, dusty form, like an old bolster on four
castors, was waiting us on the landing stage. All together we
passed, single file, through the oak copse, and came out again

into the kitchen garden. Arrived in the stable yard beyond, "Well! Here are the patent hen-houses!"

Cork sat down in the open stable doorway in the sunshine. He began scratching behind his ear with his hind leg. The hen-houses were no more than three foot square, a tattered cabbage dangled on a string from the roof of each, and a mediocre brown hen with drooping head stood in the far corner of one of them. My godmother explained: "This cabbage dangles just out of reach of the hen from this hook on the ceiling you see, thus compelling the hen to leap up and snatch at the cabbage if she desires to eat. Well then, you're supposed to scatter the grain all amongst this patent grille affair on the floor, makin' it exceedingly difficult to scratch it out again; and thus giving the hens a lot more exercise that way also! In fact, one may truly say", finished off my godmother, with satisfaction, shutting the hen-house door again, "that the hens, although cooped up in no more than a bare three foot square space, are under this patent system enabled to spend their entire lives in alternately hoppin' and scratchin'."

My godmother was obliged to leave me after the coach-house tea, in her charabanc of village children, as I still stood waiting on the doorstep for the car to take me to the station.

Colourless in the chill autumn dusk she sat, in her old curled sheepskin overcoat, in the middle of the charabanc, which stood, gently roaring on the drive, chock-a-block with little round heads. Suddenly there came a much louder roar, a shriek from the gears, and the carload shot forward, and stopped dead. Hundreds of shrill titters rose up instantaneously from the charabanc, like the sound of a bush full of birds disturbed suddenly in the night.

"Good-bye again!" called out my godmother. "Don't forget to tell your mother that I accept her offer to buy Kitty's old sewin' machine. I am comin' up Friday week, and will fetch it away with me in the Daimler. . . ." The charabanc hove slowly away round the corner, and I was left staring at the darkening laurel bushes.   [*1933*]

G. W. Stonier

NOLLEKENS

PADDLING, not long ago, down the stream of a very agreeable fiction—Mr. Evelyn Waugh's *Put Out More Flags*, I fancy—I had my hat lifted by a branch. Unexpectedly, in the middle of adventures, came a reference to "the best biography in the English language". One of the characters had picked up a book, if I remember, and this was Mr. Waugh's terse description of it. And the book's title? There, of course, was the surprise; twenty shots, if the answer had been put off to a footnote, wouldn't have enabled the reader to score a hit. The best biography was—have you guessed?—*Nollekens and His Times*.

I wonder how many this whacking recommendation sent running to a book they had never heard of; how many also, among those who had known *Nollekens* and its author J. T. Smith for years, were disconcerted to find a favourite thus dragged into the daylight. Part of its charm lay in the fact that it had *not* been trampled over by too large a public; it was a minor classic, decently obscure, permanently (so it seemed) undervalued; one read it, one reread it, one exalted it in conversation, but rarely, if ever, in print. For one thing, it was a book of uneven and curious virtues, and its appeal was local; only those who knew well, or wanted to know well, eighteenth-century London would find its divagations amusing. It comes somewhat after Boswell in time (Johnson and Boswell make a couple of lively appearances in the early pages), and a long way after in literary merit. If there's to be a competition for the "best biography", here is, perhaps, a likely dolphin to set beside the great white whale. Nollekens is a good, a first-rate catch; he isn't the Doctor. He can pull faces, dance, growl, startle, amuse by an unabashed display of human slovenliness; he is not more on guard in the presence of his biographer (or of anyone else, for that matter) than a mongrel that sits on a doorstep to scratch itself. But he could never fill page after page with greatness, and the part he plays in the book bearing his name, though central, is comparatively slight. Gossip and town lore provide the all-important background.

As an "original", though, a rare and perfect specimen, how cunningly he has been caught! One thinks of some burrowing animal, with unbelievable habits, surprised by the photographer. Fuseli or Blake seen in the distance, appear the most ordinary of mortals by comparison. The acquaintance if not the friend, of Reynolds, Johnson and Garrick, yet in talk and behaviour "little more than one remove from an idiot". Most fashionable sculptor of his day, and living in circumstances of unexampled squalor. A miser, with a fortune of £200,000. Stole the nutmegs year after year—a sight grown familiar to those who attended—at Royal Academy banquets. Never known to mention Shakespeare. Bow-legged, hook-nosed, pitiably clad, common in his speech, dirty in an age not over-sensitive to dirt.

When he first was a frequenter of the Opera, which he never missed when "*bones*" of admission were sent to him, gentlemen were obliged to go in swords and bags in full-dress, which custom, however, was dropped, on removal to the Pantheon; so that Nollekens was more at home, as he was now and then seen to take out a worsted stocking and tie it round his neck, whenever he had a sore throat, to which he was often subject. James Boswell, the faithful biographer of Dr. Johnson, meeting him in the pits of the Pantheon, loudly exclaimed, "Why, Nollekens, how dirty you go now! I recollect when you were the gayest dressed of any in the house." To whom Nollekens made, for once in his life, the retort-courteous of "That's more than I could ever say of you". Boswell certainly looked very badly when dressed; for, as he seldom washed himself, his clean ruffles served as a striking contrast to his dirty flesh.

Almost every glimpse of this strange individual, chiselling a correct Venus or a portrait bust, freezing a celebrated sitter to death in fireless rooms, giving orders that a hungry beggar should have "the bone with little or no meat on it", adds another stroke of the grotesque, and reconciles us—this is the book's touch of genius—to the unfathomable oddity of human nature.

For Nolly, despite his faults, is not unlikeable: rather the reverse. His miserliness, even, is a source of endless and delicate exploration. With such a character, it seems to me, the biographer, copying from life and face to face every day with

I

improbability, has an advantage over the novelist, who would tend to create *his* Nollekens either terrible or disgusting, futile or tragic—can one think of a single amiably life-size miser in fiction? Nollekens never towers, barely disgusts; he is certainly not pathetic; and the artful malice with which his portrait is drawn whets curiosity and even affection. His biographer, instead of trying to build up his subject, lets slip from a wealth of knowledge the most surprising and comic details, as though by accident. Take, for example, the paragraphs depicting Mrs. Nollekens at her wedding. She was rather too tall, he says, *scorney* (in her husband's phrase), but graceful, with a fresh complexion and beautiful hair. He goes on to describe her wedding-dress in detail, ending:

. . . Her beautiful auburn hair, which she never disguised by the use of powder, according to the fashion of the day, was, upon this occasion, arranged over a cushion made to fit the head to a considerable height, with large round curls on either side; the whole being surmounted by a small cap of point-lace, with plaited flaps, to correspond with the apron and ruffles. Her shoes were composed of the same material as her dress, ornamented with silver spangles and square Bristol buckles, with heels three inches and a half in height; as if she meant to exult in out-topping her little husband, whose head, even when he had his hat on, reached no higher than her shoulder.

To relish the full force of that last sentence, with its magical presentation of the little man at the end—hey, presto!—one must have read the elaborate page and a half of description that goes before.

There are other moments almost as breath-taking, usually in the loving depiction of miserliness ("parsimonious habits, *passim*", says the index), in which Mrs. Nollekens learnt from her husband and ended by surpassing him. While at Academy banquets he slipped the nutmegs into his pocket, and even crawled under the table to retrieve one that had fallen, she made the excuse to lift a clove or a pinch of cinnamon at the grocer's. He "was very fond of his ruffles, and continued to wear them long after they had become unfashionable—indeed, until they were worn out"; she was clad always in such rags that at the doctor's she succeeded in passing herself off as a poor patient until recognized and denounced.

So the revelations in Mortimer Street—morsel after decaying dainty morsel served up on the platter of reminiscence—go on. Delicious to watch this pair on a Sunday morning setting off for church; calipers (in Smith's phrase) and compasses; long legs and little bow-legs side by side; until at the corner, without a word, they part, one to attend chapel, the other to go Rome-wards. Occasionally—and it's an occasion, indeed—there may be company to dinner and then, whatever the lack of wine or viands, there will be words about a lost back-scratch ("Where was it? Why, under the pillow of your bed!") and about the servant Bronze ("I never like that woman—her mouth looks so much like the rump of a chicken"). Once, to the general astonishment, some new furniture makes its appearance in the drawing-room; and Mrs. Nollekens allows visitors to peep, holding the door ajar for the purpose. Or a caller sits shivering in another room where (says Nolly, bustling in and genially rubbing his hands) there hasn't been a fire for forty years. Or Nolly sits with his spouse and reads, in his broken English, a newspaper aloud, "beginning with the playbills and ending with the Editor's address". . . . No wonder Fuseli, encountering him one day, cries from the other pavement, "Nollekens, Nollekens! why do you walk in the sun? If you have no love for your few brains, you should not melt your coat-buttons."

Happy Nollekens! For, of course, he must have been, com-paratively, a happy man. The successful and eccentric usually are. And lucky Smith! Their friendship certainly struck a spark in the otherwise gossipy and sedate keeper of the Prints at the British Museum. Nothing eccentric about *him*, except the fact, duly tabulated on the back of the title-page, that he was born in a hackney-coach in London on 23 June 1766. He rambles to and fro over the London of his times, noting the street cries, an old house gone, a shop famous for its lemon curd, Sir Joshua's carriage drawn up by a sidewalk, the newly exhibited Elgin marbles, the scandal over Angelica Kauffmann and the living male model (nothing in it, one is glad to hear), but coming back always for refreshment to the incomparable freak-show in Mortimer Street. No detail or happening, no change in the townscape, but seems to possess a friendly inter-est. London was small enough for those living in it to feel they belonged there, and a beggar might become as famous in his way as the Lord Chief Justice. The street names still possessed a meaning; pavements weren't yet, as in a nightmare, projected to infinity; one step would take you out of town and into country. Smith gives a delightful picture of a London that to-day must be hunted down in odd corners and old prints; coming and going, he gathers his material with the leisurely preoccupation of a park-keeper doing the rounds with a spiked stick. The charm of this, the greater part of his book, may or may not attract readers: the more we feel for local history and gossip, the more we are likely to enjoy *Nollekens and His Times* as a whole. [*1943*]

LAST WORDS OF LOGAN PEARSALL SMITH

PENS, pencils, scissors, great paper-cutters, umbrellas, and friends as large as life—the things I keep losing grow bigger day by day, and one day soon I shall lose the big world itself.

We need two kinds of acquaintances, one to complain to, while to the others we boast.

What I like in a good author is not what he says, but what he whispers.

To deprive elderly people of their bogies is as brutal as snatching from babies their big stuffed bears.

In the Great World you must wear your heart on your sleeve, but it must be a sham one.

It is the grave drawback of these Hard Times that it costs so much to die.

How much of our disparagement is the talk of foxes who have lost their tails!

The fundamental distinction between the good and bad eggs of the world is a distinction which people of the world find it convenient to ignore.

The charitable attempt not to smell the smell of a bad egg only makes it worse.

People have a right to be shocked; the mention of unmentionable things is a kind of participation in them.

Those who like the same things find it the hardest thing in the world not to like each other.

A friend who loved perfection would be the perfect friend, did not that love shut his door upon me.

I find a fascination, like the fascination for the moth of a star, in those who hold aloof and disdain me.

Those who are contemptuous of everyone are more than anyone terrified of contempt.

The tone of people with low aims is always a high one: the talk of those who live purely for the good is appalling.

—AND OTHERS

The man who is master of his Passions is his Reason's slave—c. c.

There is no dead horse that is not kicking somewhere.—c. c.

Better to write for yourself and have no public, than to write for the public and have no self.—c. c.

We all find faults, but those who look for gratitude find the ugliest.—c. c.

We do not die in other people's arms if we can help it.—c. c.

Youth feels everywhere the presence of Mortality, but nowhere the reality of Death.—c. c.

Credit is the poor man's opium.—c. c.

To bestow a caress may be more wounding than to deny one, as those who have been in love may, perhaps, remember.—d. m.

In order to know yourself you must first let others know you. —d. m.

What we really want with all our hearts we obtain, except perhaps in love.—d. m.

Brilliancy in youth is only almond-blossom, and gives no promise of fruition. But how lovely, how amazing almond-blossom is!—d. m.

"Love's not Time's fool," the text of Shakespeare's sonnet reads; but there must be a misprint.—s. p.

Rich people would not so enjoy their little meannesses if they knew how much their friends enjoy them.—s. p.

Don't let young people confide in you their aspirations: when they drop them, they will drop you.—s. p.

If married people lost their unthinkable belief that they can change their wives or husbands, marriage would collapse at once.—s. p.

Don't tell your friends their social faults: they will cure the faults and never forgive you.—s. p.

Why do people lament their follies for which their friends adore them?—g. h.

If people say, I don't know why it is that I can't like so-and-so, the answer is—try envy.—m. m.

In England things are never as bad as they seem.—g. g.

[*1933*]

INDEX OF AUTHORS